Managing Projects With PMBOK 7

Managing Projects With PMBOK 7

Connecting New Principles With Old Standards

James W. Marion and Tracey Richardson

BEP

BUSINESS EXPERT PRESS

Leader in applied, concise business books

Managing Projects With PMBOK 7:
Connecting New Principles With Old Standards

Cover design by Charlene Kronstedt

Interior design by Exeter Premedia Services Private Ltd., Chennai, India

First published in 2022 by
Business Expert Press, LLC
222 East 46th Street, New York, NY 10017
www.businessexpertpress.com

ISBN-13: 978-1-63742-298-4 (hardback)
ISBN-13: 978-1-63742-294-6 (paperback)
ISBN-13: 978-1-63742-295-3 (e-book)

Business Expert Press Portfolio and Project Management Collection

First edition: 2022

10 9 8 7 6 5 4 3 2 1

Description

The Guide to the Project Management Body of Knowledge (PMBOK) published by the Project Management Institute provides a roadmap of performance domains designed to support project managers in all phases of project management. The sheer number of models, methods, and artifacts may leave project managers in a quandary about where to start and how to apply the many components. This book provides a simple explanatory guide for the layman that clarifies the "big picture" of the PMBOK.

Keywords

project management; PMBOK; uncertainty; project performance domains

Contents

CHAPTER 1

Introduction

The seventh edition of the Guide to the Project Management Body of Knowledge (PMBOK) (PMBOK® Guide 2021) ushered in a new era for the practice of project management. The traditional focus of the PMBOK was on processes and process guidance: project manager's approach to work—be it project phases or entire projects using the sequential elements of the five process groups (initiating, planning, executing, monitoring, and controlling, and closing). Also, traditionally, the ten knowledge areas included guidance for creating and managing all the subplans which together formed an overall project plan. PMBOK 7 approaches the challenges associated with managing projects with a different way of thinking. The first noticeable change is the integration of The Project Management Standard (2021) into the PMBOK. Instead of dictating processes to follow, The Project Management Standard emphasizes eleven principles to consider when managing projects: Stewardship, Team, Stakeholders, Value, Systems Thinking, Leadership, Tailoring, Quality, Complexity, Risk, Adaptability and Resiliency, and Change. PMBOK 7 includes eight performance domains that describe elements which are considered essential for successfully managing a project. The principles are said to guide the behavior of project managers as they carry out the project performance domains. The eight performance domains are Stakeholders, Team, Development Approach and Life Cycle, Planning, Project Work, Delivery, Measurement, and Uncertainty. Finally, in addition to performance domains, PMBOK 7 provides an encyclopedic list of "Models, Methods, and Artifacts" that are employed to manage projects and manage within the given performance domains.

The advantage to taking a "principle" versus a "process" approach is that The Project Management Standard and The PMBOK Guide are no longer prescriptive in its guidance. This is considered important in an era where many methodologies and approaches to managing projects are employed. In this way, projects managers can feel free to draw upon guidance that works for them as they tailor project management to their individual organization and culture. On the other hand, there is a disadvantage to this approach. While it may be beneficial to learn "about" project management and draw upon general principles to inform practice—the novice may lack a clear understanding about where to begin and exactly what to do to get started. Learning about project management is not the same as being provided specific guidance on how to do it and where to begin. Regardless of principle and the specific way in which organizations carry out projects, the work itself needs to get done—and the work typically encountered in projects was effectively modeling in the sixth edition of the PMBOK.

The PMI "Standards +" (www.pmi.org/pmbok-guide-standards/standards-plus) initiative helps in this regard by maintaining a database of standards, guides, articles, and general advice that is accessible by project managers. While useful though—it is challenging to form a big picture view regarding how the practices of previous standards relate to the new material. The purpose of this text is to clarify how to manage projects by drawing upon both PMBOK 7 as well as previously published process guidance. When used together in a big picture view, project managers can not only grasp foundational concepts, but can also follow step-by-step guidance for managing projects.

Where to Begin? The Principles

Previous editions of the PMBOK begin with a discussion of strategy and the context of project management. The apparent main point of the new material is to consider how the culture, processes, strategy, and structure relate to what projects are selected for resulting planning and execution.

The principles of The Project Management Standard are illustrated by combining them within a framework that includes the PMBOK 6 process framework and the project performance domains. In Figure 1.1, the principles are highlighted while the performance domains are greyed out for ease of viewing. From inspection of the comprehensive framework, the principles succinctly depict the strategic view of project management that is captured more generally in the early chapters of PMBOK 6. The

	Initiating	Planning	Executing	M & C	Closing
Stewardship					
Value		System for value delivery			
Systems thinking					
Leadership					
Tailoring	Adaptability	Resiliency	Change	Complexity	
	Development approach/life cycle				
	Initiating	Planning	Executing	M & C	Closing
Integration		Planning	Project work	Measurement	Delivery
Scope		Planning			
Schedule		Planning			
Cost		Planning			
Quality	Quality	Planning			
Resources	Team	Planning	Team		
Communications		Planning			
Risk	Risk	Planning	Uncertainty		
Procurement		Planning			
Stakeholders	Stakeholders	Planning	Stakeholders		
	Methods/models/artifacts				

Figure 1.1 The principles

principles can be organized into three sections and committed to memory using mnemonic devices so that the principles are always on the minds of the project managers and team members assigned to projects.

Principles Section #1—"ARCC": Adaptability, Resiliency, Change, and Complexity

The fundamental context of the principles is on the "system for value delivery." Projects cost money and are organized to produce specific deliverables. The deliverables are expected to add value by advancing the strategy and competitive advantage of the company. Projects add value—and the systems and frameworks supporting project management are in effect a system for delivering value. What produces value however is a moving target. The market can change rapidly. New competitors and standards arise— and economies and businesses rise and fall. Meeting this challenge requires that companies be "fleet of foot" and very nimble. This is where the adaptability, resiliency, change, and complexity guidance associated with The Project Management Standard principles' guidance comes into play. The governance and oversight of project management thereby requires focus on producing even in the case of dramatic change. Furthermore, projects themselves may be chartered to develop a strategy or to carry our strategic initiatives and change management efforts. The value delivery system of project management is therefore a mechanism for meeting the challenge of change and responding to it in an effective manner.

Principles Section #2—"SVSL": Stewardship, Value, Systems Thinking, and Leadership

Individuals assigned to manage projects are in many ways like mini-general managers or CEOs. They lead project teams and influence and engage stakeholders. Ideally, when such leaders act, they understand how the pieces of the project fit together and can trace out causal linkages between effort and result as well as risk and impact. Project managers are expected to take ownership of the endeavor and stay focused on the goal—even when the path is difficult. The Project Management Institute's (PMI) "Talent Triangle," Figure 1.2, depicts these qualities in the ideal characteristics of a project manager.

The triangle includes Business Acumen, Power Skills, and Ways of Working. The first two legs of the triangle that incorporate strategic and leadership abilities are a key focus of project management principles. This rings true as over the last 50 years, project management has emerged as a formal profession and the importance of business, strategic, and soft skills has risen to prominence.

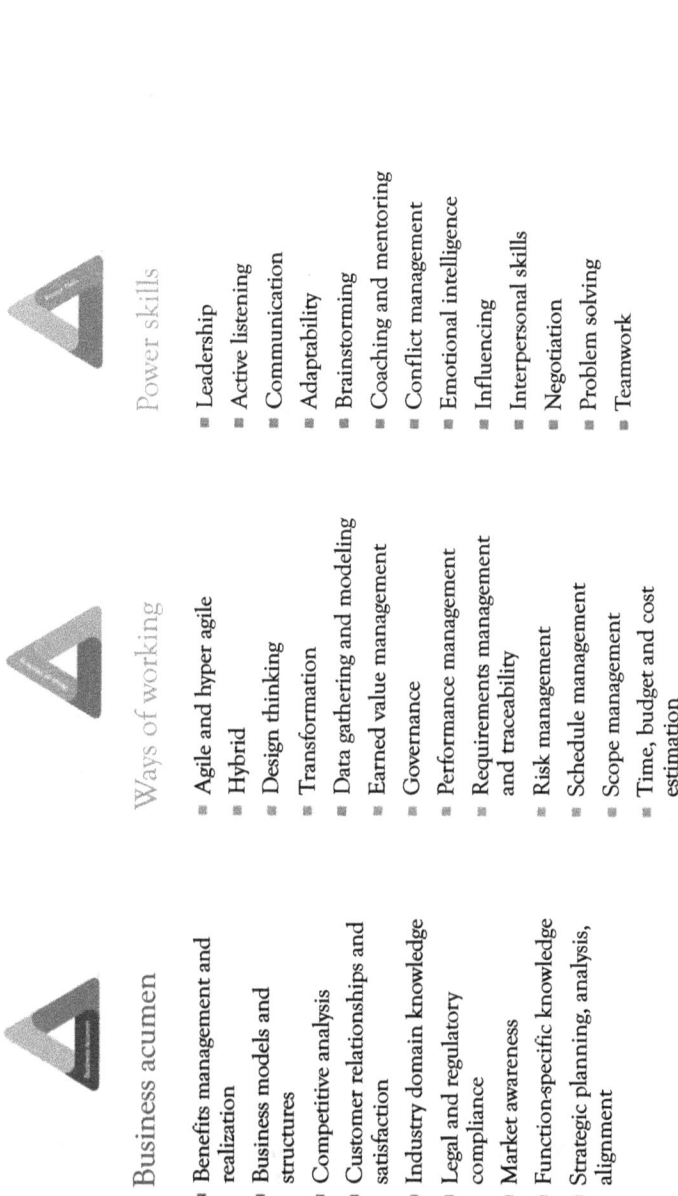

Business acumen

- Benefits management and realization
- Business models and structures
- Competitive analysis
- Customer relationships and satisfaction
- Industry domain knowledge
- Legal and regulatory compliance
- Market awareness
- Function-specific knowledge
- Strategic planning, analysis, alignment

Ways of working

- Agile and hyper agile
- Hybrid
- Design thinking
- Transformation
- Data gathering and modeling
- Earned value management
- Governance
- Performance management
- Requirements management and traceability
- Risk management
- Schedule management
- Scope management
- Time, budget and cost estimation

Power skills

- Leadership
- Active listening
- Communication
- Adaptability
- Brainstorming
- Coaching and mentoring
- Conflict management
- Emotional intelligence
- Influencing
- Interpersonal skills
- Negotiation
- Problem solving
- Teamwork

Figure 1.2 PMI talent triangle

Source: https://www.pmi.org/-/media/pmi/documents/public/pdf/certifications/talent-triangle-flyer.pdf

Principles Section #3—"QTRS": Quality, Team, Risk, and Stakeholders

Ultimately, the project management principles return from the strategic and leadership arena to more of the nuts and bolts of project management. Project management as a system of value delivery pays close attention to the performance of the deliverables it produces as it seeks to satisfy client requirements. Principles from quality management inform this activity. These principles are understood by project managers—but, it is not the project manager in isolation that performs the work of the project. Projects are systems that involve stakeholders—be they team members, clients, suppliers, or members of the industry and community. Finally, projects always operate in an environment of uncertainty. Estimates and plans are developed—but things happen—and often initial assumptions do not pan out. Risk management principles inform project managers as they navigate through uncertainty and carefully manage value delivery through to completion.

Tying Principles to Actual Project Work

The project management principles associated with value delivery are compelling. However, they are not necessarily actionable until these principles are married to the initial strategic steps of project management. Where does strategy reside in traditional project management? Typically, it resides in the activities of portfolio management and governance. These principles are put into practice prior to the start of the project and the result of which is the choice of project that the organization will undertake.

Project Management—And Its Evolution: Why Study Previous Versions of the PMBOK?

Completing a project plan as described by the PMI is different today than it was 10 to 20 years ago. The processes associated with the development of a project plan have been updated over the years since the first PMBOK guide was published. Understanding how to develop a project plan today requires an understanding of the current PMBOK framework. In 2017, the PMI published PMBOK 6. When encountering this process framework for the first time, the 49 different processes, including five process groups in 10 knowledge areas, will likely seem difficult to wade through and apply at first. However, if the rationale behind the framework as well as how the framework has evolved over time is better understood, developing a project plan using the PMBOK will likely make more sense. This is made especially clear when the current PMBOK is compared to the fourth edition launched 25 years ago. Examining the *PMBOK*® from the fourth through sixth edition will aid in understanding what the framework does, and why it does what it does as well as its underlying intent so you can best understand the leap to the seventh edition and the usefulness of the Standards+.

What Is It?

What is the project management framework anyway? It is a process-oriented series of guidelines for project managers. One of the reasons that the PMBOK framework started out being process oriented is that the management of projects occurs outside the normal ebb and flow of ongoing operations. It therefore requires policies, procedures, and processes to govern it. The fact that projects are different than ongoing operations becomes obvious when examining the framework beginning at the top left-hand corner of the framework (Table 1.1) at the intersection of the "Project Integration Knowledge Area" and the "Initiating Process Group." Integration implies "summing up" or tying things together—and this is exactly what is done when the project charter is created. The project charter authorizes the project using formal documentation that advises all project team members (as well as all who have an interest in the outcome of the project) of the authority granted to the project team to carry out its mission. In an ongoing operation, the head of the department may verbally assign work to individuals or teams without a documented charter. The department and hierarchy of leadership are already authorized to do their ongoing work—so only in the project context is such an authorization truly necessary. The project team once assigned may draw people from different functional groups and interact with different departments—and the charter enables this. This one simple example helps explain the need for a project management framework that governs the sequence of events from starting a project, planning it, carrying it out, finishing it, as well as listing the subject areas project managers need to know within these processes. The framework is not only useful—it is a necessity for planning and executing project work.

The Starting Point for Using Project Management

The project charter example implicitly illustrates how to go about using the framework. Rather than thinking of it as "49 processes," think in terms of the five process groups. Every project must be started, planned, carried out, followed-through, and finished. This commonsense series of steps for completing any type of work is captured in the five process groups that are labeled "Initiating, Planning, Executing, Monitoring and Controlling, and Closing." The five process groups did not change between the fourth and sixth editions of the PMBOK (Table 1.2). But the processes that exist in the sixth edition within each of the process groups have evolved considerably. The process changes are found within the knowledge areas of the PMBOK 6.

Knowledge areas are those specific skills, knowledge, or domain expertise that must be applied in the process groups to get the work of the project accomplished. While the process groups clarify the order of events or the steps in the process, the knowledge areas provide a content view—or what needs to be done at each step. The flow of PMBOK processes remains very similar when comparing PMBOK 5 and 6; but as the PMBOK has evolved, more direction is provided in knowledge areas and, in some cases, additional knowledge areas are given to support project activities. This is a consequence of the evolution of the field of project management over time. To fully understand the framework, it helps to understand what came before. The examination of the sixth edition therefore begins with understanding what changed between versions.

Table 1.1 The sixth edition of the PMBOK

Knowledge Areas	Project Management Process Groups				
	Initiating Process Group	Planning Process Group	Executing Process Group	Monitoring and Controlling Process Group	Closing Process Group
Project Integration Management	Develop Project Charter	Develop Project Management Plan	Direct and Manage Project Work	Monitor and Control Project Work Perform Integrated Change Control	Close Project or Phase
Project Scope Management		Plan Scope Management Collect Requirements Define Scope Create WBS		Validate Scope Control Scope	
Project Schedule Management		Plan Schedule Management Define Activities Sequence Activities Estimate Activity Durations Develop Schedule		Control Schedule	
Project Cost Management		Plan Cost Management Estimate Costs Determine Budget		Control Costs	
Project Quality Management		Plan Quality Management	Manage Quality	Control Quality	
Project Human Resource Management		Plan Resource Management Estimate Activity Resources	Acquire Resources Develop Team Manage Team	Control Resources	

(Continued)

Table 1.1 (Continued)

Knowledge Areas	Project Management Process Groups				
	Initiating Process Group	Planning Process Group	Executing Process Group	Monitoring and Controlling Process Group	Closing Process Group
Project Communications Management		Plan Communications Management	Manage Communications	Monitor Communications	
Project Risk Management		Plan Risk Management Identify Risks Perform Qualitative Risk Analysis Plan Risk Responses		Monitor Risks	
Project Procurement Management		Plan Procurement Management	Conduct Procurements	Control Procurements	
Project Stakeholder Management	Identify Stakeholders	Plan Stakeholder Engagement	Manage Stakeholder Engagement	Monitor Stakeholder Engagement	

Table 1.2 The fourth edition of the PMBOK

Knowledge Areas	Initiating Process group	Planning Process Group	Executing Process Group	Monitoring and Controlling Process Group	Closing Process Group
		Project Management Process Groups			
Project Integration Management	Develop Project Charter	Develop Project Management Plan	Direct and Manage Project Work	Monitor and Control Project Work Perform Integrated Change Control	Close Project Phase
Project Scope Management		Collect Requirements Define Scope Create WBS		Validate Scope Control Scope	
Project Time Management		Define Activities Sequence Activities Estimate Activity Durations Develop Schedule		Control Schedule	
Project Cost Management		Estimate Costs Determine Budget		Control Costs	
Project Quality Management		Plan Quality Management	Perform Quality Assurance	Perform Quality Control	
Project Human Resource Management		Develop Human Resource Plan	Acquire Project Team Develop Project Team Manage Project Team		

(Continued)

Table 1.2 (Continued)

Knowledge Areas	Project Management Process Groups				
	Initiating Process group	Planning Process Group	Executing Process Group	Monitoring and Controlling Process Group	Closing Process Group
Project Communications Management	Identify Stakeholders	Plan Communications Management	Distribute Information Manage Stakeholder Expectations	Report Performance	
Project Risk Management		Plan Risk Management Identify Risks Perform Qualitative Risk Analysis Plan Risk Responses		Monitor and Control Risks	
Project Procurement Management		Plan Procurement Management	Conduct Procurements	Administer Procurements	Close Procurements

Why Study Previous Versions of the PMBOK?

The fifth edition of the *PMBOK* is where a leap forward in terms of changes and increased structure is observed. What then changed between versions four and five of the PMBOK? There is a simple answer and then a complicated answer.

For the simple answer, there was an additional knowledge area added to the fifth edition (Table 1.3). Although the five process groups are the same, the communications knowledge area was divided into two: one knowledge area for project communications management, and then one referred to as project stakeholder management.

Why were project communications and project stakeholder management separated? Originally, communications and stakeholder management and engagement were closely related and therefore treated as a single aspect of managing a project. Because of the apparent similarity and the thinking at the time, the knowledge areas were therefore combined. However, in the PMBOK 5, it became evident from experience that communication is quite a bit different from the identification and in-depth engagement and management of stakeholders. Because of the complexity and level of effort required, it was determined that stakeholder management deserved its own sequence of processes to support the activity. It was therefore separated out from communications management for emphasis and attention to detail required in collaborating with managing the stakeholders who are always a critical part of managing a project.

The addition of the stakeholder management knowledge area within PMBOK 5 added five additional processes—bringing the total number of processes from 42 to 47. This number seems significant and not a simple matter for a project manager to keep up with. However, it is interesting to note that it is the planning process group where most project management processes—including many of the new processes—are found. It is within this process group where additional changes were made to the fifth edition. Approaching the understanding of the new processes in a step-by-step manner using the process groups as a guide can aid in making the framework more manageable and easier to digest.

Table 1.3 *The fifth edition of the PMBOK*

Knowledge Areas	Project Management Process Groups				
	Initiating Process group	Planning Process Group	Executing Process Group	Monitoring and Controlling Process Group	Closing Process Group
Project Integration Management	Develop Project Charter	Develop Project Management Plan	Direct and Manage Project Work	Monitor and Control Project Work Perform Integrated Change Control	Close Project Phase
Project Scope Management		Collect Requirements Define Scope Create WBS		Verify Scope Control Scope	
Project Time Management		Define Activities Sequence Activities Estimate Activity Durations Develop Schedule		Control Schedule	
Project Cost Management		Estimate Costs Determine Budget		Control Costs	
Project Quality Management		Plan Quality Management	Perform Quality Assurance	Perform Quality Control	

		Project Management Process Groups			
Knowledge Areas	Initiating Process group	Planning Process Group	Planning Process Group	Monitoring and Controlling Process Group	Closing Process Group
Project Human Resource Management		Develop Human Resource Plan	Acquire Project Team Develop Project Team Manage Project Team		
Project Communications Management		Plan Communications Management	Distribute Information Manage Stakeholder Expectations	Report Performance	
Project Risk Management		Plan Risk Management Identify Risks Perform Qualitative Risk Analysis Plan Risk Responses		Monitor and Control Risks	
Project Procurement Management		Plan Procurement Management	Conduct Procurements	Administer Procurements	Close Procurements

Changes to Planning in PMBOK 5

"Plan first, then do" is a central principle with project management practice. Most knowledge areas from PMBOK 4 and earlier did focus on planning prior to doing. But—noticing in the planning process group in PMBOK 4 (Table 1.2), starting from the top with the project integration management knowledge area and moving from top to bottom—it can be observed that some knowledge areas begin with a plan, whereas others do not. For example, quality begins with plan quality, communications begin with plan communications, and risk begins with plan risk management; however, others do not. Scope, time, and cost—considered the most important aspects of managing a project since they relate to "How much?" and "When?" and "What?" is to be delivered—do not begin with a "plan" step. There is therefore an inconsistency observed in the planning process group with respect to several important knowledge areas. In the PMBOK 5 (Table 1.3), it can be noticed now that scope, time, cost, quality, human resources, communications, and risk begin with the development of a plan. What this suggests is that every process in project management is going to be approached in the same way. Project managers can therefore follow a rhythm of planning what is going to be done first before doing it. Once the plan for the activities is done, the project manager follows up to confirm its completion.

A Plan for a Plan?

Beginning each knowledge area with a plan begs the question, "The planning process group inherently involves plan—so what in addition needs to be planned at the beginning of each knowledge area within the planning process group?" The rationale behind beginning with a plan in PMBOK 5 is that it is important for project manager to clearly think through and lay out the basic approach to managing each knowledge area. For example, scope, schedule, cost, quality, resource, communications, procurement, and stakeholder management begin with a plan as outlined in Table 1.4.

In short, PMBOK 5 now guides project managers to determine the basic approach or strategy to be taken as they carry out each of the

Table 1.4 Each knowledge area begins with a "plan"

Knowledge Area	Planning Process Group Initial Activity
Project Scope Management	Plan Scope Management
Project Time Management	Plan Schedule Management
Project Cost Management	Plan Cost Management
Project Quality Management	Plan Quality Management
Project Human Resource Management	Plan Human Resource Management
Project Communications Management	Plan Communications Management
Project Risk Management	Plan Risk Management
Project Procurement Management	Plan Procurement Management
Project Stakeholder Management	Plan Stakeholder Management

knowledge areas found in the planning process group. To give an example, the direction "Plan scope management" does not infer the actual planning and managing scope—but rather, how scope management will be approached. This is a strategy—or a "plan for a plan." This encourages project managers to think before doing and avoid ad hoc actions and decision making. This process-focused approach to getting work done is a mark of mature, disciplined organizations.

As previously mentioned, the stakeholder management knowledge area was separated from communications management. With this change in knowledge areas, more process support and details on stakeholder management including management engagement and controlling stakeholder engagement are now found in the newly created stakeholder management group. These supporting processes go far beyond the communications knowledge area. For example, presenting reports, holding meetings, and carrying out activities other than simple communication are needed to keep stakeholders involved in the project and be supportive. The project stakeholder management knowledge area therefore illustrates the degree to which project teams collaborate with stakeholders while carrying out the work of the project.

Complex Changes in PMBOK 5

There are additional and more complicated differences between *PMBOK 4* and *PMBOK 5* beyond planning processes and the addition of a single knowledge area. One of these differences is involved in determining how the project ensures that it is meeting the requirements of the customer. PMBOK 4 accomplishes this through the verification of scope. This means that the scope, or WHAT the project delivers, is checked against the project specifications. In verification, it is assumed that the project specifications for the customer deliverables are correct. Verification under this scheme is an indirect method of confirming that the project deliverables meet the requirements of the client. The PMBOK 5 uses scope validation instead of verification.

What is the difference and why is this new term used? While verification is used to confirm that the deliverables meet the specifications, validation ensures that the specification itself is correct. This is a stronger form of confirming the project scope. To clarify the difference between the two terms, it could be argued that validation is equated to "doing the right things" whereas verification equates to "doing things right." In PMBOK 4, the focus on scope was on verification, or "doing things right." In PMBOK 5, it is proposed that validation or "doing the right thing" is more important in terms of process emphasis. Put another way, it does no good to simply focus on producing deliverables that match the specifications developed by the project. Instead, it is more important that the project specification matches what the client wanted in the first place. This is validation and it is found in the scope management knowledge area beginning with PMBOK 5.

Consistency in Process Flow

The changes to the planning process group have consistency with other fields within operations management. For example, Deming's plan, do, check, and act cycle is closely mirrored in the *PMBOK* as initiate, plan, execute, control, and close. The idea being expressed is to develop a consistent management rhythm and do the same things in the same way each time (Table 1.5). When processes are approached in the same way each time, the steps are not forgotten or left out. It is important in "the thick of battle" in the midst of a project when things get difficult to have a process flow that, to the project manager, may act as an "internal compass."

Table 1.5 The Deming cycle and the process groups

Plan	Do	Check	Act
Initiate/plan	Execute	Control	Close

The DIKW Model

PMBOK 5 provides a model for managing data produced by the project. Data that comes from managing work and collecting information on the progress of project work is used for analysis in project monitoring and control. How data becomes information and knowledge after the analysis of such data is described in the data model introduced in the PMBOK 5. This model is known as the DIKW model, or data, information, knowledge, and wisdom model (Figure 1.3). This model illustrates that data becomes information when work is applied to it. Once the information is used and incorporated repeatedly in projects, it becomes knowledge. Finally, the application and refinement of knowledge over time eventually becomes wisdom. This model sets the stage for managing knowledge within a project, capturing the data that the project produces, and then refining it, applying it in future projects, storing it, and retaining it. The introduction and clarification of the DIKW model led to the incorporation of knowledge management in the subsequent PMBOK 6.

The DIKW model

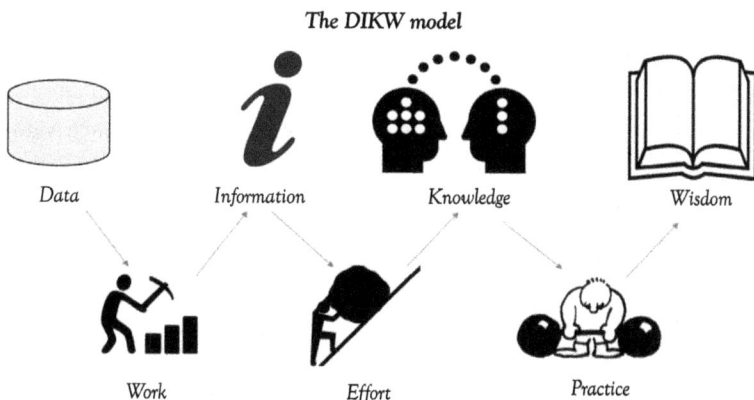

Figure 1.3 The DIKW model

Table 1.6 Planning as the largest process group

Process Group	Processes	Percentage (%)
Initiating	2	4.08
Planning	24	48.98
Executing	10	20.41
Monitoring and Controlling	12	24.49
Closing	1	2.04
Total	49	100

PMBOK 6 and the Planning Process Group

A simple count of processes within the PMBOK 6 illustrates that the planning process group includes more processes than any other (Table 1.6). This is followed by monitoring and controlling, executing, and finally initiating and closing.

When PMBOK 5 changed over to PMBOK 6 in 2017, several changes were made to the planning process group. The changes included some changes in nomenclature to reflect more accurately what was being managed. Instead of referring to "time," the process group previously labeled as "Project Time Management" is now referred to as "Project Schedule Management." This makes sense as, although time is certainly involved, what results from these activities within this knowledge area within the project planning process group is a schedule. Further, the estimation of activity resources process is moved from "Project Schedule Management" to "Project Resource Management." Although resources and resource constraints impact a schedule, the activities of estimating and planning resources are a natural fit within the newly named "Project Resource Management" knowledge area. Why the change from "Human Resources" to "Resources"? Because resources used on a project do not have to be human resources. Resources could be machines, equipment, and even funding.

PMBOK 6 and the Executing Process Group

The executing process group in PMBOK 6 places formal emphasis on knowledge management. This is the first time that knowledge management has appeared within the PMBOK framework. Knowledge in the context of a project involves the retention of lessons learned in such a way that it is organized and made available for use in future projects. While lessons learned have appeared within earlier versions of the PMBOK, knowledge management infers a more active development and application of project lessons learned. Note that the DIKW model infers that work must be performed on data to create knowledge. The creation and management of knowledge developed, suggested by the new "Manage Project Knowledge" processes, assumes the transition of data through information and knowledge and uses the DIKW model as its foundation. Notably, these are placed within the executing process group so that emphasis on lessons learned is placed throughout the project while the work of the project is getting done and problems are encountered and solved.

Risk And Quality Processes

The executing process group has also been expanded in PMBOK 6 to include additional processes in risk and quality. Quality is now managed in the executing process group. Quality management contrasts with "Perform Quality Assurance" as given in PMBOK 5. Managing the quality of project deliverables is now considered a more all-encompassing effort that goes beyond the narrower focus on quality assurance alone. Finally, an additional process is added to the project risk management knowledge area within PMBOK 6. The PMBOK 5 emphasized risk identification, assessment, and the planning of risk responses. PMBOK 6 includes the "Implement Risk Responses" process that supports escalating and managing risks that become issues. This process guidance for risks adds execution focus beyond the heavy emphasis on risk planning observed in both PMBOK 5 and 6. This is a bit of a "gray area" in risk management. Technically, when a risk is realized (i.e., occurs), then it is no longer a risk—but an issue. Despite this technicality, the resulting issues linked to risks will naturally map to the risk response plans.

PMBOK 6 Tools and Techniques Summary

PMBOK 6 includes a comprehensive listing of tools and techniques that are mapped to each of the knowledge areas. This mapping of 132 tools and techniques is illustrated in a series of tables located in Appendix X6 of the sixth edition of the PMBOK. This reference tool allows project managers to briefly see the tools and processes associated with each knowledge area. Project managers are advised to bookmark this comprehensive reference when dealing with challenging situations in which unique approaches may be required. Further, this final toolset summary can act as an index to save time in locating the right tool or process when needed. Project teams, even after significant exposure to the PMBOK framework through training and application, can still at times become a bit overwhelmed by project events. When in doubt and need some immediate project advice, jump to Appendix X6.

PMBOK 6 and Agile

PMBOK 6 emphasizes agile methodologies throughout. The sixth edition combines both project management and agile guidance within a single publication. The reason for this is that agile is becoming increasingly utilized throughout industry. The idea behind agile is to produce tangible deliverables quickly that the customers can evaluate, and break larger projects into smaller pieces, so that the larger project deliverables may be built up using an iterative sequence of smaller deliverable subprojects or "sprints." Agile is therefore focused on simplifying processes, moving quickly to produce tangible outcomes, and breaking larger projects into smaller pieces. This methodology is become more widely used beyond its origins in software development. Agile methods are incorporated throughout PMBOK 6 to give better visibility to project managers that this is an important way that projects are being managed today. Finally, it bears remembering that the process groups may be applied not only to the overall project but also to project subdeliverables and any complex deliverables. The process groups may be used iteratively and therefore fit well with the agile methodology.

What is the difference between Agile methods and traditional project management processes? To begin with, it is important to recognize that Agile is a methodology born out of software development processes. In software development, requirements often change quickly. Further, when traditional project management methods are used, the result of the software development is not obvious until the very end. For this reason, it is not uncommon to end up with a final "big bang" software integration that does not initially work and is riddled with significant defects. By way of contrast, Agile methodology focuses on completing a project in small increments that are characterized by tangible deliverables that the client can evaluate. One of the benefits of Agile is the ability to incorporate changes in requirements and to react to technical difficulties and scope changes as they arise. Further, progress measurement is considerably improved when the project produces deliverables along the road to completion. Agile represents a significant change in culture. Its very name evokes the ability to move quickly and flexibly with minimal process overhead. The inclusion of Agile methods in the PMBOK reflects the significant incorporation and popularity of this methodology. Project managers are advised to be aware of Agile nomenclature and to understand its fundamental operating principles. Finally, note that no matter what overall processes are employed, they all must be initiated, planned, executed, monitored, and controlled, and closed.

CHAPTER 2

Stakeholder Performance Domain

One of the first steps undertaken in any project is the identification of project stakeholders. On the face of it, this would appear to be a simple matter given that a stakeholder may be defined as "anyone who has an interest in the outcome of the project." Stakeholder identification, however, is complicated by the fact that stakeholders exist who may not initially be considered. Take for example an office relocation project. The immediate concern of the project would be the employees involved in the move, the landlord of the existing and the new building, and finally other tenants in each building. A deeper consideration of stakeholders goes beyond this narrow view and considers individuals such as family members employees, members of the community, local establishments such as restaurants and fast-food outlets, and finally local and regional government officials. In practice, it is not the stakeholders that the project team considers that are likely to become a problem—but rather those whom the project team fails to consider. When it comes to stakeholder identification, it pays to cast a wide net.

Stakeholders: Who Are They and Why Think About Them?

Once a project is formally authorized, it is time for the project team to pause and consider who are the players involved in the project. It may be tempting for the project team to think in terms of only two sets of "players" (or, "stakeholders") involved in the project—the project team and the client. However, this is far too narrow a view of the overall dynamics of the project. While the project team and the client both have an interest in the outcome of the project and are therefore considered stakeholders, it is important to consider other possible stakeholders. Additional stakeholders to consider might include managers and employees in the company who are not a part of the project directly, managers and employees in the client's company who are not a part of the project directly, the project sponsor(s), and members of the community outside of the community—to name but a few.

Why should a project team think about individuals who are not directly involved in the project? The reasons for this are many. To begin with, the project team will likely need support from individuals who are not directly a part of the project team or the client. Support could range from simple cooperation to occasional collaboration, to moral support. Also, stakeholders, who have an interest in the outcome of the project, will desire information updates on a periodic basis. Finally, some stakeholders or stakeholder groups may have the power to influence the outcome of a project—either positively or negatively. It is for these reasons that it is incumbent upon the project team to know who the project stakeholders are, to understand how they may interact with or influence the outcome of the project, and finally, to understand the overall level of potential impact. It is important to remember that not all stakeholders will want to see your project succeed. For instance, internal and external competitors for project funding or client business may well have a greater interest in the failure of the project rather than its success. The project team must be especially aware of this stakeholder group.

Analyzing Your Stakeholders

The analysis of stakeholders is a relatively simple process that is carried out using the following steps:

1. Identify stakeholders: Project team brainstorming is recommended to ensure that all relevant stakeholders are captured and recorded.
2. Interest ranking: Rank all identified stakeholders in terms of the perceived level of interest of each stakeholder.
3. Power ranking: Rank all identified stakeholders in terms of the power to affect the outcome of (or otherwise interfere with) the project.

The power or interest ranking helps the project team understand briefly which project stakeholders need most attention—and which may be addressed with routine communication and engagement efforts.

Table 2.1 Stakeholder register example

Name	Title	Role	Contact information	Concerns	Power	Interest
John Jones	GM	Sponsor	Jjon1@xyz. com	Budget	H	H
Bill Smith	VP	Client	Bsmit95@ abc. com	Schedule	H	H
Jill Ong	IT Dir.	Support	Jo45@123. com	Network	L	H
Sue Huff	HR	Staffing	Sh100@ 456. com	Team	L	H
Ed Pkunk	Man-ager	Mainte-nance	EP85@ xyz. com	Offices	L	L

There are two practical outcomes of the stakeholder analysis process. The first output of the process is known as a stakeholder register. The stakeholder register is a list of stakeholders presented in the order of importance with associated details that are of interest to the project team. Think of the stakeholder register as a table or spreadsheet that is maintained and updated as the project progresses. The stakeholder register is in essence a directory of project stakeholders. A simple example of a stakeholder register is provided in Table 2.1.

The second output of the stakeholder analysis process that is very useful for the project manager is the stakeholder "Power or Interest" grid. The "Y" grid axis ranges from low to high power. The "X" grid axis ranges from low to high interest. Stakeholders are placed onto this grid according to their respective rankings carried out in the initial stakeholder power or interest analysis. For example, a stakeholder with an "HH" ranking (High power, High interest) would appear in the upper right-hand corner of the grid. Likewise, a stakeholder with an "LL" (Low power, Low interest) ranking would appear in the lower left-hand corner of the grid. Intermediate rankings such as HL and LH would appear in the upper left hand and lower right hand of the grid, respectively (Table 2.2).

A new project manager may well ask the question, "Why go to all of this trouble—especially at the beginning of the project? After all, we have so much work to get started on!" Although stakeholder analysis does seem to be quite a bit of apparently nonessential work—the need for these efforts comes into clear focus as the project progresses. Fundamentally,

Table 2.2 Stakeholder power-interest grid

High power		John Jones
		Bill Smith
Low power	Ed Pkunk	Jill Ong
		Sue Huff
	Low interest	High interest

project managers must understand who the project serves and with whom the project will interact. Also, stakeholders, by definition, have an interest in the outcome of the project. Because of this, they are likely to be interested to hear progress updates on a regular basis. This leads to the conclusion that stakeholder will need communication and will need to be engaged. It takes resources to do this—so a good understanding of who the players are as well as their information needs is essential in planning out the overall project workload. Finally, tools such as the stakeholder register, and the power or interest grid help ensure that the appropriate focus and attention of the project team is placed where it is most needed.

Stakeholder Impact

Project stakeholders may be numerous, but not all project stakeholders have the same ability to impact the project. Furthermore, the limited resources within the project team make it incumbent upon the project manager to pay closer attention to the stakeholders with the greatest ability to affect the project. It is for this reason that stakeholder identification does not end with a listing of project stakeholders. Rather, stakeholder identification includes the analysis of stakeholders so that the level of stakeholder management effort may be prioritized. Such analysis includes a determination of the power of each stakeholder along with the relative interest of the stakeholder in the outcome of the project. Naturally, the project team will spend more time and effort engaging with the stakeholders who hold sway over the resources or outcomes of the project as well as those who are highly interested in the project result. The list of project stakeholders is therefore supplemented by a "Power/Interest" ranking ranging from high to low for each factor (Figure 2.1).

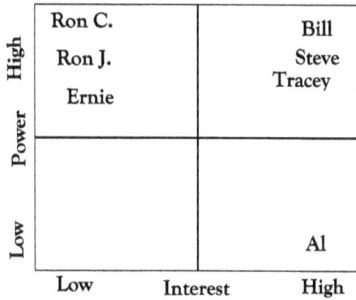

	Low		Interest	High
High	Ron C. Ron J. Ernie		Bill Steve Tracey	
Low			Al	

Name	Title	Project Role	Contact Info	Notes	Power	Interest	Ranking
Al Wilson	Prop. Manager-Old	Supplier	123@456.com	Final inspection	L	H	3
Steve Shen	Prop. Manager-New	Supplier	456@789.com	Move-in support	H	H	1
Ron Jones	Local Newspaper	Communications	abc@def.com	Inform community	H	L	2
Ernie Smith	Local Radio	Communications	ghi@jkl.com	Inform community	H	L	2
Ron Cabernet	Local TV	Communications	ghi@jkl.com	Inform community	H	L	2
Bill Edwards	City Mayor	Support	ghi@jkl.com	Inform community	H	H	1
Tracey John	Chamber of Commerce	Support	ghi@jkl.com	Networking	H	H	1

Figure 2.1 Stakeholder analysis

When carrying out this analysis, it is important to remember that not all stakeholders with an interest in the project support the project. Some interested stakeholders may desire to see the project fail. This is especially true in large-scale public projects that engage with a wide array of stakeholder constituencies. Identifying "negative" stakeholders is a factor to be taken into consideration when developing project communication and engagement strategies.

Stakeholder Engagement

The term "engagement," according to Dictionary.com, can refer to an encounter or, in the sense of mechanical mechanisms, the state of being interlocked. This definition provides a glimpse of the rationale behind project stakeholder domain as described within the PMBOK. Project teams work closely together with stakeholders—and particularly those who rank most highly in terms of "power/interest." Yet, an effective project plan will lay out the strategy for "how" project stakeholders are to be engaged. An engagement plan may be multifaceted and make use of several approaches. For example, it is common to assign project team members specific stakeholders with which to engage. The engagement itself will likely take many forms ranging from formal and informal face-to-face meetings, ongoing conference calls or videoconferences, or gatherings at annual events such as industry conferences. Regardless of the chosen engagement strategy, in keeping with the fundamental approach of "planning before doing," it is important to think through the engagement and to formally document it.

Managing and Monitoring Engagement

After the stakeholder engagement plan is documented, the project manager then engages assigned stakeholders and further takes steps to ensure that the engagement plan is being carried out. The execution of the plan may be carried out using the preferred tools and techniques of assigned team members. However, the progress to plan of stakeholder engagement, as well as any exceptional issues, should be reported out regularly in team meetings and project reviews. In the same way that stakeholder identification and analysis go together, managing and monitoring stakeholder engagement are linked. To ensure ongoing engagement and monitoring of the interaction with key stakeholders, it is suggested that each team member assigned to engage a stakeholder should be referred to as a "stakeholder manager." In addition to acting as a project team member, the adoption of the role of a project "stakeholder manager" brings clarity to the role and aids in the ongoing management and monitoring of the process.

The Elements of Stakeholder Management

What elements should be included in the stakeholder management? The stakeholder management for a project should answer the following questions:

1. Who are the project stakeholders?
2. How will the project team determine management and engagement priority of project stakeholders?
3. How will project stakeholders be engaged?
4. Who on the project team is responsible for stakeholder engagement?
5. How are stakeholder managers assigned?

CHAPTER 3

Team Performance Domain

Before studying project teams, it is necessary to examine the organizations in which they work. Traditionally, organizations have used a hierarchical and functional structure to organize and direct the various disciplines employed within the company. Using the principle of the division of labor, resources associated with each discipline are grouped together. This allows individuals trained in each discipline to work together with others who have the same training and carry out similar job functions (Figure 3.1). The benefits of this type of organization result from efficiencies of grouping like employees together to accomplish similar functions. Also, the reporting structure is clear and unambiguous. Individual employees report to supervisors, who report to managers, who report to directors and, eventually, the vice president or general manager.

The flow of authority within the hierarchy from the top of the organization to the bottom is reinforced by the reporting structure. Once a decision is made at the top, the orders may be quickly executed.

The problem with this type of organization however is multifold. Although execution occurs quickly once a decision is made, it may take quite a bit of time to decide. This is because activities requiring decisions must "bubble up" to the top prior to being made and then "pushed down" to the levels within the organization that execute the decision (Figure 3.2). Further, although employees within the same functional group may work together well and communicate frequently, they may not readily communicate with individuals in different functional groups. As an example, employees trained in finance may not fully grasp details within the engineering functional group—and vice versa. Project management seeks to bring together the different disciplines and domains so the problems may be solved in a holistic manner. There is nothing like working closely together on a team to encourage the emergence of a common understanding—despite the difference in domain expertise and associated worldviews.

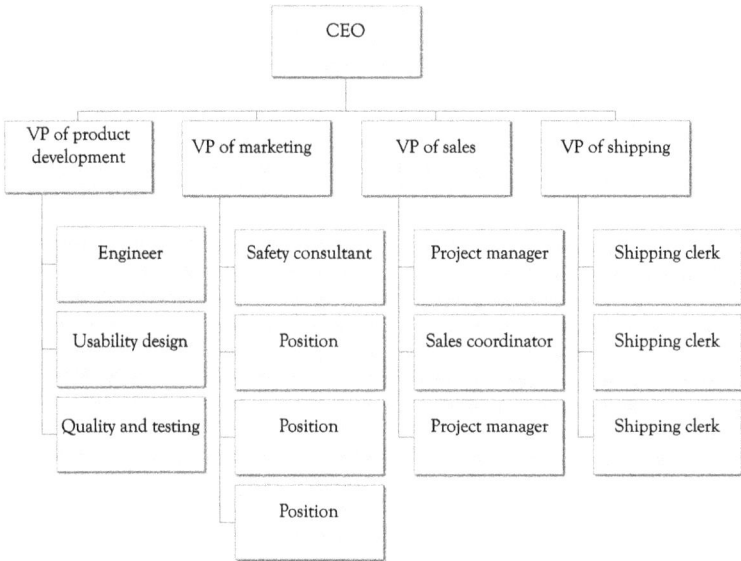

Figure 3.1 Functional organization example

Cross-Functional Teams

Project teams are formed to produce deliverables to stakeholders (such as clients) who are outside of the organization or the firm. The deliverables that project teams produce are usually the result of the skill and know-how from several technical and business disciplines within the

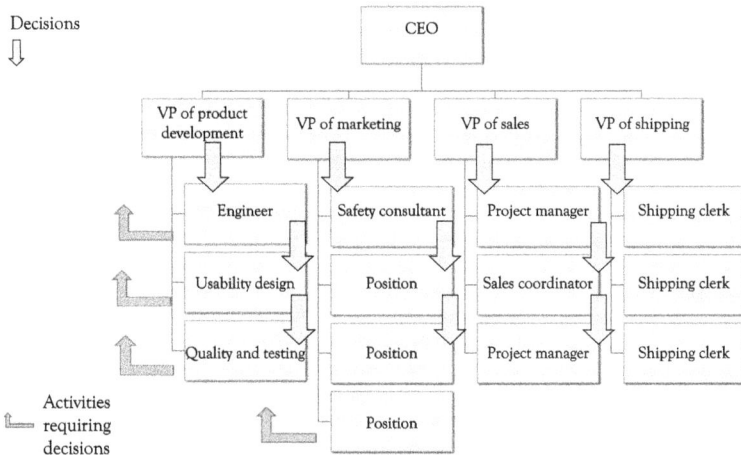

Figure 3.2 Functional decision making

organization. Because of this, such project teams are cross-functional in that they are composed of members drawn from multiple functional groups (Figure 3.3). Multiple functions are required to work together as a team to develop and produce deliverables composed of contributions from each represented discipline. The cross-functional structure also enables project teams to act quickly, make decisions, and work together across multiple disciplines in a holistic manner.

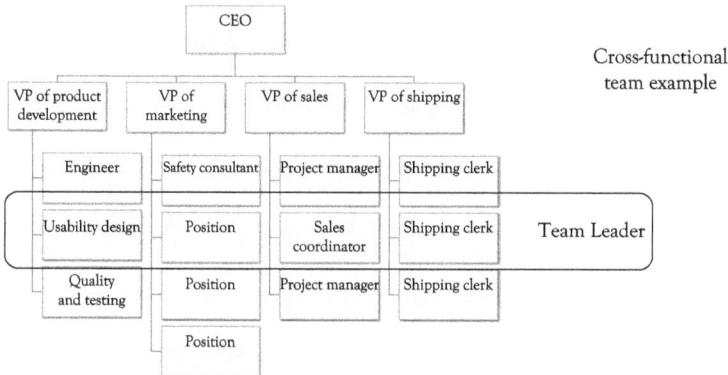

Figure 3.3 Cross-functional team

How then do project teams acquire team members from functional organizations?

Typically, this is accomplished by negotiating with functional managers. Project team members first contact each functional manager overseeing the disciplines that are required by the project. The project manager then demonstrates the authority to "borrow" resources required by the project by reviewing the project charter with the functional manager. Finally, the project manager discusses with the project manager which skill sets are required to complete activities associated with project deliverables.

The functional manager then lends resources to the project team and collects the accounting code for charging labor expense of the resources to the project. This is because during the time that the employee is working on project work, the expense of the employee is allocated to the project. Keep in mind though that, in some organizations, all resources in the organization may be centrally controlled by an organization known as the project office. Although resource assignment is coordinated between the project office, project manager, and functional management, the project office maintains the control of resources so that available skill sets may be tracked organization wide.

The Problem of Two "Bosses"

Once an employee is assigned to work on a project team, the employee now effectively has two reporting lines that include both the project manager and the functional manager (Figure 3.4). This complication does not exist in a purely functional organization. How does the employee keep track of two bosses?

Recall that a project team exists only to product deliverables. The project team is therefore concerned primarily with WHAT is being delivered (the project scope) as well as WHEN the deliverables are to be completed. The functional departments within an organization are effectively islands of specialized disciplines.

Functional managers are therefore primarily concerned with HOW things are done. The HOW relates to the process disciplines governed by the functional managers. Functional managers are also aware of which employees have the specialized skill sets required by the project team. For this reason, the functional manager is in command of WHO is assigned to do work within the project team. To simplify the chain of command

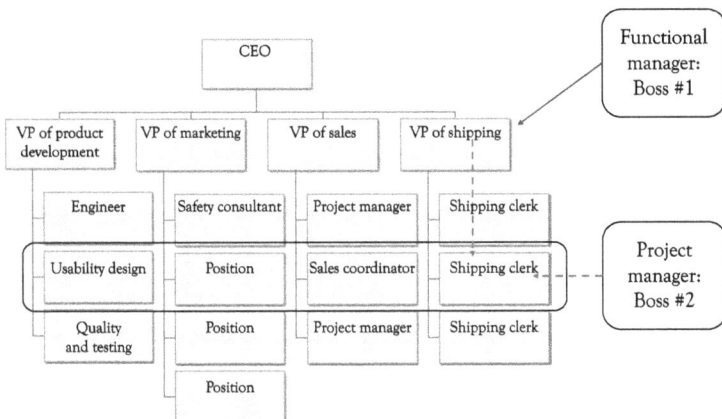

Figure 3.4 The two-boss problem

in the project team, the employee is advised that the project manager is responsible for providing direction and making decisions for WHAT and WHEN, while the employee's functional manager governs WHO does the work and HOW it is to be done.

Functional manager	Project manager
WHO	WHAT
HOW	WHEN

The Balance of Power

The process of negotiating resources from the functional manager may be only an occasional activity in many functional organizations. The functional organization may carry out most of the work of the organization, and, when needed, the executive may charter a project as a kind of "tiger team" to deliver something outside of the scope of the functional organization and in a rapid and efficient manner. In this type of organization, the process for negotiating resources may not be clearly documented and may be carried out in an informal, ad hoc manner. Further, the project manager and associated team may be considered by the rest of the organization to have less authority than the functional groups within the organization. Further, rarely do documented policies and procedures exist to organizationwide governance for managing temporary team activities.

By way of contrast, some organizations may carry out projects on an ongoing basis as the primary means for producing external deliverables. This might include producing contractual deliverables for a client, or product development projects for the open market. Organizations such as these that use project teams as their primary vehicle for producing deliverables along with supporting functional groups are referred to as matrix organizations. A matrix organization, in the same way as a functional organization, groups together disciplines as functions, but includes a substantial governance and process framework for commissioning projects, assigning resources from functional groups to project teams, and coordinating all project activities. The matrix organization maintains the integrity of the functional disciplines while, at the same time, providing a vehicle for targeted cross-functional activity. The matrix project organization is said to provide "the best of both worlds" offering the advantages of both a project team and a functional organization.

While there are advantages associated with the matrix organization, managing within a matrix organization tends to be more complex than a functional organization. While a functional organization employs the traditional structure of hierarchy and clear lines of reporting to accomplish organizational goals and complete deliverables, a matrix organization relies on highly refined and documented processes and procedures. While working within a functional organization may seem "natural" to an employee carrying out instructions from a supervisor, an employee within a matrix organization must rely on training and process discipline. It may take time and effort before working within such an operation becomes "second nature." On the other hand, many technical organizations, due to the complexity of the project deliverables, have long since adopted the matrix organization structure. Given that technical organizations were some of the first to adopt the matrix organization, employees working in such organizations may well consider matrix organizations—including the "two-boss" problem—to be second nature and the normal way of getting things done.

Evolution of the Matrix Organization

Organizations that operate matrix organizations deploy them differently depending upon the needs of the organization as well as the company strategy. Often, organizations that have traditionally operated within a functional structure see the benefits of project teams as well as the cross-functional coordination that is made possible by the project manager. Instead of formally chartering a project, a strong functional organization may begin migrating toward a matrix organization by assigning a project coordinator to lead various cross-functional activities.

Examples of such activities include the expediting of a significant order or the coordinating of the development and launch of a project. Over time, the coordinator position may evolve to a more concrete project management role with an assigned team and the title of project manager. In the project coordinator stage of evolution, the functional organization has existed for a longer period and carries more weight in operational decision making. This may shift over time depending upon how often project teams are formed as well as the relative importance of the deliverables they are chartered to produce.

The Weak and the Strong Matrix

In some organizations, the project manager is chartered to request resources from the functional managers—but the functional managers may opt to decline such request. The functional managers are therefore observed to hold more power than the project manager. This type of project/matrix organization is known as a "Weak Matrix." The weak matrix is one step removed from a project coordinator style organization in which the functional managers hold the largest share of power. However, the project manager, unlike the project coordinator, typically has project team members assigned to report to the project manager for the duration of the project to produce the project deliverables.

The weak matrix structure may operate well in circumstances in which the project team produces highly technical deliverables that need strong participation and decision making from functional domain experts. Recall that functional groups are owners of the technologies, processes, and know-how contributed to the project. The more that the project needs advice and support from domain experts, the more that the functional managers will have a say in how the technical work of the project is carried out. In contrast to the weak matrix organizational structure, the "Strong Matrix" uses a project manager that holds more power than the functional manager. In this situation, although resources report to the functional manager between projects, the functional manager is more of an administrative leader who develops resources with the right domain expertise so that the resources are ready and available to contribute to projects. The functional manager hires resources, trains them, and conducts annual performance reviews. When it comes to satisfying customers and producing deliverables to the outside world, the role of functional managers is not "where the action is."

The strong matrix is ideal for situations in which clarity of requirements, deliverables, and milestones is of primary importance to the project, the sponsoring organization, and the client. Recall that project managers govern WHAT and WHEN; so, if these goals are high in priority in projects, it is reasonable to expect that a strong matrix organization will be in place. Finally, many companies seek to optimize matrix organizations by seeking to foster equal collaboration between functional and project managers. It is in this organization that the project manager and the functional manager are assigned equal power. The resulting matrix organization is referred to as a "Balanced Matrix (Figure 3.5)." The balanced matrix organization is a good fit for situations where WHAT, WHEN, WHO, and HOW need tight synchronization—thereby requiring significant ongoing collaboration between the project manager and the functional manager.

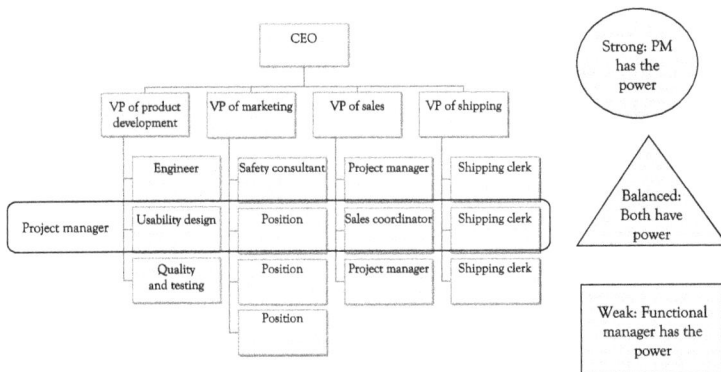

Figure 3.5 Balanced matrix

The Project Organization

By way of contrast with the evolution of a traditionally functional operation, some companies, because of the nature of the product or service offered, were structured from the beginning as a project operation. A project operation features dedicated project teams. A typical example of such an operation includes a construction company (Figure 3.6).

A construction company may have dedicated project teams for commercial construction as well as other teams for residential construction. Since all products that are delivered are delivered by project teams, it

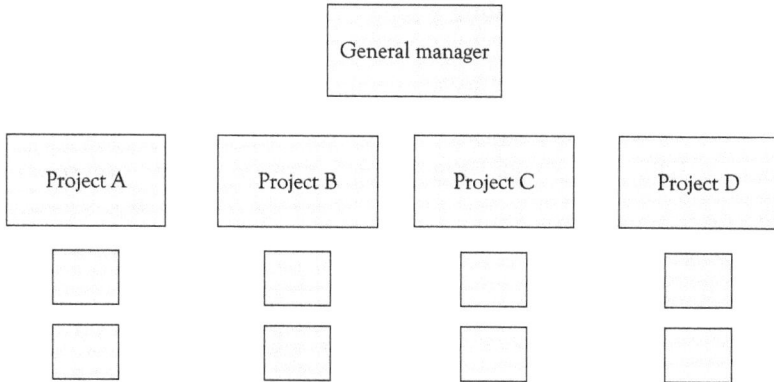

The project organization has self-contained teams but no functional structure.

Figure 3.6 The project organization

makes sense to organize the company as a collection of project teams. One negative aspect of the project organization is that projects tend to focus on project scope and schedule—potentially, at the expense of the technical disciplines that tend to be reinforced within functional organizations. Project organizations therefore need to have policies in place that prevent schedule and budget concerns to override important technical and process decisions.

Resources and Outsourcing

Regardless of the organizational structure, it is not uncommon for project teams to fail to acquire resources needed for the project solely from internal sources. The reasons for this are many including the need to staff more internal projects than the total number of internal resources can support. Further, the need for specialized expertise may lead the project team to consider alternatives beyond the existing organization. In these situations, project managers may seek to acquire resources outside of the organization. This may involve the use of contract workers (or rental equipment in the case of nonhuman resources), and it may involve contracting out portions of work. Both outsourcing options require management expertise to ensure that the acquired resources perform according to internal standards, and as well produce work products in such a way that, upon completion of the work, the deliverables are easily integrated into the overall body of work of the project team. Such concerns are rarely simple to resolve when developing the resource plan. This requires developing an understanding of the internal policies, procedures, and processes of the outside source of resources. Often, this may not be fully determined until the project team and the outside partner begin working together. By this time, if a significant mismatch in capability is uncovered, it is often too late to do anything about it.

Managing and Developing Resources

The temporary nature of the project suggests that in practice the team members assigned to the project from departments throughout the organization will often be working together as a team for the first time. Newly formed teams are not likely to perform at maximum levels. It therefore falls to the project manager to steer the team through the difficulties that teams face as they work though roles, responsibilities, and working relationships. The guidance that the project manager provides the team is born of a good understanding of how individuals are motivated as well as the process that teams go through as they evolve from a collection of individuals to a unified whole. This is a highly nuanced management process, and much has been written about it in organizational behavior literature. Nevertheless, the project plan should include at least some high-level strategy for developing a highly functional and productive project team.

Motivation

Motivational theorists such as Maslow, Herzberg, and McGregor (to name but a few) have proposed models during the last century that describe how humans in organization are motivated (Figure 3.7). Project managers are encouraged to draw upon these theories and consider how to apply them when managing project teams. Since the project resource plan outlines the strategy for how the project manager will acquire, develop, manage,

Motivational theorists

Maslow	Herzberg	McGregor

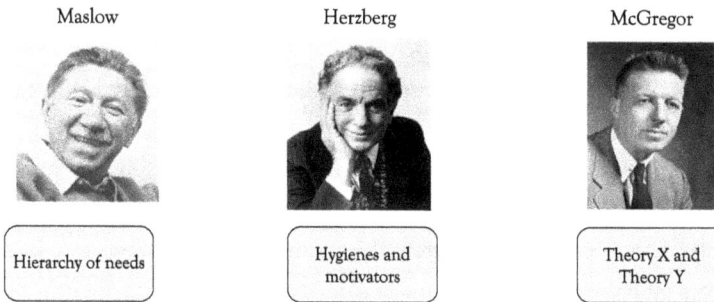

Hierarchy of needs	Hygienes and motivators	Theory X and Theory Y

Figure 3.7 Maslow, Herzberg, and McGregor in project organizations

lead, and motivate the team, the project manager should consider what team motivation and leadership techniques will be applied within the project. In practice, project teams often build their motivational strategy on the foundation of a good start. This usually involves an initial project kickoff meeting along with several team-building activities.

Another central consideration for team motivation is to involve the members of the team in the development of all project plans. The team project planning effort could be organized during the initial project kick-off and team meetings. A team planning workshop pays dividends later in the project as it is far easier to motivate individuals to execute a plan that they developed rather than to ask the team to carry out an idea crafted by someone else. Another important principle is to keep in mind that the project manager should never ask a team member to do something that the project manager would not do. When it comes to the difficult tasks of capturing project cost and schedule estimates, or dealing with difficult client, sponsor, or client negotiations, it is recommended that the project manager participate and lead rather than entirely assign the work to other team members.

Taking Conflict Into Account

One possible factor that often gets in the way of individual and team motivation is conflict. When developing the resource plan, the effective project manager will recognize the human tendency for "no two people to see things the same way." Project team members will have differences of opinion. This is a natural outcome of a diverse cross-functional team. Team members drawn from different functional areas will tend to, in the day-to-day context, focus on narrow technical issues associated with their domain of expertise.

When team members are collected in the project team, the project effectively acts as a small business that has as its goals producing the deliverables associated with its charter. This requires team members to take on a more global view and to communicate, discuss, and negotiate how best to proceed. Additionally, conflict may arise not as the result of differing perspectives resulting from different technical expertise—but rather from differences in outlook related to personality differences. There are several tools that may be used to assess personality differences. These include, but are not limited to:

- The MBTI: The Myers-Briggs Type Indicator
- The Big Five analysis of personality traits
- The Birkman personality assessment
- The DISC personality assessment

Each of these personality assessment tools has strengths and weaknesses. Cases may be made for or against each with respect to their overall validity. However, applying a personality assessment tool at minimum gets team members talking about themselves and how they think, and additionally helps each person to better understand how others approach teamwork and decision making. Regardless of the validity measures of each test, making the effort to understand and discuss personality differences at the beginning of a project goes a long way toward minimizing personality-related conflict.

Healthy Conflict

Differences of opinion will always exist within a project, but this will often be a good thing. Conflict tends to prevent project teams from making decisions too quickly and, in addition, avoids the problem of groupthink that is characteristic of less diverse teams. Although conflict can be

Figure 3.8 *Healthy and unhealthy project team conflict*

healthy, the project manager leading the effort to develop the overall project plan will need to be aware that conflicts will take time to resolve, and this will likely lead to the need for additional time. Finally, it is important to remember that there are forms of conflict that may be unhealthy for a project team. In general, conflict over strategy and methods for producing deliverables often leads to stronger decisions. Conflict of a personal nature, however, can be detrimental to a well-functioning team. This is an area that the project manager should be alert for so that it could be dealt with by employing a conflict resolution process in the overall project resource plan (Figure 3.8).

The Team Development Life Cycle

The fact that teams take time to "gel" and become effective over time has inspired researchers and human resource specialists to attempt describe the process of team development. Two notable models are often cited to attempt to explain the team development process. The rationale behind providing such models is to provide guidance to managers of all categories—and especially project managers since all project work is executed in the context of the team environment. The model which most managers will be familiar is Tuckman's "Forming-Storming-Norming-Performing" model. In practice, this model suggests that, after teams are initially brought together (forming), they then discuss, debate, and negotiate issues such as team responsibilities, decision making, roles, and

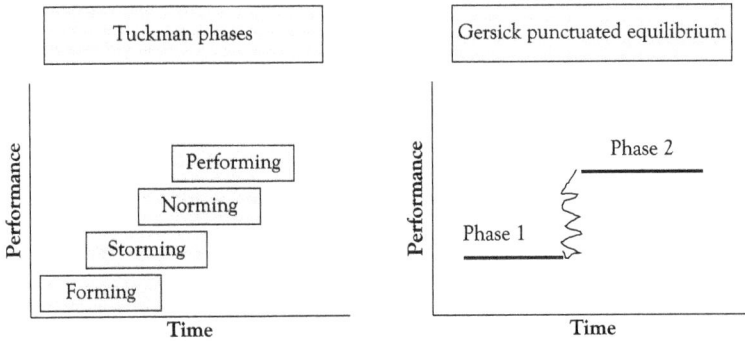

Figure 3.9 Tuckman, Gersick, and team development

processes. Often, disagreements and arguments ensue—and this is the reason that this stage is referred to as "storming." Eventually, the issues are worked through, and team members reach an agreement on the structure of the team and the rules that will be followed (norming). After this stage is experienced, the team is said to reach a level in which it can execute together in an effective manner (performing). Project managers observe that it takes time for a team to evolve—and the stages of the Tuckman model are likely to seem intuitive to experienced project managers.

A competing model of team development is Gersick's "Punctuated Equilibrium Model" (Figure 3.9). This model suggests that teams do not smoothly transition between discrete stages—but rather tend to begin performing when it is recognized that deadlines loom on the horizon. The essence of this model is that teams do not perform at maximum levels until the team reaches the approximate halfway point of the project timeline. It is theorized that, at this point, the team is forced to gel and then experiences a step function in performance through the end of the project.

What do these models mean for the project manager and the project team? First, it must be understood that theoretical frameworks are attempts to model reality. Models only imperfectly describe reality—and any given project is likely to vary from any given academic model. The underlying principle that nearly always applies is that there is no such thing as an "instant team." Teams take time to evolve and to reach a point when they are performing well together—and project managers are encouraged to take this into account in the resource plan and consider how the project team will be led so that its formative period may be accelerated.

CHAPTER 4

Development Approach and the Life Cycle Performance Domain

The very fact that projects begin, they evolve as deliverables are developed, and then end at some point suggests that projects may be characterized by a life cycle. The project life cycle is typically described in terms of phases as the purpose of the project is articulated, plans are developed and then executed, and finally, the project deliverables are launched. The common-sense sequence of the development cycle sounds rather like the sequence of steps that might be taken to deliver an entire project from beginning to end—Feasibility, Design, Build, Test, Deploy, and Close. Projects after all, begin, and like the sequence of phases, they end.

When companies execute projects, they do so for any number of reasons including developing unique products or services to deliver to the market, developing strategic plans, or implementing strategic initiatives—to name but a few. When companies manage projects, they typically start by performing activities such as defining what they intend to deliver, refining the product concept, or conducting a feasibility study. As a result, typical project life cycles may evolve with a stage referred to as "Design." The PMBOK, industry practice, and many other texts refer to similar generic project life cycles. Given that there are various approaches to governing a project from start to finish using a life cycle—where then do the PMBOK phases come into play? The phases are used to execute any work that is complex, uses resources, is unique, and takes multiple steps to complete. In fact, project life cycle stages fit this definition—and as a result—each stage of the overall life cycle may be executed. For example, if a project life cycle begins with a phase referred to as "Feasibility" or "Concept Definition," the phase must be built, tested, deployed, and closed. The Development

Feasibility, design, build, test, deploy, close

| F | D | B | T | D | C |

| F | D | B | T | D | C |

| F | D | B | T | D | C |

| F | D | B | T | D | C |

| F | D | B | T | D | C |

| F | D | B | T | D | C |

Develop

Plan

Feasibility

Concept

A generic lifestyle governed by processes

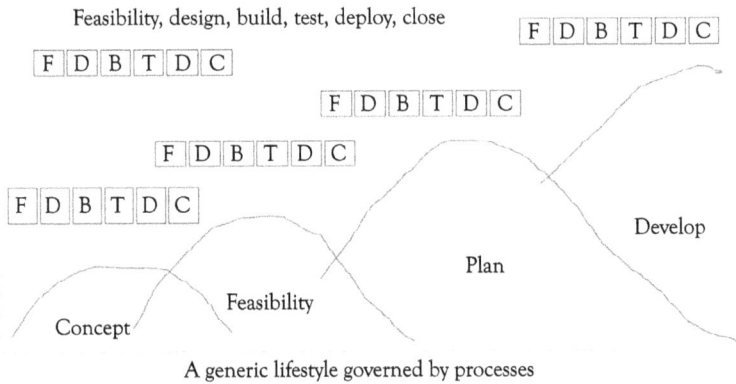

Figure 4.1 Managing the life cycle using phases

Approach will have, in effect, a bundle of related processes for carrying out specific activities as the work done by the project progresses. If the management work that is carried out in a project is thought of in terms of layers, the project management performance domains could be thought of as occupying a layer "underneath" the project life cycle layer (Figure 4.1).

Incremental Development Approach

The incremental development approach is built in integration. The term integrate generally refers to "the act of combining one thing with another so that they become a whole." This integration describes the high-level activities that tie together all aspects of the project. Integration begins in the conceptual stage and is documented in the project charter. The charter is the formal authorization of the project. Why does a project need authorization? Remember that this is because a project is a one-time only, unique sequence of activities. It, therefore, acts outside of the normal processes of the organization.

The project needs the authority to acquire resources, to spend money, and dedicate time to the work of producing the project deliverables. Since the authority given to the project relates only to what the project team is assigned to do, some brief mention of scope and constraints is included in the project charter. In some cases, the scope may not be completely clear. An example of a project such as this is a project chartered to develop a new product for launch to the market. On the other hand, a project chartered to produce deliverables according to a contractual commitment may begin with a project scope that is well understood. An example of the life cycle and phases will be fully described in Chapter 6, Project Work Performance Domain.

CHAPTER 5

Planning Performance Domain

Project selection decisions rely on limited data regarding the proposed project. Since the project has not yet started, the data used for project selection comes from estimates of the overall cost and schedule. Once the project has been selected, it is useful to confirm the overall level of financial, time, and resource commitment that will be needed to complete the project. The difficulty with such a confirmation is that at the stage of the process after the project is selected—the project scope is not well known. Scope may not be known with specificity, but some mention of what the project will be doing will be found on the project charter. This is because there must be some clarity about what it is that the project is being authorized to do. If the scope is not yet known—as in the case of a new concept or product development—the project may first be chartered to develop the project scope.

A detailed estimate of the project requires significant time and effort to produce and requires a thorough analysis and determination of scope, resources, and timing to develop. The irony of project estimating is that project sponsors, such as senior management, desire to know the required level of commitment at the earliest stage of the project. Unfortunately, this is at the point in the project when the least amount of information is available. By the time all information is available—it is likely that the time window for an advance decision has passed. How should project managers address this conundrum?

Starting a Plan With a Project Schedule: The ROM Estimate

The Rough Order of Magnitude (or ROM) estimate is a path forward for estimating projects at the earliest stages of the process. Although it is true that all estimates are wrong (otherwise, they would not be estimates!), ROM estimates are known to be more wrong than other methods of project estimates. In fact, ROM estimates may be in error by as much as 50 to 100 percent. Despite the lack of accuracy, ROM estimates are very useful for determining the scale of the overall effort. The term "order of magnitude" refers to powers of 10. For example, powers of 10 from 1 (10^1) through 6 (10^6) represent the numbers 10, 100, 1000, 10,000, 100,000, and 1,000,000. The scale of the estimate is that which proves useful to the project manager and the project sponsor in the earliest phases of the project life cycle. The scale of the project often stated in terms of order of magnitude informs sponsors and project team members alike whether the project is a commitment for $100,000.00 or a $1,000,000. Even if the estimate produced by the ROM differs significantly from the actual result—the scale of the estimate is likely to be accurate. A ROM estimate therefore answers the question, "What level of investment are we really about to sign up to?" Based on the strategic direction of the company, the result of a ROM may trigger the start of the development of a project plan.

A schedule, in contrast to a complete plan, is focused on "what?" "when?" and "how much?" The schedule therefore is a useful start for beginning the development of a complete project plan. Once the schedule is in place—the rationale for the elements of the complete project plan begins to come into clear focus. A completed schedule provides a reasonable checkpoint for making a "Go/ No-Go" decision for spending the resources for developing a complete project plan thereby providing a sound rationale for starting first with a project schedule—then continuing to a full project plan. A schedule requires more time and effort to develop than a high-level ROM estimate, but considerably less effort than a complete project plan. Also, it may be desirable to plan and complete only a phase of a project, learn more about the level of difficulty and cost, and then proceed further to develop a complete plan. In either case, laying out the "what, who, and how much" elements of a plan lay down a significant foundation to a complete planning effort.

Start It! Getting Work Started

Starting a project is straightforward when the objective is known upfront. This is a likely occurrence in a contractual situation—for example—when a client agrees to pay a specific amount over a period for the delivery of a detailed Statement of Work (SOW). Unfortunately, this is a luxury that not all project teams enjoy. In the case of a project initiated for the purpose of creating and fleshing out a product concept for the ultimate launch to the marketplace, the initial objective or project scope may initially lack clarity. In these situations, one of the first activities assigned to the project team would be to develop the project scope. The scope and the charter therefore become a "chicken-and-egg" situation. In some cases, the scope is clear; in other cases, the scope at this stage is just an idea in need of a project team to fully develop. In either case, the project begins with the project charter.

What Is a Project Charter and Why Is It Needed?

Projects, being temporary organizations, need special authorization to get the work of the project done. Projects acquire people from departments or from outside the organization, and they spend money as they develop deliverables. Since project teams are temporary organizations operating outside of the functional organization structure, they must be formally authorized. This then is the purpose of the project charter—to provide formal authorization for everything that the project will do. What would project manager expect to find on a project charter? Although the exact format of the charter is likely to vary from company to company, project charters will include, at minimum, one or more of the following elements:

- **Scope**: Scope may not be known with specificity, but some mention of what the project will be doing will be found on the project charter. This is because there must be some clarity about what it is that the project is being authorized to do. If the scope is not yet known—as in the case of a new concept or product development—the project may first be chartered to develop the project scope.
- **Timing parameters**: The charter identifies the high-level time-frame for which the project will be authorized. If the project exceeds this timeframe, the project must be reauthorized. In some cases, a larger project may be broken into smaller phases and each phase is chartered separately. Later phases are char-tered only if earlier phases are completed successfully.

- **Team**: The project manager and the core project team members are identified. The term "core" team distinguishes between team members who remain assigned to the project throughout the project life cycle and those who are assigned temporarily to complete assigned project work packages.
- **Cost parameters**: The project is authorized to operate within specific cost limits. As in the case of the overall timing parameters—if the cost parameters are exceeded, the project must be reauthorized.
- **Constraints**: Any constraints that would impact the project are noted in this section. Constraints might include dependencies, time to market, or regulatory issues to name but a few.
- **Sponsor**: The sponsor or authorizing authority of the project is identified.
- **Business case or rationale**: A simple statement or paragraph identifying the purpose of the project is included in this section.
- **Comments or notes**: Any special notes, observations, or requests by the sponsor or other interested parties are indicated here.
- **Authorization signatures**: The sponsor and the project manager sign the project charter. Also, some companies may include space for acknowledgment signatures by members of the management team who may interact with or supply resources to the project team.

Although the project charter contains several important elements, note that the primary purpose of the charter is the authorization of the project. Some project details and parameters are necessary for project authorization—but the details do not constitute a complete elaboration of scope, schedule, nor a complete project plan. The details are produced by the project team after it is authorized to do so in the charter.

The Charter as a Contract

Another way to think of the project charter is to view it as a type of contract between the executive stakeholders of the company and the project team. In essence, the executive body funds a project team to do work within the bounds of performance, schedule, and budget constraints. This arrangement is like the contractual relationship setup between the company and an outside vendor. Creating and managing the project charter as a contract has the further advantage of minimizing the management burden of the executive team. The project, under the authority of the project charter, is given full license to carry out its activities within the bounds of the constraints identified in the charter. If the project team violates one or more constraints—or recognizes the possibility that it will do so—the team calls for a formal review meeting with the executive committee to see reauthorization of the project and update of the charter. If the team remains within the bounds of the charter, the team needs no additional management oversight until the next contractual milestone. At each milestone—or special review called by the project team—the project charter is reaffirmed (and updated as necessary), or the project is redirected or terminated. The project charter from this point of view amounts to a means for implementing the delegation of authority in a structured and efficient manner. It also solves the problem of ensuring the result of the delegated effort meets the desired outcomes of the project sponsors.

Scope, Time, and Cost in Project Planning

The project is selected and authorized—and the key players are known. It is now time to think about what the project is going to deliver in detail, how the deliverables will be produced, and in what order. Further, the specific resources required to produce the produce the project deliverables must be understood. This is the fundamental building block of the larger project plan, and it begins with building a fully resourced schedule. It is important to understand though that while the plan is developed, the plan is not to be considered something that is "carved in stone." A plan could be thought of as a "plan of attack." Keeping this in mind helps the project manager appreciate that the project is dynamic and faces constant issues, changes, and barriers to success every day. The process of planning therefore does not end once the initial plan is developed. The plan is iterative—beginning with the original baseline—and modified over time as the project team manages through the dynamics of the project as it unfolds.

Why Plan?

If the plan is flexible and iterative, it raises the question of "why plan?" Planning is given high importance in the PMBOK—and this is evident by the number of artifacts in project planning. The philosophy behind the emphasis on planning is that of process maturity. Companies that rigorously follow a process are said to be more mature—and have the potential to be more successful—than those who manage their respective businesses using *ad hoc* management methods. The emphasis on planning therefore helps ensure that the project team avoids jumping directly into project execution—and instead—carefully thinks through what needs to be done, why and how. Although the plan may change—and multiple plans may be created over time—it is still preferred to acting before thinking or being in perpetual "reactive mode." A project team that takes planning seriously is one that is said to be mature in its business management outlook.

The Role of Estimates in the Project Plan

As the project team steps through each of the elements of project planning, there will be an ongoing need for cost, time, and resource estimates. Estimates are essential in planning to set expectations for timing and resource needs in addition to sequencing of activities and deliverables. After the project was selected, the entire project was estimated using a ROM estimate. When the actual work of the project begins, estimates are used for life cycle phases, for activity durations, for the cost of deliverables—in short—anything that needs to be planned. Finally, estimating is likely to be iterative in nature and repeated throughout the project to support iterative planning. Because of this, it is important to have a good understanding of practical estimating fundamentals.

Estimating the Project: Beyond the ROM

Although many techniques exist for estimating project work, there are two primary approaches-top down and bottom up. The top-down approach begins with an assumption about overall cost, time, or effort, and then proceeds to apportion the top-level number among each of the lower-level elements. As an example, in a homebuilding project, a budgetary number could be assumed for the overall cost of the house—and then, the overall home cost could be apportioned among the components of the home such as the land, the foundation, the roof, the kitchen, and so on. An example of an apportioned estimate for a home is demonstrated in Figure 5.1.

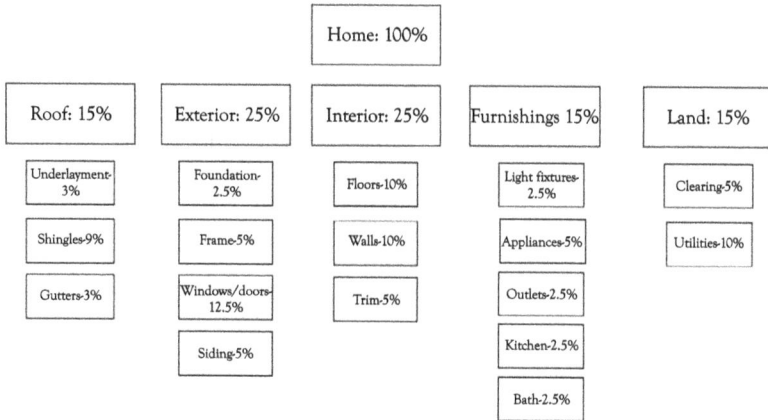

Figure 5.1 Apportioned estimate example

Top Down Versus Bottom Up

The strength of the top-down approach is its simplicity. It is logical, and it results in what amounts to budgetary targets for cost, duration, or effort. Its simplicity and its natural fit with existing budgets make the top-down approach appealing to senior management. The weakness of the top-down approach is that it begins with assumptions about total costs that may or may not reflect reality. Top-down estimates are often spearheaded by management and project sponsors who seek to fit the project into business model constraints. The top-down budget has the potential therefore to represent what the project should cost rather than what it costs.

By way of contrast, a bottom-up approach to estimating is derived from an analysis of each step within each project activity. The cost of each low-level activity is estimated and combined with other activities until a top-level number is reached. The bottom-up view is created by those who do the work. The bottom-up estimators therefore have a highly granular view of every step that needs to be completed in every activity along with its associated cost. Those who are estimating a project from the bottom up therefore often see details that managers who have the top-down view tend to miss. Since the bottom-up approach is closely grounded to the actual activities associated with each deliverable, the bottom-up number that results may be more accurate. The weakness of the bottom-up approach is that it is focused exclusive on the work itself rather and does not consider possible budgetary constraints. Further, those who are doing the work have the motivation to ensure that funding and allotted time duration is sufficient for producing the agreed upon project deliverables. As a result, the bottom-up number that is gained is usually higher than the top-down number.

Applying Expertise

Whether the top-down or the bottom-up approach is used in estimating—there are several different estimating practices that the project team may use. Such practices may be readily used without thinking of it as a specific estimating methodology—especially when highly skilled team members employ it. Estimating typically involves highly experienced professionals with expertise in completing similar project. It is this expert judgment that is applied by senior team members who have experience with the work being estimated.

Expert judgment in estimating can save considerable time and effort. However, it is essential to ensure that the expertise truly applies to the work at hand. Some previous experience may be related—but not sufficiently related such that an accurate estimate is produced. This is especially true in software or intellectual property projects where several intangibles are involved. Technologies and standards are changing rapidly, so expertise garnered from a project that took place three to five years ago may no longer be applicable. Unfortunately, flaws in estimates that are related to out of date or not adequately applicable expertise may not be discovered until it is too late. The lesson for project managers is to ensure that those who apply expert judgment have the judgment that they claim to have.

Using Analogies and Parametric Estimation

Another common estimating practice is to employ analogies. For example, an activity, a project phase, or a particular deliverable that is like something that was done within another project may be compared. The previous experience may form the basis of the current estimate. Also, the previous project experience could be scaled. As an example of this approach, the project manager's thought process might proceed as follows, "Last year we delivered this software subsystem—and what we are working on now seems to be similar—but about twice as much work." Finally, another estimating practice is the parametric approach. Parametric estimating is a time-saving device that is very simple to implement. As an example of parametric estimating, if one element of work is determined to cost $10 and this work must be completed ten times throughout the project, then the total estimated amount is 10 × $10 or $100.

Estimating and Trade-Offs

The desired result of estimating—be it time, cost, or effort—is to arrive at a number that both works for planning purposes as well as for budgeting. It is one thing to have a number that reflects the likely actual outcome—but, it is quite another to arrive at a number that the project sponsors and the client are willing to fund. For this reason, there is often considerable give and take as the estimates of the project unfold. Granted, bottom-up approaches may arrive at a number that is too high to be acceptable to management. A top-down number may be considered too small to be workable by the project team. In the end, the numbers agreed on for planning and budgetary purposes will be the result of ongoing negotiation—and trade-offs between the overall cost, schedule, and scope of the project.

Project Estimates and "The Learning Curve"

The learning curve is a mathematical formula applied in operations management that describes how efficiency improves and effort declines as the output of production doubles. The learning curve is a powerful model for describing efficiencies that are observed within a manufacturing or mass production environment.

The formula for the learning curve is:

$$y = a^*x^Ab$$

where y is the cumulative cost or outcome, a = the time or cost for the initial unit produced, x = the number of units produced, and b is the learning factor, b = (log learning rate/log 2) (Figure 5.2).

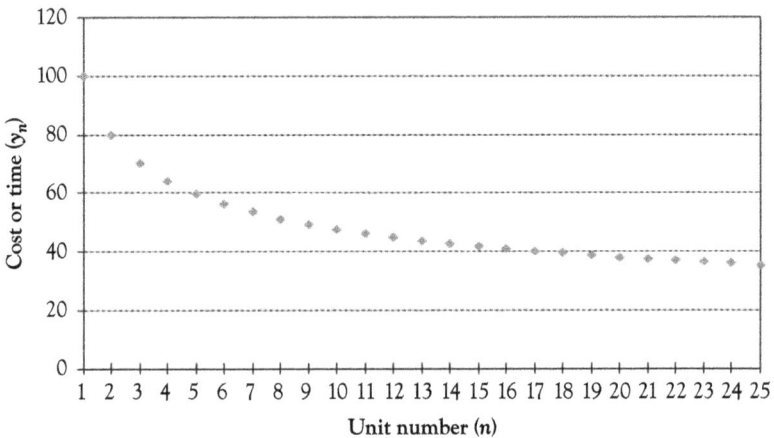

Figure 5.2 The learning curve

The mathematical expression produces a continuous curve that is characterized by the learning rate and the number of units produced. Although the term "learning curve" is often used, it is usually used informally and tied loosely to the original context of mass production.

The learning curve is also often referenced with respect to project management and estimates. The reason for this is that when estimates are generated for projects that involve work in which the project team is well experienced, it can be assumed that the effort required will diminish over time—and that this fact should be reflected in the project estimate. While it is generally true that effort tends to decrease as experience is gained, the learning curve formally generally does not apply in the project context. Recall that every project is unique and has a clear beginning and ending. For this reason, projects generally do not exhibit long production runs associated with doubling of volumes. When estimating projects, it is therefore fair to consider experience and recognize that the second and following times that a particular type of work is done—the experience of the project team will generally lead to increased efficiency and therefore lower cost estimates. For example, the second time a project team develops a particular type of information system or network—the less time and cost will be required—assuming minimal new technologies or configurations are encountered. However, it is the principle of the learning curve that is applied in estimates rather than the specific learning curve formally derived from manufacturing and operations management.

From High-Level Estimates

Estimates take time, money, and resources to complete. Still, estimates are only estimates until the project details are laid down in project plans. Also, an actual plan can still be considered an estimate since it is never truly known how much something will cost nor how long it will take until the activities are executed. The first step, however, in moving from initial estimates into a project schedule or complete plan is the definition of project scope.

Project Scope-Getting Started

Projects exist for a singular purpose—to produce deliverables. The project scope refers to *what* the project will deliver. Given that the objective of a project is limited to producing very specific things over a fixed period—the concept of project scope would appear to be straightforward. Unfortunately, it is not. Scope in project management tends to grow over time for many reasons. To begin with, each time a problem is encountered in a project, the project scope grows. This is because additional work is required to solve the problem. Depending upon the exact nature of the problem, additional resources may be assigned, and new plans generated. Also, scope can grow simply because a project takes time to deliver. Because of this, requirements, standards, markets, and so on may change—and this may require additions to the work that is already planned. Because of these and many other scope-impacting factors, the first step in the scope planning process is to step back and think about how you as project manager will approach managing it.

Planning to Plan: How to Approach Your Project Schedule

PMBOK 6 provides guidance for what amounts to the development of a "plan for a plan" in the context of scope, time, and cost management. This may be observed in the "Plan Scope Management, Plan Cost Management, and Plan Schedule Management" processes. While PMBOK 7 does not go into this type of detail, it is worth mentioning as planning tends to be a very complex activity of a project manager. On the surface, PMBOK 6 may appear to be add another layer of planning—and perhaps more planning than is even necessary.

There is another way to view this apparent additional and possibly unnecessary sequence of steps. This is to think of this step as a means to step back and consider the strategy to be taken when managing scope, time, and cost. For example, with respect to project scope, it is useful to consider the basic approach employed for dealing with the most difficult challenges in scope management—scope identification and scope control. Each of these elements of scope management could conceivably be managed in different ways. Scope identification could be implemented by means of a team brainstorming session. It could also be carried out by use of an outside facilitator with both project team and client team members present. Further, there are different tools and techniques from which to choose in managing the requirements from which the project scope is developed. Finally, different strategies for controlling scope exist—such as the implementation of a change management process or a change control board (CCB).

The "plan for a plan" approach as outlined in PMBOK 6 therefore provides project managers with the opportunity and the means to step back, think about the big picture, and establish in writing the basic strategy for managing the important elements of the project beginning with scope, time, and cost. Rather than being an unnecessary step, it is a step that once undertaken, can prevent additional planning work later in the project or the implementation of loosely defined *ad hoc* methods.

Describing Scope in Stages

Project scope starts small, and then is progressively elaborated until the entire project scope is fully understood. Projects that are fortunate enough to begin with a SOW associated with a contract have a head start in the development of project scope. However, the SOW requires further interpretation, it requires translation into specific project deliverables, and finally, it may well require some additional negotiation. Prior to the activity of fully elaborating the project scope, it is highly recommended that the project team begins with the writing of a simple scope statement. The scope statement serves multiple purposes. It captures the essence of what the project will and (equally important in the context of scope management) will not do. Also, as the elaboration of scope and the overall management of the project progresses, the scope statement is a useful point of reference for decision making as well as dispute resolution among the project team and stakeholders. To make an analogy, the government of the United States is governed by its constitution. The constitution is a highly succinct document that serves as a foundation for the extremely large body of laws that exist at all levels of government. Likewise, the scope statement is a succinct document that underpins the often elaborate full documentation of project scope.

What Should Be Included in the Scope Statement?

The scope statement is a challenge to write. There is an old saying that it is "difficult to be simple," and this saying certainly applies to the writing of the scope statement. The effort to condense the essence of the project into a few succinct paragraphs can be simplified by asking the following questions:

- What specifically will this project deliver?
- What is the primary objective of this project?
- How will the success of this project be determined and measured?
- What will not be included in this project? (Stated differently, What should be considered "out of bounds" or "out of scope?")
- What constraints should be considered in this project?
- What specific assumptions should be specifically stated?
- What are the acceptance criteria for the project deliverables?

A simple statement no more than one or a few paragraphs—not to exceed a single page—is a good start to the development of the project scope.

The WBS: What's the Point?

The scope statement is the beginning of the development of project scope. It is, however, is only the beginning of the process of the elaboration of scope. Recalling that scope is about "*what*" is to be delivered by the project, the elaboration of scope is an exercise in identifying the deliverables of the project in fine detail. It is essential though to keep the activity of scope elaboration highly organized—and to ensure that no deliverable is overlooked. It is for this reason that the next phase in scope development is the creation of the Work Breakdown Structure (WBS). The WBS is a structured outline of deliverables that is both hierarchical as well as categorical. The term "hierarchical" refers to the multiple levels of a WBS. It is the vertical (or said another way, the "top to bottom") description of the project deliverables.

Using the example of a homebuilding project, the home itself is the highest-level project deliverable. However, underneath the house in the WBS is the roof. The roof includes elements such as plywood, underlayment, shingles, and a gutter system. The sequence of house-roof-shingles-underlayment-plywood-gutter system illustrates the hierarchical view of the WBS. It is clear though that a home includes more than a roof. It also includes a foundation, exterior, interior, rooms—to name just a few. This list is an example of the horizontal or categorical view of the project that is presented in the WBS. The categories—or range of elements—that must be delivered by the project along with all levels and sublevels of deliverables include 100 percent of the scope of the project. Notice that the simple case of the "home" WBS is identical to the top-down apportioned estimate—but in this case—it lacks the percentage breakdown (Figure 5.3).

Scope = Deliverables

A description of the WBS includes frequent mention of deliverables. This is because deliverables are, in effect, the totality of the scope of the

PLANNING PERFORMANCE DOMAIN   63

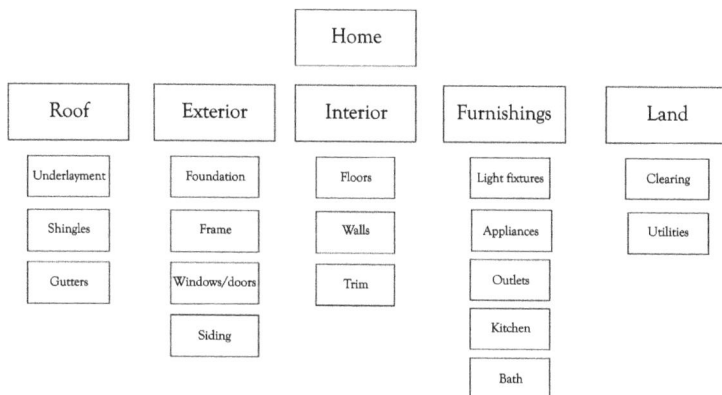

Figure 5.3 The Work Breakdown Structure (WBS)

project. It is important to note what the WBS does *not* include. The WBS does *not* include:

- Activities
- Durations
- Milestones
- Resource assignments
- Verbs (typically associated with activities)

It is recognized though that these items are important, and part of the work involved in completing a project. Why then are they not included in the WBS? This is because the WBS is an elaboration of *what* will be delivered—not who, how, or *when*. This information comes later in the project schedule. The WBS therefore is not a project schedule—and it is not a task list. It is only an outline of deliverables. However, an outline of deliverables is required to fully describe the project scope.

Why Constrain the WBS?

Given that activities, durations, and milestones are very important in projects—why should project teams be constrained to focus on only deliverables rather than activities at the early stages of scope development? There are several reasons for this. First, activities and milestones are not a part of the project scope—they are components of the project schedule. It follows then that these elements of the project plan should not be included in the WBS—which is the elaboration of scope. There is another important reason however for focusing solely on deliverables first in project planning. A project exists for a limited period and, as a result, has limited resources as authorized by the project charter. Therefore, it is important to ensure that every activity undertaken by the project must be directly linked to the deliverables that the project is expected to produce. The project must not engage in any activities that are not associated with the work of the project. The approach to project planning that first begins with the elaboration of scope as outlined in the WBS forces the project team to focus first on what needs to be delivered. Once this is complete, the project team may then focus on identifying the activities required to produce the project deliverables. In this way, no extraneous or unnecessary activities end up in the final project plan.

The Work Package: WBS or Schedule?

The WBS includes multiple levels—typically at least three. As the top-level project is broken down into the lowest level of deliverables, eventually the deliverables become of sufficient scope and scale that they could be assigned to one or more individuals for completion. The assignment of the lowest level of deliverables to project team members is typically done in the form of the work package. The work package is a management tool for assigning and tracking of work. Deliverables are included in a work package—but the work package—unlike the WBS—includes more than deliverables. The work package includes deliverables—including a description or specifications, resource assignments, duration, and budget estimates. The data that is included in the work package is administrative in nature and is designed to both assign as well as track the work that is assigned to individuals and team. Although it is often said that the work package forms the lowest level of the WBS. This is not entirely correct. The work package includes the deliverables that are specified within the lowest level of the WBS. However, the work package also includes other information that is not part of the WBS—but is a part of the schedule (such as resource assignments and task durations). Because of this, the work package should be viewed as a work assignment and administration tool that represents a transition from the development and elaboration of scope to the creation of the project schedule (Figure 5.4).

Project name:	Project manager:	Date required:
WBS code:	Activity/summary description:	Actual finish date:
Responsible team member:	Cost variance:	Time variance:
Completion comments/notes:		
Approvals/signoffs	Team lead signature/date:	Project manager signature/date:

Figure 5.4 Work package example

Time: Activities and Deliverables

The WBS identifies all project deliverables. Once the project deliverables are determined, the scope is defined and the project team begins the development of the schedule. What should the project team include in the project schedule? The activities that are required to produce the project deliverables are that which is placed in the project schedule. This requires then that the project team systematically examine the deliverables as identified in the WBS, and then identify all activities required to produce them. A test of a valid WBS is to confirm that it contains only nouns since only deliverables should be included. By way of contrast, the list of project activities that is used to populate the project schedule includes only verbs—since activities are actions that are taken to produce the deliverables outlined in the project scope. The rigorous focus on deliverables first, followed by activities helps ensure that no extraneous activities are included within the project schedule. This is a reasonable approach since the only work that is carried out within a project is that which is done to complete the fundamental mission of the project—which is to produce the project deliverables.

Putting Things in Order

This shift in focus from project deliverables to project activities signals the shift from PMBOK 6's project scope development (project scope management knowledge area), to the development of the project schedule (the project time management knowledge area). The project schedule describes how much time it takes to produce the deliverables of the project. The challenge in doing this is that the schedule requires more analysis than simply adding together the duration of each deliverable to arrive at a total time. The reason for this is that not all activities within a project schedule will follow in sequence one after another. Some activities will follow each other while others will unfold in parallel with each other. A good way to think of the series and parallel nature of project activities is to think of making a pot of coffee as a project. Several of the activities associated with making coffee must be carried out in sequence. For example, coffee may not be added to the pot until the filter is installed. Also, the brewing cycle may not start until both the water is poured and the coffee is put into the coffee maker. These activities are sequential, and one must be done before the other. Once the brewing starts, several activities may be carried out in parallel. For example, during coffee brewing—this is a good time to retrieve the cup, the spoon, the sugar, and the cream. For some who prefer this, it is also possible to add cream and sugar to the cup during the brewing cycle.

To further examine the simple example of brewing coffee, it is possible to estimate the total time, in seconds, required to brew coffee (Figure 5.5).

In this example, the time required for all coffee-brewing activities are added together. The total time required to brew the pot of coffee is determined to be 630 seconds. As mentioned previously, this time is clearly not correct since some activities fall in sequence one after the other—whereas some are in parallel. Once the parallel activities are identified, the actual time required to brew the coffee comes into clearer focus, as follows in Figure 5.6.

From inspection of the highlighted activities in the coffee example, the total brewing time becomes 605 rather than 630 seconds since Activities D, E, F, and G are carried out during the time that Activity L, "Brew Coffee" is carried out. In fact, Activities D, E, F, and G may be delayed for a significant period without delaying the overall coffee preparation time. For example, Activity D, "Get cup" requires 5 seconds. Activity L, "Brew coffee" requires 500 seconds. Because of this, it is possible to delay "Get cup" for 495 seconds and the cup will still be ready for use at exactly the right

	Activity	Seconds
A	Get coffee grounds	10
B	Get pitcher of water	10
C	Get coffee filter	5
D	Get cup	5
E	Get cream	10
F	Get sugar	5
G	Get spoon	5
H	Pour water	15
I	Put in filter	5
J	Put in coffee grounds	20
K	Turn on coffee maker	5
L	Brew coffee	500
M	Pour coffee	15
N	Add cream	5
O	Add Sugar	5
P	Stir	10
		630

Figure 5.5 Coffee-brewing activities

	Activity	Seconds
A	Get coffee grounds	10
B	Get pitcher of water	10
C	Get coffee filter	5
D	Get cup	5
E	Get cream	10
F	Get sugar	5
G	Get spoon	5
H	Pour water	15
I	Put in filter	5
J	Put in coffee grounds	20
K	Turn on coffee maker	5
L	Brew coffee	500
M	Pour coffee	15
N	Add cream	5
O	Add Sugar	5
P	Stir	10
		630

```
                          L
                          D
A B C I J H E M N O P
                          F
                          G
```

Figure 5.6 Coffee brewing with activities in parallel

moment when the coffee brewing ends. Activity D is therefore said to have 495 seconds of "slack" or "float" in the overall coffee-brewing "project."

In addition to overall project timing and slack, another important principle may be gained from inspecting the sequence of events associated with coffee brewing. Since Activities D, E, F, and G are in parallel with a much longer activity (Activity L, Brew coffee), it is observed that these activities are not on the longest path or sequence of project events. The sequence of events leading up to, including, and following Activity L make up the longest path of the project. The longest path in the project is the shortest possible period in which the brewing of coffee may be completed. The longest path in a project is referred to as the project "critical path." It is referred to as critical because a delay of any activity on the critical path will cause a delay in the overall project, see Figure 5.6. This does not infer that other activities are not important. It simply means that activities that are not on the critical path may be delayed—by the amount of slack in the activity—without delaying the overall project.

From Simple, to Complex

Brewing coffee is a relatively simple endeavor and therefore does not represent the complexity observed in most projects managed by project managers and project teams. However, the same scheduling principles are applied to all projects—regardless of complexity. They are as follows:

1. List all activities required to produce the project deliverables.
2. Order them in such a way that sequential and parallel activities are identified.
3. Identify the longest path in the project (the sequence of project activities that do not have slack—or "those activities that cannot be moved without delaying the overall project").

After Steps 1 to 3 are completed, the project manager and project team are now able to determine how much time it will take to complete all project activities, and as well, identify which activities may not be delayed without delaying the overall project. In the case of brewing coffee, these steps may be completed by inspection. A more complex and more typical project will require the use of a structured methodology that makes use of network diagrams.

What Is a Network Diagram?

A network diagram is a method for recording and analyzing the sequence of project activities and their relationships to each other. The type of network diagram most frequently employed by project managements and project management software is known as the "Activity on Node" or AON method. In this type of diagram, activities are identified by a series of boxes that are connected to each other with lines. The nodes, or boxes, contain information about the activity including the activity identifier, the duration of the activity, the amount of slack associated with the activity (SL)—as well as the earliest and latest start (ES and LS) and finish (EF and LF) time of the activity (Figure 5.7).

The information contained in each node is extensive, but it is there for a specific purpose. Each node in a network diagram contains the information required to determine the project critical path using the "Forward and Backward pass" algorithm. This analysis is known as CPM, or the "Critical Path Method." It is also sometimes referred to as PDM or the "Precedence Diagramming Method." Both labels describe the basic function of network diagrams in terms of putting the activities in order and determining the critical path.

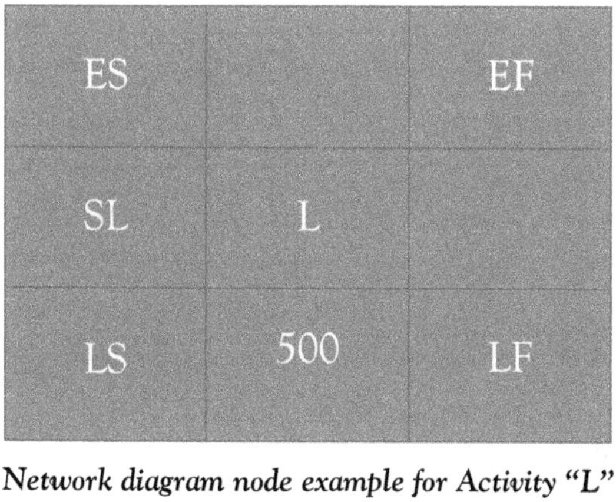

ES		EF
SL	L	
LS	500	LF

Figure 5.7 Network diagram node example for Activity "L" in coffee-brewing example

Activity on Arrow: A Different
Type of Network Diagram

The AON network with its connecting boxes complete with activity information is most commonly observed in project management software packages. It is also the most intuitive method to use when project networks are developed and analyzed manually. However, Activity on Arrow (AOA) networks are sometimes seen in projects, and they are useful for software optimization packages that seek to optimize projects for minimum duration and costs. AOA networks include activity labels on the arrows themselves instead of on the network nodes. Unlike the AON method, the nodes act simply as connectors for the arrows and may contain node labels (Figure 5.8).

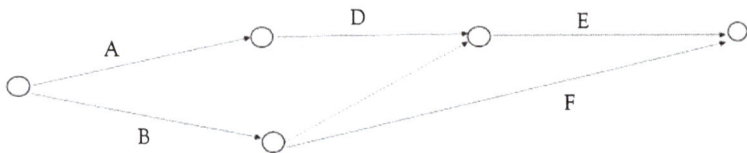

Figure 5.8 AOA network diagram

One reason that AOA diagrams are not frequently used (unless for specialized mathematical optimization applications) is the presence of "dummy" activities. In AOA, since each arrow includes both activity and duration information, there may be situations where the project manager needs to indicate a sequence of events that end at the same time—but not all previous activities are predecessors. In the earlier example, Activity E follows both B and D—but only D is an activity predecessor. Project managers should be aware of AOA networks even though as a practical matter, such project networks are developed only for specialized applications by those who understand and can interpret them. It might be asked, "If AOA networks can be misinterpreted—why use them?" The rationale behind the AOA network is simply that the connector nodes used in an AOA network make it easy to include constraint equations into an optimization package such as a spreadsheet solver (Figure 5.9).

As a simple example, the Connector Node "5" could be represented with the expression:

$$\text{``5''} < E + F$$

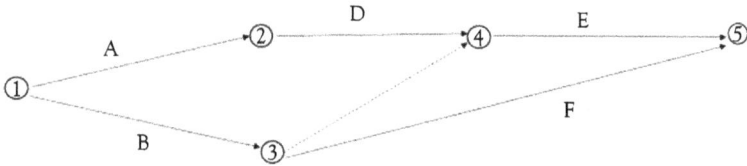

Figure 5.9 AOA *network diagram with dummy activity*

Analyzing Project Duration Using a Network Diagram

The benefits of using network diagrams to determine the critical path become clear when the critical path is not easily determined by simple inspection. A typical project scenario using CPM illustrates this.

CPM Scenario

Assume that you are a project manager within a small computer system and networking and installation company. Your company has been awarded a contract to upgrade a network of computers in a call center environment. The upgrades in the contract consist of updating the operating system and call center application residing in each of each of the computers, performing memory upgrades to those desktops that require it, and converting to a wireless LAN network. Once the contract has been analyzed and the scope statement and the WBS for the project have been created, the high-level activities required to produce the deliverables are identified and listed. The first step therefore in creating the network diagram for CPM analysis begins with the list of activities.

Activity List

1. Desktop PC evaluation
2. Call center bandwidth estimation
3. Upgrade plan
4. Procure computer memory
5. Procure wireless access equipment
6. Procure system software
7. Install wireless access equipment
8. Install PC memory and wireless cards

9. Install OS and Applications

10. Develop training materials and user guide

11. Train end users and administrator

12. Launch new system

Activity Precedence

The task list is then prepared for the development of the network diagram by establishing the order of precedence of all tasks. Establishing precedence simply involves determining what activities come before, after, or in parallel with another activity. Stated another way, this step in the processes identifies the logical progression of project activities. Each activity is labeled with an identifier as well as a predecessor (if applicable) in a corresponding table (Table 5.1).

The Network Diagram

The precedence table is then employed to create a network diagram. Each activity forms a node in the network, and the nodes are connected using lines to indicate graphically the logical flow of task (Figure 5.10).

As anticipated, a typical "real world" schedule is considerably more difficult to analyze than the simple coffee-brewing project example. From

Table 5.1 Task list for call center scenario

Identifier	Task description	Predecessor
1	Desktop PC evaluation	-
2	Call center bandwidth estimation	-
3	Upgrade plan	1
4	Procure computer memory	3
5	Procure wireless access equipment	2,3
6	Procure system software	3
7	Install wireless access equipment	5
8	Install PC memory and wireless cards	4,5
9	Install OS and Applications	6,8
10	Develop training materials and user guide	6
11	Training	7,9,10
12	Launch new system	11

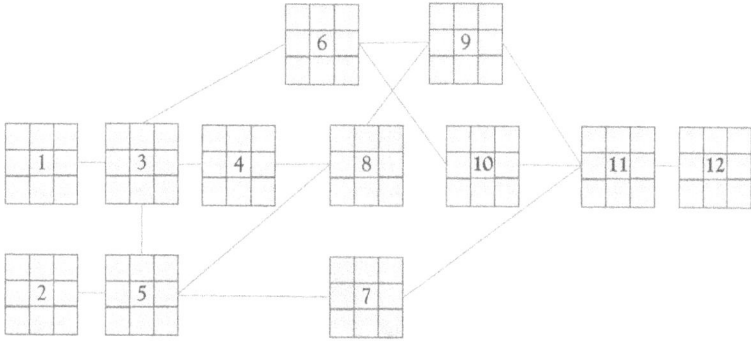

Figure 5.10 Network diagram for call center scenario

inspection of the network diagram, the logical progression of activities is clear. Several activities follow in sequence one after another, while some activities are carried out in parallel. However, the longest, or critical path in the project is by no means obvious. To continue with the CPM analysis, now that the activities are in logical order, the next step is to include the duration of each activity on the diagram. The duration of each activity was not previously stated—but is first added to the project activity list using a series of estimated durations using the expert judgment of the project manager and project team (Table 5.2).

The network diagram is then updated with the duration of each activity (Figure 5.11).

Table 5.2 Call center activities and durations

Identifier	Task description	Predecessor	Duration
1	Desktop PC evaluation	-	10
2	Call center bandwidth estimation	-	5
3	Upgrade plan	1	7
4	Procure computer memory	3	3
5	Procure wireless access equipment	2,3	4
6	Procure system software	3	3
7	Install wireless access equipment	5	10
8	Install PC memory and wireless cards	4,5	10
9	Install OS and Applications	6,8	7
10	Develop training materials and user guide	6	15
11	Training	7,9,10	7
12	Launch new system	11	1

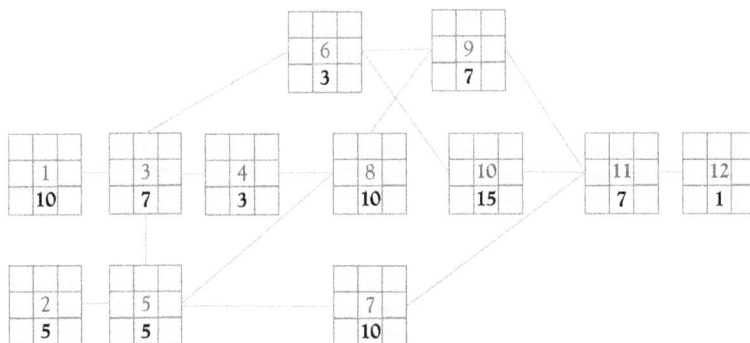

Figure 5.11 Call center network diagram with activity durations

With the duration of each activity in place, it is observed that some activities take more time than others, but the project critical path remains hidden. The CPM "Forward and Backward Pass" algorithm is the necessary next step required to reveal which activities include slack and which do not.

The Forward Pass

The forward pass calculation begins by populating the early start (or ES) box in the first node, adding the duration, and inputting the total (ES + Duration) into the early finish (or EF) box (Figure 5.12).

In the case of this sample project, Activities 1 and 2 do not have predecessors. Because of this, they both begin at time "0." To complete a forward pass for each element, take the ES time, add the duration, and

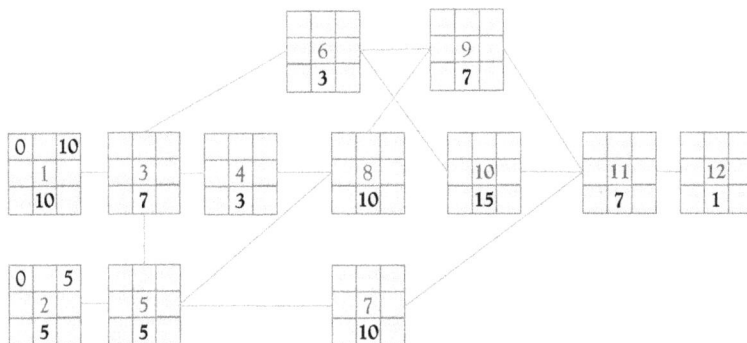

Figure 5.12 Beginning the forward pass calculation

place the total into the EF box. The general formula for the forward pass for each element is:

$$EF = ES + Activity\ Duration$$

This formula has been completed for Activities 1 and 2 in Figure 5.12.

The next step of the forward pass is carried out by moving the EF from the completed nodes and using this number as the ES of the immediately following node (Figure 5.13).

This process continues throughout the network diagram until any node is reached that is connected to two predecessors. This occurs first in Activity 5.

Forward Pass With Merging Activities

In activities in which more than one predecessor merges (such as Activity 8), the ES date is no longer a simple matter of "carrying over" the EF date of the previous node. There is, however, a common-sense approach to determining the ES date. This is done by asking the following question, "According to the diagram, when is the earliest that Activity 5 may start?" The simple answer is that "Activity 5 begins when *both* Activity 3 *and* Activity 2 are completed." At what time are both Activities 3 and 2 complete? At time 13 (the EF for Activity 3). Prior to this time, Activity 2 may be complete—but not both Activities 2 and 3. This leads to a general rule for calculating the forward pass ES times for activities with more than one predecessor (Figure 5.14):

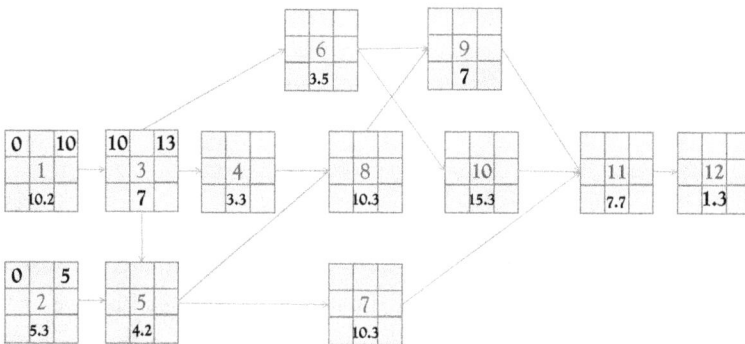

Figure 5.13 Continuing the forward pass calculation

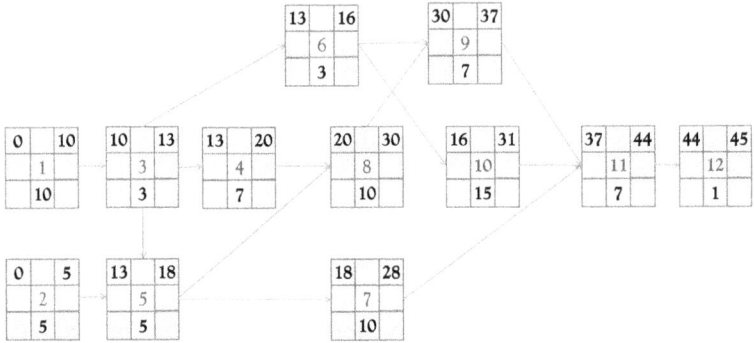

Figure 5.14 Forward pass with merge activities

When more than one activity precedes an activity in the forward pass calculation, the highest early finish date is used as the early start for the successor activity.

Using these two rules, the forward pass is completed for the network (Figure 5.15).

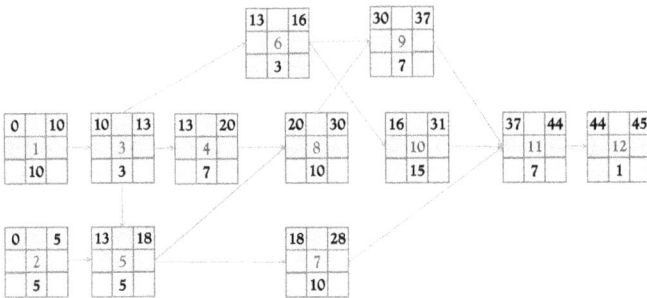

Figure 5.15 Completed forward pass calculation

The Backward Pass

The backward pass begins at the end of the network diagram and works forward toward the beginning of the schedule by taking successive Late Finish (LF) times, subtracting the duration, and arriving at the Late Start (LS) time. As a first step, the EF time of the final activity is moved "down"

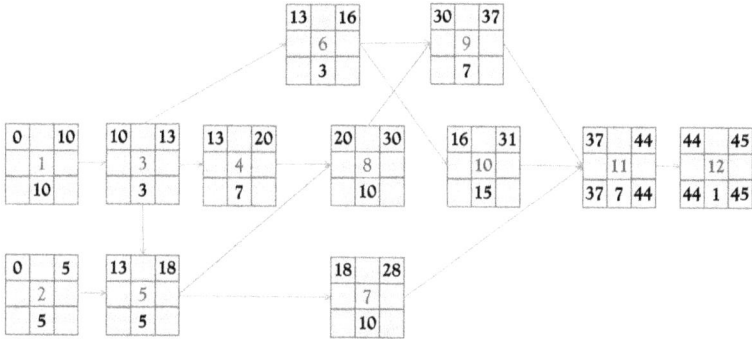

Figure 5.16 Backward pass for Activities 11 and 12

to the LF square in the final activity node. The rationale for doing this is that when the final activity has ended, the activity can finish no later than when the project is completed. For this reason, in the final project activity, the LF equals the EF. For activities directly in sequence, the backward pass process is straightforward. This process is completed for Activities 11 and 12 (Figure 5.16).

In Figure 5.17, it is observed that Activity 11 connects to Activities 7, 9, and 10 when moving from the end of the schedule to the beginning. The LS date of 37-time units is then moved forward to the LF finish date of Activities 7 through 10 as indicated in Figure 5.17.

Once again, the duration is subtracted from the LF date—in this case 37—to arrive at the LS for Activities 7 to 10 (Figure 5.18).

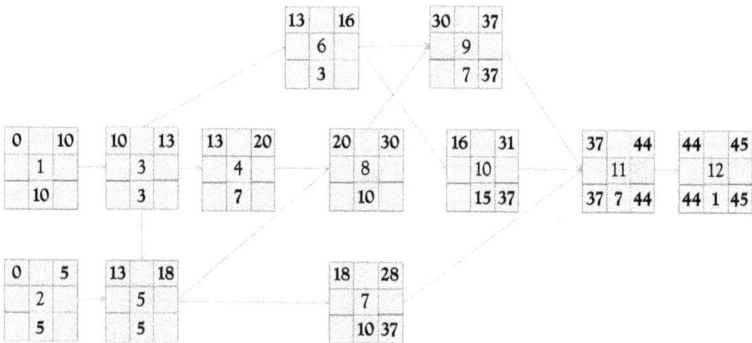

Figure 5.17 Backward pass calculation with merge activities

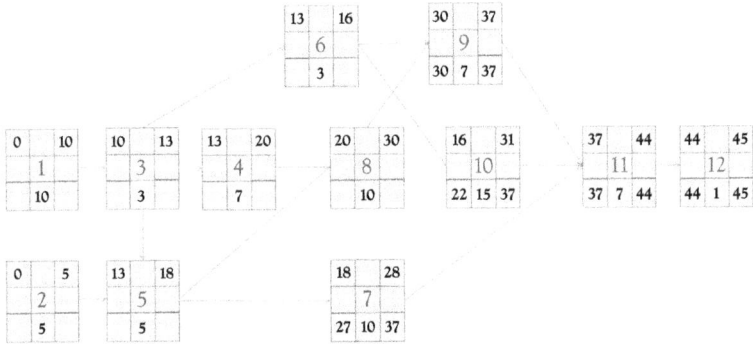

Figure 5.18 Backward pass including Activities 7–10

In the next step of the backward pass process, it is observed that Activities 9 and 10 both connect to Activity 6. Which LS date should then be carried over to become the LF date of Activity 6? This question may be answered by asking the question, "What is the latest date—in terms of time units—that Activity 6 can finish—without delaying any succeeding activities?" The answer is the date of 22 units of time. Although Activity 9 would not be delayed if Activity 6 were delayed beyond 22 units— Activity 10 would be delayed (Figure 5.19).

This leads to the next rule for the backward pass algorithm:

When more than one activity succeeds an activity in the backward pass calculation, the smallest late start date is used as the late finish for the predecessor activity.

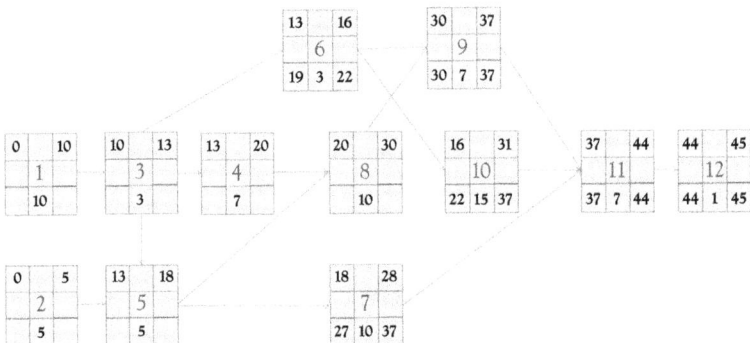

Figure 5.19 Backward pass calculation through Activity 6

The backward pass is completed in Figure 5.20.

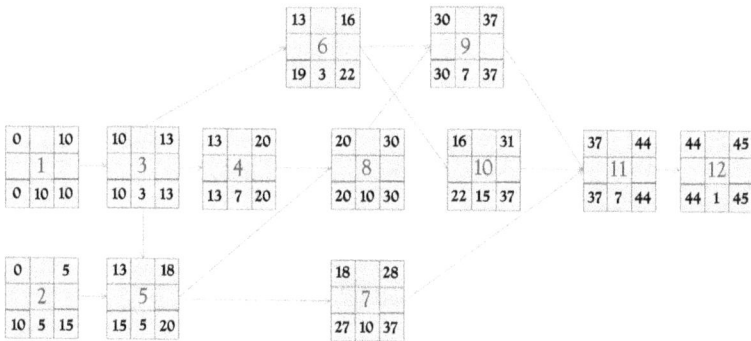

Figure 5.20 Completed backward pass calculation

The purpose of this exercise becomes clear when the difference between the ES and the LS is determined via subtraction. If there is no difference—that is—a difference of zero, then the activity is said to be on the project critical path. Why should this be so? Consider that a property of activities found on the project critical path is that any delay of that activity would delay the overall project end date. An activity with a difference of zero between the ES and LS indicates that the LS is the same as the ES. Said another way—there is no room to maneuver, and the activity cannot be delayed without delaying the overall project. To find the project critical path, simply identify all activities where the difference between the ES and LS is zero. This is completed in Figure 5.21 with the critical path highlighted in red.

Activity Slack

The term "slack" or float is used to describe the difference between the ES and LS. It is observed that activities with zero slack may not be delayed. How then should activities with positive slack be interpreted? The amount of slack indicates the period by which the activity may be delayed without delaying the overall project. Slack is found in activities that are in parallel with activities that are on the critical path. As an example, Activities 2 and 5 are in parallel with Activities 1, 3, and 4. If Activities 2 and 5 are delayed by the amount of slack in each activity, then Activity 5 would finish at the

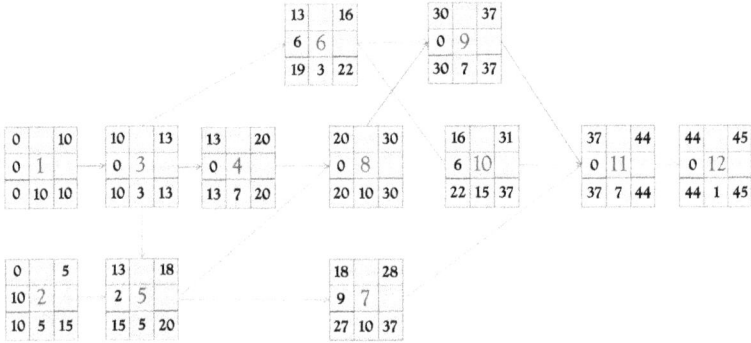

Figure 5.21 Critical path identified

LF of time 20. Since Activity 4 on the critical path also finishes at time 20, then the delay equal to the amount of slack in Activities 2 and 5 does not delay the overall schedule (Figure 5.22).

If Activities 2 and 5 did exceed the slack for both activities, the sequence would finish later than 20 units of time and would then delay Activity 8. Since Activity 8 is on the critical path, this delay would then delay the overall project. Slack therefore allows for delays in activities corresponding to the amount of slack—but—exceeding the amount of available slack delays the entire project.

The critical path activities are now highlighted in tabular form along with the total project duration equating to the duration of all activities on the critical path (Table 5.3).

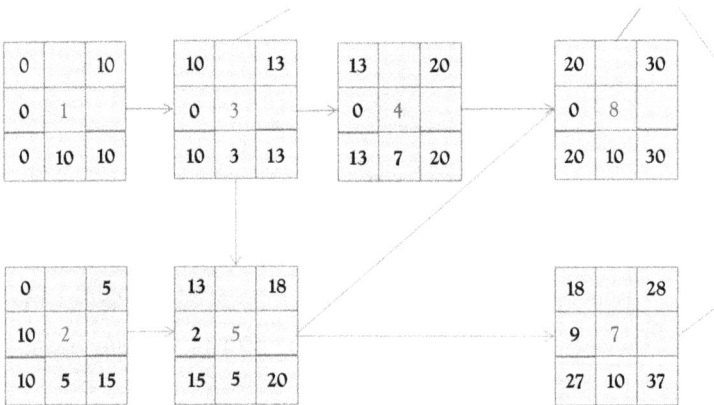

Figure 5.22 Slack in parallel activities

Table 5.3 Critical path in tabular form

Identifier	Task description	Predecessor	Duration
1	Desktop PC evaluation	-	10
2	Call center bandwidth estimation	-	5
3	Upgrade plan	1	7
4	Procure computer memory	3	3
5	Procure wireless access equipment	2,3	4
6	Procure system software	3	3
7	Install wireless access equipment	5	10
8	Install PC memory and wireless cards	4,5	10
9	Install OS and Applications	6,8	7
10	Develop training materials and user guide	6	15
11	Training	7,9,10	7
12	Launch new system	11	1
Total		45	

CPM and Sensitivity

The term "sensitivity" refers to the critical path and its propensity to "wander" as the project moves from planning and into project execution. As each activity in the project is carried out, some activities take longer than planned—while others may take less time than initially envisioned. Because of the natural fluctuation in project execution, the path that was initially identified as the critical path may no longer be the critical path. A different path may have taken the place of the original critical path. The degree to which this is more or less likely to occur is referred to as the project sensitivity. If the duration of the project critical path is close to the duration of a noncritical path, the project is said to be highly sensitive. If the critical path is significantly different in duration from other paths in the project, then the project network is not sensitive.

Overall Observations on the CPM

The purpose of the network diagram within the CPM is to organize all activities in the logical order of activity precedence so that the project critical path—the longest path in the project—may be determined. Knowing which specific sequence of activities in the network that may not be delayed is important for management purposes—but, it also definitively determines the overall project duration. Without the analysis of the critical path, the overall project duration would not be obvious. For instance, the multiple parallel paths along with the two activities in parallel at the beginning of the network diagram in this example illustrate the difficulty of assessing the project duration by simple inspection of a list of activities and predecessors. The CPM also informs the project manager regarding how much room to maneuver exists when scheduling activities that are not on the critical path. Finally, it should be noted that the forward and backward pass algorithm is a manual process that is completed automatically in project management software packages—providing that the activities, duration, and activity precedence are entered correctly. When project schedules are developed manually, the CPM using the forward and backward pass algorithm is the most straightforward approach.

Going Beyond CPM: The PERT Method

An implicit assumption throughout the development of a schedule using the CPM is that the duration of all activities in the project are well understood. Another way to say this is that CPM is "deterministic"—the activity of each duration is known, and it is fixed. Unfortunately, this is not an ideal model for developing project schedules in the real world. Real projects consist of activities with durations that are estimated rather than certain and are not fixed. This is true for many reasons including normal variation, unanticipated difficulty in completing the activity, or unexpected work interruption. The Program Evaluation and Review Technique, or PERT, methodology provides tools for considering the expected variation in the duration of project activities. Additionally, PERT provides statistical techniques for calculating the probability of achieving a specific target schedule duration. Finally, the PERT method of using estimates instead of fixed activity durations is ideal for garnering support and buy-in from sponsors, clients, and other senior-level stakeholders. For example, a project manager is free to poll senior management for PERT estimates instead of being the sole source of project duration estimates.

Different, Yet Similar

PERT analysis does differ from the CPM by virtue of its statistical approach including three-point estimates that are combined using a type of weighted average. However, PERT analysis follows the same approach that is employed by CPM. Both methods use network diagrams, and both use the forward and backward pass algorithm to identify the project critical path. Since in most cases project durations are not known with certainty, and so much is common to both CPM and PERT analysis, many project managers will often use the two terms interchangeably.

Beginning a PERT Analysis

The PERT is a method used to examine the tasks in a schedule and determine a CPM variation. The first step in PERT analysis is the same as the CPM. The list of activities required to produce deliverables in the WBS along with the accompanying logical predecessors is collected in a list or table. The PERT methodology can be illustrated using the CPM scenario described earlier and beginning with the activity and predecessor list (Table 5.4).

Table 5.4 Activity list for PERT analysis

Identifier	Task description	Predecessor
1	Desktop PC evaluation	-
2	Call center bandwidth estimation	-
3	Upgrade plan	1
4	Procure computer memory	3
5	Procure wireless access equipment	2,3
6	Procure system software	3
7	Install wireless access equipment	5
8	Install PC memory and wireless cards	4,5
9	Install OS and Applications	6,8
10	Develop training materials and user guide	6
11	Training	7,9,10
12	Launch new system	11

Unlike CPM, the duration of each activity is not assumed to be known with certainty. Instead of fixed durations, PERT incorporates three estimates including the best-case (BC) estimate, the worst-case (WC) estimate, and finally, the most-likely (ML) estimate for each project activity. The three estimates are combined using a form of weighted average. The weighted average formula used for these estimates is:

$$\frac{BC + 4\,ML + WC}{6}$$

Why use this specific formula for the weighted average? This formula is derived from a special statistical distribution known as the "Beta Distribution." It is useful in PERT analysis for its ability to incorporate both BC and WC estimates while weighting the ML estimate more strongly. Knowledge of this distribution as well as other statistical distributions that might be employed are necessary only for the most advanced analysis. Therefore, the implementation of the simple formula is all that is needed to use PERT in practice.

From Where Are the Estimates Obtained?

Estimates often flow naturally from the application of expert judgment of project team members. On the other hand, the PERT estimating process provides an avenue for senior level stakeholders to become directly involved in estimating the project duration. This can be important for project managers since in most cases, the target schedule results from a negotiation between the project team, the client, and project sponsors. One means for doing this is to bring together senior stakeholders by holding a high-level schedule estimation meeting. When high-level activity duration input is collected from senior stakeholders within the setting of a schedule development workshop meeting, the risks, and implications of the agreed on final project schedule dates may become more obvious. The ability of the PERT methodology to quickly provide probability calculations for achieving a schedule on a particular date offers feedback to senior sponsors on the schedule risk that often would not be otherwise forthcoming.

Building the Estimated PERT Schedule

Once the PERT estimates are acquired—either through project team member expert judgment—or in the ideal case of a stakeholder schedule development workshop—the BC, WC, and ML estimates are collected in tabular form in the same way as the CPM. For the sake of simplicity, the ML durations are taken from the fixed durations used in the CPM scenario (Table 5.5).

As a next step, the three estimates for each activity are combined using the PERT weighted average formula (Table 5.6).

Table 5.5 PERT activity estimates

Identifier	Task description	Predecessor	BC	ML	WC
1	Desktop PC evaluation	-	7	10	14
2	Call center bandwidth estimation	-	3	5	10
3	Upgrade plan	1	4	7	10
4	Procure computer memory	3	2	3	7
5	Procure wireless access equipment	2, 3	3	4	8
6	Procure system software	3	2	3	7
7	Install wireless access equipment	5	7	10	14
8	Install PC memory and wireless cards	4, 5	7	10	14
9	Install OS and Applications	6, 8	3	7	10
10	Develop training materials and user guide	6	10	15	21
11	Training	7, 9, 10	4	7	14
12	Launch new system	11	1	1	3

Table 5.6 PERT weighted average of activity estimates

Identifier	Task description	Predecessor	Duration
1	Desktop PC evaluation		10.2
2	Call center bandwidth estimation		5.5
3	Upgrade plan	1	7

(Continued)

Table 5.6 (Continued)

4	Procure computer memory	3	3.5
5	Procure wireless access equipment	2,3	4.5
6	Procure system software	3	3.5
7	Install wireless access equipment	5	10.2
8	Install PC memory and wireless cards	4,5	10.2
9	Install OS and Applications	6,8	6.8
10	Develop training materials and user guide	6	15.2
11	Training	7,9,10	7.7
12	Launch new system	11	1.3

It is observed that the calculation of the weighted average results in fractional time periods. What do fractional time durations mean to a project manager? This will depend upon what units of time are being used in the project. However, in PERT analysis, it is recommended that fractional durations be evaluated once the final analysis is complete. If the fractional unit of time is sufficiently important to the project, it may be retained in the project schedule. Alternatively, the fractional time units might be rounded up to the next period. When PERT analysis is carried out using a spreadsheet (and it often is), fractional durations are easily managed.

The PERT Network Diagram

Once the durations are calculated, the network diagram may be analyzed in the same manner as the CPM by means of the forward and backward pass algorithm. The network diagram is initially constructed using the PERT weighted average durations (Figure 5.23).

Once the initial network diagram with PERT durations is constructed, the forward pass algorithm is applied (Figure 5.24).

The backward pass algorithm is applied in the same manner as the CPM method. It is important to remember, for correct analysis, the two rules of thumb for the forward and backward pass algorithm (Figure 5.25).

Forward pass: The largest EF duration for multiple activities converging into a single activity is "carried over" to become the ES of the succeeding activity.

Backward pass: The smallest LS duration for multiple activities converging into a single activity is "carried over" to become the LF of the preceding activity.

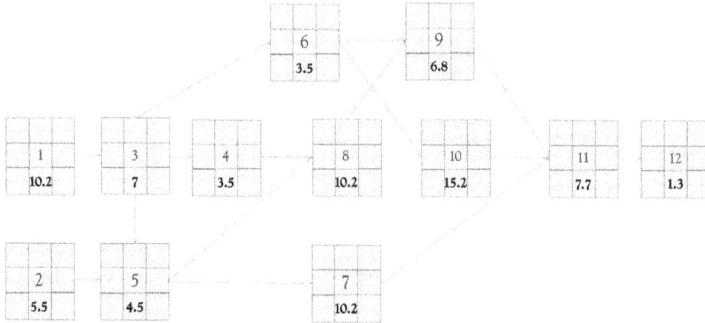

Figure 5.23 PERT network diagram

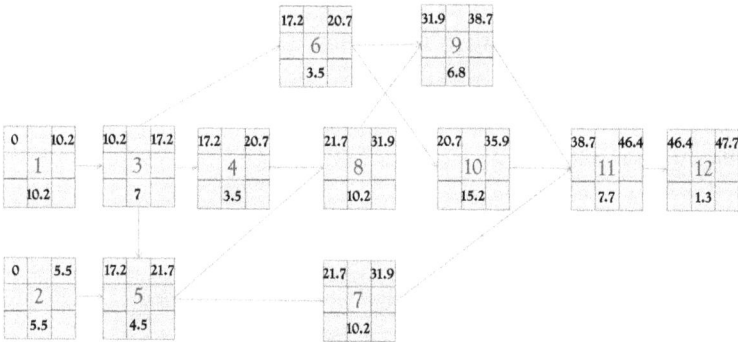

Figure 5.24 PERT forward pass calculation

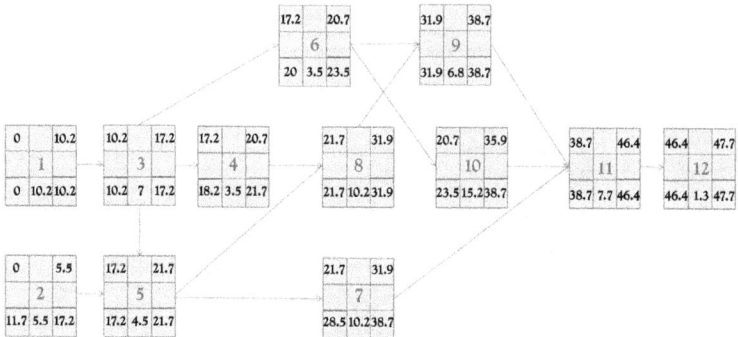

Figure 5.25 PERT backward pass calculation

The project critical path is then identified by taking the difference between the ES and the LS. The project critical path based on the PERT activity estimates is shown in Figure 5.26.

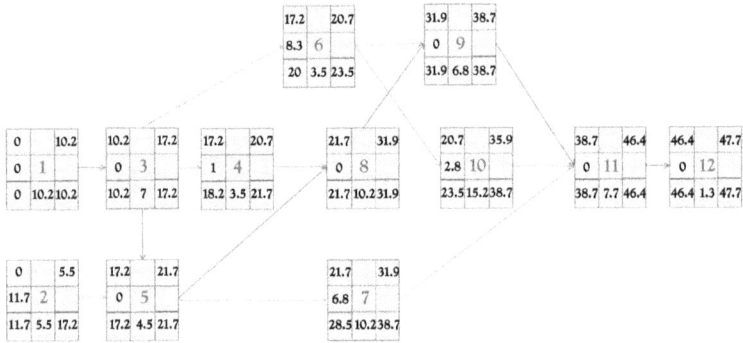

Figure 5.26 **PERT critical path identification**

The PERT critical path is highlighted in a tabular view of the project activities. The critical path analysis using the PERT estimates changed many of the overall activity durations and changed the critical path sequence. Further, the overall project length was extended by almost three units of time (Table 5.7).

Table 5.7 **PERT critical path in tabular form**

Identifier	Task description	Predecessor	Duration
1	Desktop PC evaluation	-	10.2
2	Call center bandwidth estimation	-	5.5
3	Upgrade plan	1	7
4	Procure computer memory	3	3.5
5	Procure wireless access equipment	2,3	4.5
6	Procure system software	3	3.5
7	Install wireless access equipment	5	10.2
8	Install PC memory and wireless cards	4,5	10.2
9	Install OS and Applications	6,8	6.8
10	Develop training materials and user guide	6	15.2
11	Training	7,9,10	7.7
12	Launch new system	11	1.3
Total		47.7	

At this stage of the PERT analysis process, it would appear that PERT has accomplished only three things:

1. Provided a means for collecting and using estimates from key stakeholders.
2. Created a schedule with a more realistic overall duration.
3. The sensitivity of the critical path to changes in activity durations for noncritical path activities was uncovered. (This is evident given the shift of the critical path observed once the project activity durations were changed based upon the weighted average of duration estimates.)

Although the PERT estimated schedule is an improvement, the most important benefit of applying this form of analysis is the ability to predict the probability of achieving a specific project target date. Using these features of PERT analysis, however, requires some familiarity with basic statistics.

The Weighted Average and the Project Average

The important benefits of PERT analysis derive from the fact that activity duration estimates are formed using weighted averages. Although the weighted averages of the activities individually use the beta distribution rather than the normal distribution—known as "the normal curve"—the collection of all weighted averages of activities found on the critical path do approximate the normal distribution, and when summed, form an overall project mean. The reasons for this are theoretical and go beyond the topic of project probability estimation. What is important is that the PERT estimated weighted averages of critical path activities lead to a project mean that corresponds with the common normal curve. This is significant in project duration estimating due to the link between the normal curve and probability estimation.

The Normal Curve and Probability

Properties that are sampled in nature often follow the normal curve. For example, demographic characteristics such as height, age, and income are normally distributed (Figure 5.27).

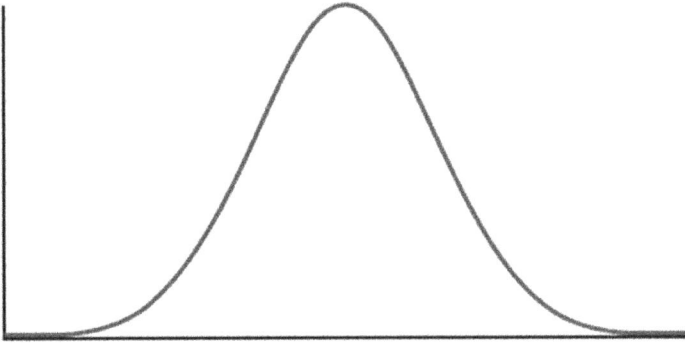

Figure 5.27 The normal curve

This is because when measuring such characteristics, the probability of falling near the center of the curve (average or mean) is higher than falling far from the center. Samples that occur far from the center are often referred to as outliers. This phenomenon may be observed in the distribution formed by dropping marbles through a series of pegs. As can be seen in Figure 5.28, most marbles tend to gather around the center of the distribution (Figure 5.28).

Figure 5.28 Marble distribution normal curve

It is less likely, or probable, for marbles to fall far from the center of the distribution. The property of being near or far from the mean can be viewed as a measure of its probability. An inspection of the marble game illustrates how the area of the curve (i.e., sections that contain more versus less marbles) relates to the likelihood of marbles being found in each individual slot. Calculating probability however requires some method of measuring the distance from the center of the normal curve. Distance in terms of the normal curve is given by a measure known as the standard deviation. The standard deviation is referred to by the Greek letter sigma (σ). Project managers may be familiar with the term "Six Sigma" commonly used in industry. This refers to "six standard deviations from the mean"—or, from the center of the normal curve—since the mean is located at the center of the normal curve. Six standard deviations are distant from the mean and would be representative of values that are associated with a very low probability of occurrence. This is the point of six sigma quality management—to achieve an extremely small number of defects.

Units of Project Time and Probability

Project management makes use of the center of the normal curve and the standard deviation in PERT analysis to determine if the units of time established for the target schedule duration are likely or unlikely to be achieved. The probability of the project duration being achieved is based upon their distance from the center or mean of the normal curve. The essence then of PERT probability analysis is to convert project units of time into "number of standard deviations" so that project target dates may be envisioned in terms of standard deviations from the mean. Once this is done, the probability associated with that distance from the mean may be calculated. If the project mean ("average") and standard deviation ("how wide the project normal curve is in terms of time units") are known, the probability of achieving the project schedule target date may then be calculated.

Measuring Standard Deviations

The exact measure of probability associated with the number of standard deviations is provided by a reference known as a "Z table." The "Z" in the Z table is interpreted as "number of standard deviations"—and typically "number of standard deviations from the mean." The number associated with each Z value within a Z table corresponds to the probability value associated with a particular Z value. Another way to think of the Z value in this case is that it answers the question, "What is the probability that a marble will be found 'Z' number of standard deviations from the center, or mean of the distribution?" For example, a Z value of "1.5" refers to "1.5 standard deviations above the mean." Likewise, a Z value of –1.5 refers to "1.5 standard deviations below the mean." Referring to the marble game, the greater the distance from the center, the less likely it is that marbles will be found. Likewise, when measuring properties in nature such as height, once the mean height and standard deviation of the population is known, it is possible to calculate the probability of having a height measurement that exist in standard deviation multiples (such as +/- 1.5 Z) above or below the population mean.

Using the Z Table

A Z table consists of rows and columns each beginning with zero and increasing in decimal increments. To use a Z table, the Z probability is found by combining the first two Z digits in the column to the far left with the last two Z digits in the row across the top of the table. Then, the probability is found at the intersection of row and column. For example, a Z value of 1.000 (Row value of 1.0 plus column value of .00) corresponds with a probability of approximately 34 percent (.3413). Likewise, a Z value of 1.55 (Row value of 1.5 plus column value of .05) equates to a probability of approximately 44 percent (.4394), and finally, a Z value of 2.000 (Row value of 2.0 plus column value of .00) corresponds to a probability of approximately 48 percent (.4772) (Figure 5.29).

Approximating Probabilities

While a Z table provides exact probabilities, it is not typical for project managers or team members to have a Z table readily available. Probabilities however may be estimated directly from the normal curve. This is because there are simple rules of thumb that may be used to approximate normal curve, and therefore, schedule probabilities. Referring to the Z table, note that a Z value of 1, or +1 SD is associated with 94 • Project Management a probability of approximately 34 percent. Taken together

	.00	.01	.02	.03	.04	.05	.06	.07	.08	.09
0.0	.0000	.0040	.0080	.0120	.0160	.0199	.0239	.0279	.0319	.0359
0.1	.0398	.0438	.0478	.0517	.0557	.0596	.0636	.0675	.0714	.0753
0.2	.0793	.0832	.0871	.0910	.0948	.0987	.1026	.1064	.1103	.1141
0.3	.1179	.1217	.1255	.1293	.1331	.1700	.1406	.1443	.1480	.1517
0.4	.1554	.1591	.1628	.1664	.1700	.1736	.1772	.1808	.1844	.1879
0.5	.1915	.1950	.1985	.2019	.2054	.2088	.2123	.2157	.2190	.2224
0.6	.2257	.2291	.2324	.2357	.2389	.2422	.2454	.2486	.2517	.2549
0.7	.2580	.2611	.2642	.2673	.2704	.2734	.2764	.2794	.2823	.2852
0.8	.2881	.2910	.2939	.2967	.2995	.3023	.3051	.3078	.3106	.3133
0.9	.3159	.3186	.3212	.3238	.3264	.3289	.3315	.3340	.3365	.3389
1.0	.3413	.3438	.3461	.3485	.3508	.3531	.3554	.3577	.3599	.3621
1.1	.3643	.3665	.3686	.3708	3729	.3749	.3770	.3790	.3810	.3830
1.2	.3849	.3869	.3888	.3907	.3925	.3944	.3962	.3980	.3997	.4015
1.3	.4032	.4049	.4066	.4082	.4099	.4115	.4131	.4147	.4162	.4177
1.4	.4192	.4207	.4222	.4236	.4251	.4265	.4279	.4292	.4306	.4319
1.5	.4332	.4345	.4357	.4370	.4382	.4394	.4406	.4418	.4429	.4441
1.6	.4452	.4463	.4474	.4484	.4495	.4505	.4515	.4525	.4535	.4545
1.7	.4554	.4564	.4573	.4582	.4591	.4599	.4608	.4616	.4625	.4633
1.8	.4641	.4649	.4656	.4664	.4671	.4678	.4686	.4693	.4699	.4706
1.9	.4713	.4719	.4726	.4732	.4738	.4744	.4750	.4756	.4761	.4767
2.0	.4772	.4778	.4783	.4788	.4793	.4798	.4803	.4808	4812	.4817
2.1	.4821	.4826	.4830	.4834	.4838	.4842	.4846	.4850	.4854	.4857
2.2	.4861	.4864	.4868	.4871	.4875	.4878	.4881	.4884	.4887	.4890
2.3	.4893	.4896	.4898	.4901	.4904	.4906	.4909	.4911	.4913	.4916
2.4	.4918	.4920	.4922	.4925	.4927	.4929	.4931	.4932	.4934	.4936
2.5	.4938	.4940	.4941	.4943	.4945	.4946	.4948	.4949	.4951	.4952
2.6	.4953	.4955	.4956	.4957	.4959	.4960	.4961	.4962	.4963	.4964
2.7	.4965	.4966	.4967	.4968	.4969	.4970	.4971	.4972	.4973	.4974
2.8	.4974	.4975	.4976	.4977	.4977	.4978	.4979	.4979	.4980	.4981
2.9	.4981	.4982	.4982	.4983	.4984	.4984	.4985	.4985	.4986	.4986
3.0	.4987	.4987	.4987	.4988	.4988	.4989	.4989	.4989	.4990	.4988
3.1	.4990	4991	.4991	.4991	.4992	.4992	.4992	.4992	.4993	.4993
3.2	.4993	.4993	.4994	.4994	.4994	.4994	.4994	.4995	.4995	.4995
3.3	.4995	.4995	.4995	.4996	.4996	.4996	.4996	.4996	.4996	.4997
3.4	.4997	.4997	.4997	.4997	.4997	.4997	.4997	.4997	.4997	.4998
3.5	.4998	.4998	.4998	.4998	.4998	.4998	.4998	.4998	.4998	.4998
	.00	.01	.02	.03	.04	.05	.06	.07	.08	.09

Figure 5.29 Z table

with −1 SD, it may be observed that +/− 1 SD corresponds with (2*34) or 68 percent of the area of the curve. Stated another way, "there is a 68 percent chance in the marble game for a marble to be found between +/− 1 SD of the center" or "there is a 68 percent chance that an individual will have a height measurement falling between +/− 1 SD of the population mean (Figure 5.30)."

Likewise, it is observed that a Z value of 2.000 corresponds to a probability of approximately 45 percent (0.4772). Taken together with −2SD, it can be seen that +/− 2 SD corresponds with approximately 95 percent of the area

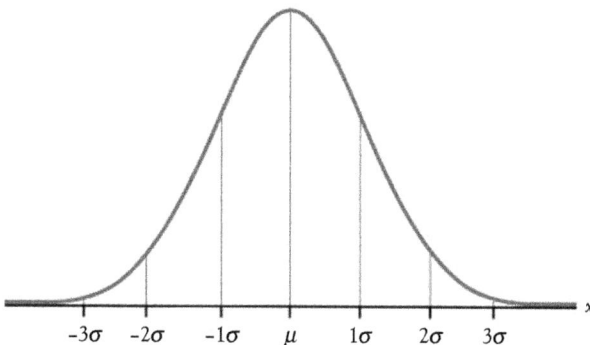

Figure 5.30 Normal curve with "rules of thumb"

of the curve. Finally, by inspection of the normal curve, +/– 3 SD corresponds with approximately 99 percent of the area of the normal curve (Table 5.8).

Table 5.8 *The normal curve rules of thumb*

Standard deviation	Probability
+/– 1 SD	≈68%
+/– 2 SD	≈95%
+/– 3 SD	≈99%

The "50 Percent Rule"

The "68–95–99" rule of thumb is used to approximate project schedule probability by using this in conjunction with the "50 percent rule" for the mean. The mean falls in the center of the normal curve. It is therefore at the 50 percent point of the area of the curve being one-half of the area of the curve when starting from zero. Using this property of the normal curve, a point of +1 SD from the beginning of the normal curve is found to correspond with a probability of approximately 84 percent. This is because from zero to the mean or midpoint of the curve is 50 percent of the area, and from the mean to +1 SD equates to 34 percent of the area of the normal curve. Therefore, 50 percent plus 34 percent is 84 percent of the area of the curve. Likewise, a point corresponding to –1 SD is equivalent to 50 percent (the distance from 0 to the mean) minus 1 SD—or –34 percent of the area of the normal curve. As a result, 50 percent minus 34 percent corresponds with a probability of approximately 16 percent. Using these properties of the normal curve, and extrapolating between points on the normal curve, the schedule probability may be estimated for any number of project standard deviations calculated in PERT analysis (Figure 5.31).

Converting Schedule Time Units to Standard Deviations

Returning to the PERT call center schedule scenario, observe that the PERT process progressed through the following steps:

1. Identify project activities (activities required to produce the deliverables in the work breakdown structure).
2. Identify the logical sequence of activities (activity predecessors and successors).

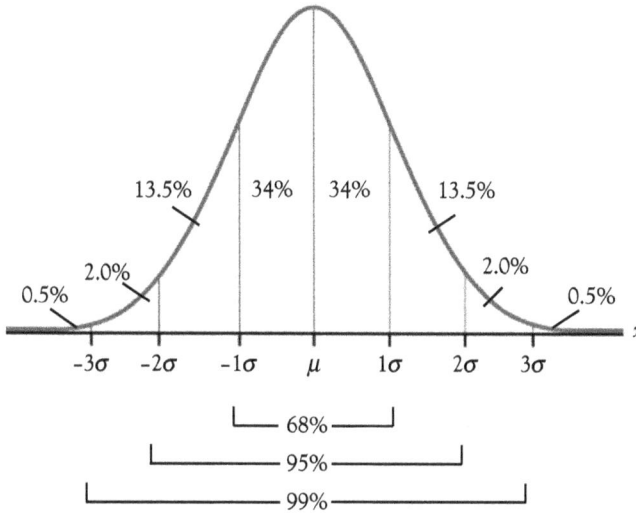

Figure 5.31 Rules of thumb illustrated

3. Determine the PERT weighted average estimates of each activity by:
   (a) Obtaining an estimate for the BC, ML, and WC duration for each activity.
   (b) Calculating the weighted average for each estimate using the Beta Distribution (carried out in practice by the formula):

$$\frac{BC + 4 * ML + WC}{6}$$

4. Create a network diagram using the logical sequence of activities and PERT durations.
5. Determine the critical path using the forward and backward pass algorithm.

The only difference observed between CPM and PERT analysis is Step 3, the duration calculation. Other than this difference, PERT is approached in the same way as CPM.

The Significance of the Project Mean

Once Step 5 in the PERT analysis process is complete, the estimated schedule duration is known. This is because of the summing of the three-point duration estimates of the critical path activities. It is of interest to note that the duration of the PERT estimated schedule corresponds with a 50 percent probability. This is because the duration is a mean resulting from the summation of the weighted averages (i.e., means) of the critical path activity durations. The mean resides at the midpoint of the normal curve and, as observed in the analysis of the normal curve rules of thumb, corresponds to a 50 percent area under the curve—or probability. Project managers would be prudent to highlight this fact when using a team of stakeholders to derive project estimates (Figure 5.32).

The result of the best guesses of the project duration has only a 50-50 chance of being realized. A project with only a 50 percent chance of successfully meeting its duration estimate is no better than the flip of a coin and is generally too risky to undertake for most projects. Further, it is clear that the duration should not be reduced. A proposed schedule reduction would guarantee a project date achievement probability of less than 50 percent. This is because a proposed schedule reduction results in a duration that is less than the project mean. Moving from the project mean toward the origin of the normal curve moves the schedule probability from 50 percent to a value that quickly approaches zero. The project manager is in a good position therefore to suggest that the probability of schedule completion be increased. How would the probability be increased? It could be increased by adding additional time to the schedule. Doing so increases the project schedule probability from 50 percent to a value that quickly approaches 100 percent. Adding time to a schedule is best done systematically—with a typical target probability

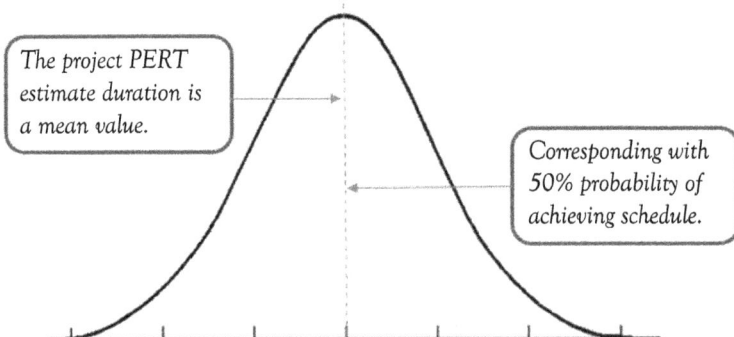

Figure 5.32 Project mean significance

of achievement in mind. A typical target achievement probability used in project management is 95 percent. When the project manager seeks to achieve a specific schedule duration probability, this requires that the project manager and team be able to associate project units of time with normal curve standard deviations. Then, a target duration such as 95 percent is accomplished by adding time to the project consistent with the right standard deviation multiplier.

Determining the Project Standard Deviation

The first step in finding the project standard deviation is taken by finding the variance of each activity on the critical path. Although this may appear to be a rather daunting prospect, the variance of each critical path activity is determined by using a very simple formula:

$$\left(\frac{WC - BC}{6}\right)^2$$

The variances of each critical path activity are then added together:

$$\sum\left(\frac{WC - BC}{6}\right)^2$$

Then, the square root is taken of the sum of the variances:

$$\sqrt{\left(\sum\left(\frac{WC - BC}{6}\right)^2\right)}$$

Notice that only the variances for the critical path activities are calculated. The critical path determines the overall project duration—so, the variances of additional activities are not required. Therefore, the critical path is identified prior to the variance and standard deviation calculation work is performed. By focusing on the only path that counts—the critical path—unnecessary work is avoided.

Variance Calculations

The variance calculations for the call center scenario are given in Table 5.9. It is evident that the simple "square root of the sum of the variances" formula lends itself to spreadsheet formulas (Table 5.9).

Table 5.9 Variance calculations

Identifier	Task description	Predecessor	BC	ML	WC	Var
1	Desktop PC evaluation	-	7	10	14	1.36
2	Call center bandwidth estimation	-	3	5	10	
3	Upgrade plan	1	4	7	10	1
4	Procure computer memory	3	2	3	7	
5	Procure wireless access equipment	2,3	3	4	8	
6	Procure system software	3	2	3	7	
7	Install wireless access equipment	5	7	10	14	
8	Install PC memory and wireless cards	4,5	7	10	14	1.36
9	Install OS and Applications	6,8	3	7	10	1.36
10	Develop training materials and user guide	6	10	15	21	
11	Training	7,9,10	4	7	14	2.78
12	Launch new system	11	1	1	3	0.11
Sum						7.97
SD						2.82

The project SD is 2.82, and, referring again to the duration of the call center project, the project mean, or PERT estimated time, is 47.7 units of time (Table 5.10).

Given the understanding of the rules of thumb for calculating probability from the normal curve, the following immediate observations arise from the project standard deviation calculation:

Observation 1: The project has a 50-50 chance of completion by 47.7 units of time.

Observation 2: The project has an approximately 68 percent chance of being completed between 50.52 and 44.88 units of time. (+/– 1 SD, or, as determined by the project PERT calculations, +/– 2.82 days). *Observation 3:* The project has a 95 percent chance of being completed between 53.35 and 42.05 units of time. (+/– 2 SD, or, as determined by the project PERT calculations, 2* (+/– 2.82) units of time).

Table 5.10 PERT duration estimate

Identifier	Task description	Predecessor	Duration
1	Desktop PC evaluation	-	10.2
2	Call center bandwidth estimation	-	5.5
3	Upgrade plan	1	7
4	Procure computer memory	3	3.5
5	Procure wireless access equipment	2,3	4.5
6	Procure system software	3	3.5
7	Install wireless access equipment	5	10.2
8	Install PC memory and wireless cards	4,5	10.2
9	Install OS and Applications	6,8	6.8
10	Develop training materials and user guide	6	15.2
11	Training	7,9,10	7.7
12	Launch new system	11	1.3
Total		47.7	

Practical Use of PERT Analysis

Although this is interesting information produced by PERT analysis, what is more useful is to understand the impact of reducing the schedule from the PERT estimate and to know the project duration associated with a 95 percent probability target date. Often, after working with stakeholders to obtain PERT estimates and arriving at the mean, or "50 percent probability schedule," the first request from senior stakeholders is to reduce the project by a certain number of days or time units. The project manager can address such a request by:

1. Converting the units of time into "number of project standard deviations;" and
2. Subtracting the resulting probability from 50 percent—since 50 percent is the starting point for PERT schedule probability.

Using the call center schedule example, assume that stakeholders have requested that the project team commit to finishing the schedule five days—or five units of time—early. Five units is a round number and typical of a schedule reduction request. Since the project SD was determined to be 2.82 units, reducing the schedule by five units of time is equivalent to reducing the schedule by:

$$\frac{5}{2.82} = 1.77 \ SD$$

This is almost 2 SD. Referring to the 68–95–99 rules of thumb for the normal curve, it is observed that –1 SD is approximately equal to 16 percent probability, and –2 SD is associated with an approximately 2.5 percent probability. Using the rules of thumb does not lead to exact probabilities—but in the context of schedule negotiation—the point is clearly made in this context that reducing the schedule by five days leads to a schedule that has only a very limited probability of successfully achieving the reduced schedule (in this case, between 2.5 and 16 percent by observation of the normal curve rules of thumb).

What Is an Acceptable Duration?

Once stakeholders are informed of the reduced schedule probability, the question arises, "What project duration would we be certain to achieve?" While no project duration may be guaranteed with complete certainty, a 95 percent probability is considered desirable for planning purposes. The challenge for the project manager is to point out to stakeholders what project duration would lead to a 95 percent probability. This may be done by finding the number of standard deviations on a Z Table that corresponds with a 95 percent probability. From inspection of the Z table, a Z value of 1.65 leads is associated with an approximate 95 percent probability (Figure 5.33).

This is determined by cross-referencing Row 1.6 with Column .05 and noting the intersection of .4505. By inspection, this appears to be only 45 percent. However, recall that this percentage represents the area between the mean and 1.65 SD above the mean. When the area between 0 and the mean is included, .5 is added to .4505 thereby resulting in 95.05 percent. The 1.65 number is a good one for project managers to remember given the desirability of a 95 percent schedule probability. However, the 95 percent target can also be approximated from the normal curve rules of thumb. Recalling that +1 SD equates to an 84 percent (50 percent

	.00	.01	.02	.03	.04	.05	.06	.07	.08	.09
0.0	.0000	.0040	.0080	.0120	.0160	.0199	.0239	.0279	.0319	.0359
0.1	.0398	.0438	.0478	.0517	.0557	.0596	.0636	.0675	.0714	.0753
0.2	.0793	.0832	.0871	.0910	.0948	.0987	.1026	.1064	.1103	.1141
0.3	.1179	.1217	.1255	.1293	.1331	.1368	.1406	.1443	.1480	.1517
0.4	.1554	.1591	.1628	.1664	.1700	.1736	.1772	.1808	.1844	.1879
0.5	.1915	.1950	.1985	.2019	.2054	.2088	.2123	.2157	.2190	.2224
0.6	.2257	.2291	.2324	.2357	.2389	.2422	.2454	.2486	.2517	.2549
0.7	.2580	.2611	.2642	.2673	.2704	.2734	.2764	.2794	.2823	.2852
0.8	.2881	.2910	.2939	.2967	.2995	.3023	.3051	.3078	.3106	.3133
0.9	.3159	.3186	.3212	.3238	.3264	.3289	.3315	.3340	.3365	.3389
1.0	.3413	.3438	.3461	.3485	.3508	.3531	.3554	.3577	.3599	.3621
1.1	.3643	.3665	.3686	.3708	.3729	.3749	.3770	.3790	.3810	.3830
1.2	.3849	.3869	.3888	.3907	.3925	.3944	.3962	.3980	.3997	.4015
1.3	.4032	.4049	.4066	.4082	.4099	.4115	.4131	.4147	.4162	.4177
1.4	.4192	.4207	.4222	.4236	.4251	.4265	.4279	.4292	.4306	.4319
1.5	.4332	.4345	.4357	.4370	.4382	.4394	.4406	.4418	.4429	.4441
1.6	.4452	.4463	.4474	.4484	.4495	.4505	.4515	.4525	.4535	.4545
1.7	.4554	.4564	.4573	.4582	.4591	.4599	.4608	.4616	.4625	.4633
1.8	.4641	.4649	.4656	.4664	.4671	.4678	.4686	.4693	.4699	.4706
1.9	.4713	.4719	.4726	.4732	.4738	.4744	.4750	.4756	.4761	.4767
2.0	.4772	.4778	.4783	.4788	.4793	.4798	.4803	.4808	.4812	.4817
2.1	.4821	.4826	.4830	.4834	.4838	.4842	.4846	.4850	.4854	.4857
2.2	.4861	.4864	.4868	.4871	.4875	.4878	.4881	.4884	.4887	.4890
2.3	.4893	.4896	.4898	.4901	.4904	.4906	.4909	.4911	.4913	.4916
2.4	.4918	.4920	.4922	.4925	.4927	.4929	.4931	.4932	.4934	.4936
2.5	.4938	.4940	.4941	.4943	.4945	.4946	.4948	.4949	.4951	.4952
2.6	.4953	.4955	.4956	.4957	.4959	.4960	.4961	.4962	.4963	.4964
2.7	.4965	.4966	.4967	.4968	.4969	.4970	.4971	.4972	.4973	.4974
2.8	.4974	.4975	.4976	.4977	.4977	.4978	.4979	.4979	.4980	.4981
2.9	.4981	.4982	.4982	.4983	.4984	.4984	.4985	.4985	.4986	.4986
3.0	.4987	.4987	.4987	.4988	.4988	.4989	.4989	.4989	.4990	.4990
3.1	.4990	.4991	.4991	.4991	.4992	.4992	.4992	.4992	.4993	.4993
3.2	.4993	.4993	.4994	.4994	.4994	.4994	.4994	.4995	.4995	.4995
3.3	.4995	.4995	.4995	.4995	.4996	.4996	.4996	.4996	.4996	.4997
3.4	.4997	.4997	.4997	.4997	.4997	.4997	.4997	.4997	.4997	.4998
3.5	.4998	.4998	.4998	.4998	.4998	.4998	.4998	.4998	.4998	.4998
	.00	.01	.02	.03	.04	.05	.06	.07	.08	.09

Figure 5.33 Z table with 95 percent probability

+34 percent) probability, and the +2 SD point equates to a probability of 97.5 percent (50 percent + 47.5 percent), it is clear that the SD multiple for a 95 percent schedule is somewhere between +1 and +2 SDs.

It should be noted that not all Z tables provides the probability figure in the same way. Some, for example, provide Z values assuming "0" as the starting point rather than the mean. This type of Z table is a useful shortcut. In this type of table format, one would be able to read .9505 directly at 1.65 SD instead of .4505. Project managers would benefit from being familiar with both Z table formats—but when in doubt—remember the 68–95–99 rule.

An Additional Number to Remember

The 1.65 value is therefore another rule of thumb to remember, and it is multiplied by the duration of time associated with the project SD, and then added to the project duration estimate. For the call center project scenario, the 95 percent probability duration is found to be:

$$47.7 + (1.65*2.82) = 52.35$$

The general formula for the 95 percent probability calculation is therefore:

Project PERT Duration + (*1.65* * Project SD)

Recalling the PERT Analysis Sequence

There are many steps involved in developing the project PERT estimates. But remembering and applying the steps to determine the project estimated duration as well as the probability of achieving given schedules is a powerful technique for both schedule estimating as well as managing the expectations of project stakeholders.

The PERT sequence previously described is repeated in a concise series of steps.

1. Find durations for all high-level project tasks using estimates from key stakeholders.
2. Find the weighted average ("Beta Distribution") duration for each activity using the following formula:

Activity Weighted Average Estimate = $\dfrac{\text{(Best Case} + (4^* \text{ Most Likely)} + \text{Worst Case)}}{6}$

3. Create the network diagram using the PERT activity estimates.
4. Find the project critical path and determine the overall estimated PERT duration.
5. Find the variance for all tasks on the project critical path using the following formula:

$$((\text{Worst Case–Best Case})/6)^2$$

6. Find project standard deviation using the following formula:

$$(\sqrt{\textit{Variance 1} + \textit{Variance 2} + \textit{Variance 3} \ldots \textit{Variance n}})$$

7. The project duration is sum of the durations on the critical path—and the probability of achieving this is 50 percent.

8. Find the 95 percent probability duration. This probability is found at the project duration associated with 1.65 standard deviations.

9. Find other project duration probabilities using the normal curve "rules of thumb" (68–95–99 percent) rule, or by consulting a Z table to cross-reference Z values and probability values.

Finally, this series of steps may be easily carried out by setting up a spreadsheet with formulas to carry out statistical operations such as finding the weighted average of activity durations as well as the project standard deviation. Once the formulas are put into a spreadsheet, it can be reused in future projects as a project probability calculation tool. In this way, the project team can focus on the data and the result rather than the associated statistics.

PERT Versus Monte Carlo Analysis

The term "Monte Carlo" may evoke images of a roulette wheel—and this is not far off from the meaning of Monte Carlo analysis. Unlike PERT analysis, Monte Carlo analysis does not compute weighted averages of each critical path activity, and compute the PERT expected time and standard deviation. Instead, Monte Carlo analysis uses computerized "brute force" methods to simulate thousands of project schedule trial runs to develop a statistical profile of the expected project duration. For example, in Monte Carlo analysis, the project manager may assign a three-point duration estimate for every activity in the project schedule. When Monte Carlo analysis is run, the software carrying out the simulation will use, at random, one of the three-point estimates for each activity in the project for each trial run. Over thousands of iterations—and thousands of random selections of three-point estimates—the Monte Carlo software builds up a statistical distribution of duration outcomes. Monte Carlo analysis has become more popular with the advent of power applications that may be added on to popular project management software tools.

Is Monte Carlo Better?

The project manager may well ask, "Does Monte Carlo analysis produce different results than PERT analysis?" The answer is, like many things in project management, "maybe." Since Monte Carlo incorporates all project paths in its analysis—rather than just the critical path as is the case in PERT analysis—results may differ when the critical path is considered "sensitive." Recall that the critical path is said to be sensitive when other paths in the project are very close to the critical path in duration. When this is the case, the random selection of three-point estimate values may produce many project durations that exhibit a critical path that is different from the original plan. PERT analysis would not necessarily capture these dynamics since PERT focuses only on the critical path. Finally, it should be considered that both PERT and CPM have their place in project management.

Whether to use PERT of Monte Carlo analysis could well depend upon what the project team is attempting to achieve. PERT works well in negotiating high-level project schedules within a schedule workshop environment. This is in part due to its simplicity and its focus on the project critical path. Monte Carlo analysis might be preferred for large complex projects where using manual PERT calculations would neither be realistic nor feasible. Also, Monte Carlo analysis would be useful when the project team and project stakeholders are able to understand and interpret the statistical distributions that Monte Carlo analysis produces.

How Long Does the Project "Really" Take?

Both CPM and PERT implicitly assume that the resources required to get the work of the project completed will be available. When determining the logical order of events and the critical path, resources are therefore not taken into consideration. However, in practice, resources, which may involve people, equipment, and even funding have practical limits. For example, project activities include work that requires unique skill sets. The rarer the skill set, the more challenging it is to schedule. Project teams often find that multiple activities that need to occur at the same time must be performed by the same resource. What happens then to the project schedule when resources are found to be lacking? In most cases, this will result in the schedule being delayed beyond the original plan. It is essential then for project managers to analyze resources are considered so that the final schedule is executable and is realistic in duration.

The Schedule Duration and Resource Limitations

In the same way as CPM and PERT analysis, factoring in the impact of resources into the schedule is carried out using a series of steps. As a first step, the task list table with duration and predecessors is expanded to include the resources that are to be used for carrying out each activity. This is presented in Table 5.11 using the call center scenario developed for the PERT analysis.

Step 1: Activity and resource table with assigned resources.

Step 2: Determine possible resource overlaps.

When resources are constrained—as is usually the case in project management—the overlap in resource assignment may be observed by plotting the resource needed at every given unit of time using the logical sequence of activities presented in the project network diagram. By comparing the activities and assigned resources from Table 5.11 with the PERT network diagram repeated in Figure 5.34, the resources are plotted over units of project time in the correct units (Figure 5.35).

From inspection of the resources versus project units of time chart, it is observed that resource bottlenecks exist in purchasing as well as in the desktop technician resource.

Step 3: Resolve the resource overlaps using workaround strategies.

Project managers may employ different strategies for resolving resource bottlenecks depending upon the priorities of the project and the overall strategy of the company. For example, if the goal of the project manager is to achieve the schedule and to avoid delays to the greatest extent possible, then the possible options for the project manager include:

- Increasing the available project resources;
- More fully utilize existing resources;
- "Fast Track" by carrying out activities in parallel that are designed to be completed in sequence;
- Scope reduction: Negotiate the reduction of scope for project deliverables.

Table 5.11 Activities with resources assigned

Identifier	Task description	Predecessor	Duration	Resource
1	Desktop PC evaluation	-	10.2	Desktop Tech
2	Call center bandwidth estimation	-	5.5	System Engineer
3	Upgrade plan	1	7	System Engineer
4	Procure computer memory	3	3.5	Purchasing Rep
5	Procure wireless access equipment	2,3	4.5	Purchasing Rep
6	Procure system software	3	3.5	Purchasing Rep
7	Install wireless access equipment	5	10.2	Desktop Tech
8	Install PC memory and wireless cards	4,5	10.2	Desktop Tech
9	Install OS and Applications	6,8	6.8	Desktop Tech
10	Develop training materials and user guide	6	15.2	Trainer
11	Training	7,9,10	7.7	Trainer
12	Launch new system	11	1.3	System Engineer
Total			47.7	

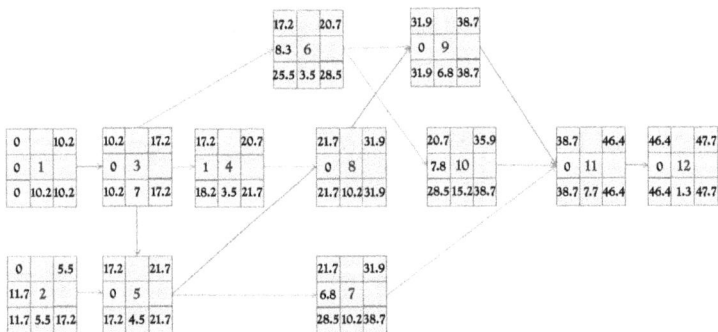

Figure 5.34 PERT network diagram

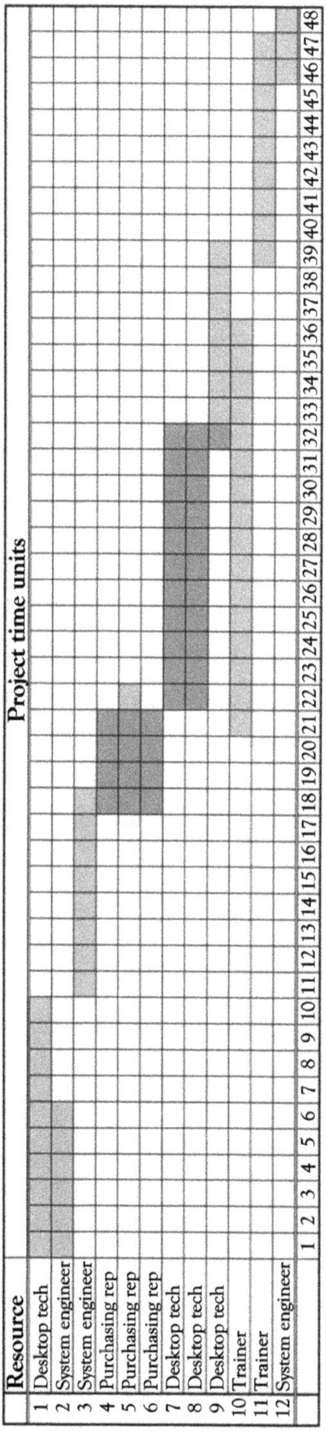

Project time units

	Resource	1	2	3	4	5	6	7	8	9	10	11	12	13	14	15	16	17	18	19	20	21	22	23	24	25	26	27	28	29	30	31	32	33	34	35	36	37	38	39	40	41	42	43	44	45	46	47	48
1	Desktop tech																																																
2	System engineer																																																
3	System engineer																																																
4	Purchasing rep																																																
5	Purchasing rep																																																
6	Purchasing rep																																																
7	Desktop tech																																																
8	Desktop tech																																																
9	Desktop tech																																																
10	Trainer																																																
11	Trainer																																																
12	System engineer																																																

Figure 5.35 Resources plotted per unit of time

Each of these options along with their relative merits and associated risks are outlined as follows.

Increasing Resources

Increasing resources requires bringing in new people and often additional equipment to the project. This requires possible training as well as additional management oversight. Further, complex projects benefit from team members who are intimately aware of the context of the project—and resources joining the project late in the schedule tend to lack such awareness. Because of this, it is natural to expect a lag time between the addition of a new resource and the resource's ability to make a positive contribution to the project schedule. Last minute newcomers need time to understand how the project deliverables fit together.

In practice, adding significant numbers of resources late in the project may not improve the schedule. This raises the question of initial resource numbers. If additional resources are found to be needed, why then aren't they included at the beginning of the schedule? The typical answer is that resources are not usually included because the initial project did not allow for it. The only reason that they should be considered late in the game is due to the attempt to maintain the commitment to the project schedule given few desirable alternatives.

Utilizing Resources

In lieu of adding resources, project managers seeking to stay on schedule when faced with constrained resources may push the team to take on longer hours and extended work schedules. When resources are utilized beyond the standard schedule, project managers may expect diminishing returns. Occasional overtime and weekend work may be assigned in exceptional circumstances—but, overscheduling resources may lead to mistakes, additional rework, and poor team morale. As a practical matter in highly complex projects, increasing work hours is commonplace. There is risk of morale and potential quality problems—but, this must be balanced against other limited alternatives that exhibit equal if not more risk.

Fast-Tracking

Fast-tracking activities are possible means for working around the need to additional resources—or additional utilization of existing resources. It is however a less than ideal solution. Fast-tracking assumes that activities that were originally scheduled in sequence be instead executed in parallel— or at the least—a somewhat overlapping sequence. The problem is that activities originally scheduled in sequence were arranged that way for a reason. As an example, consider the development of a user manual for a software application. Such a manual would typically be developed after the application development was finished. Conceivably, the manual could be "fast-tracked" and started prior to the completion of the development of the application. Additionally, software testing might be started prior to the completion of the development. This strategy might work—and if it does—the schedule will be expedited. On the other hand, fast-tracking could lead to rework of both the software and the manual should. This is likely to occur if the application under development changes unexpectedly. Also, problems revealed in testing could also lead to changes required in both the software as well as the user manual. As in nearly all attempts at reducing the project schedule by working around resource constraints, the possibility exists that the project could experience further delays instead of being reduced (Figure 5.36).

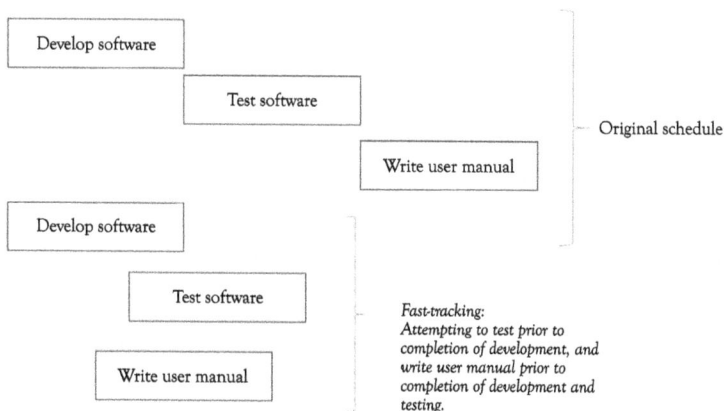

Figure 5.36 Fast-tracking illustration

Scope Reduction

One possible response to resource constraints is to seek to reduce the overall number of deliverables—or the level of performance of some of the scheduled deliverables. This is only possible if the client agrees to it and typically involves significant negotiations. Further, if the project is producing a product for sale in the market—a reduction of features could lead to problems with product acceptance. In the case of the software development fast-tracking example, the development of the application could be terminated early by removing key features. This would result in a lower development, testing, and documentation burden. The combined effect of reducing the project scope in this example would be to reduce the overall project duration regardless of the constrained resources. The danger is that the client fails to agree to scope reduction—or that sales in the marketplace collapse due to feature reductions. Regardless of the observed drawbacks—scope reduction is often done in the market—particularly when software is involved. It is not uncommon, for example, to purchase a software application only to receive repeated feature updates long after the initial launch.

Schedule Delay

It is evident that each of the possible strategies for working around resource constraints correspond with significant management risks. Further, even if the risks are managed—it is entirely possible that the project may be delayed—even with significant management efforts. Also, the delay comes at the expense of additional resources and possible goodwill in the marketplace, stakeholders, and finally, the client. Because of this, the project manager will have no choice at times but to eliminate resource overlaps by means of delaying the overall schedule. This final undesirable alternative may be carried out in a systematic manner. In fact, the schedule delay option is planned and efficiently executed as a series of tasks that could be considered a subproject. The project manager will employ guidelines or rules of thumb to minimize schedule delays while rearranging activities in such a way as to eliminate the resource bottlenecks.

Step 4: Resolving resource overlaps by delaying activities.

Referring again to Figure 5.36, Activities 4 to 6 as well as 7 to 9 are highlighted in red due to resource conflicts with the purchasing representative (4–6), and the desktop technician (7 to 9) resource. Since these resources are scheduled to carry out multiple activities at once, and additional resources or alternative solutions are not available, a resolution of the conflict requires that one or more activities be moved. The question for the project manager is, "Which one(s)?" Fortunately, common sense can be applied to this problem. Recall that the project critical path determines the overall duration of the project. All activities on the critical path have zero slack since they cannot be delayed without delaying the overall project. The first rule therefore for resolving resource conflict is to move activities that are not on the critical path by applying available resources first to those activities that *are* on the critical path. This rule may be generalized as:

> *Apply available resources first to those activities with the least available slack.*

Beginning with Activities 4 to 6 and referring again to Figure 5.36, it is observed that, of the three activities, only Activity 5 is on the critical path. Therefore, this is the activity that should be first in line for resource assignments. If this activity is resourced, then the two parallel activities requiring the same resource must be moved out. As can be seen in the revised resource plot, the movement of these activities creates a ripple effect in which other resources come into conflict. In this case, Activities 7, 8, and 9 as well as the desktop technician resource remain in conflict. Further, the purchasing representative resource associated with Activities 4 and 6 continues to be in conflict (Figure 5.37).

The call center resourcing example illustrates how incomplete a project schedule is without consideration of resources. A single movement of an activity to address a resource conflict reveals several other underlying conflicts. This is not always immediately obvious since, during the first step in resolving resource conflict, only the initial conflict is the point of focus. To fully appreciate the impact, the network diagram is revised to include the new starts for each activity (Figure 5.38).

The Critical Chain

The problem of resource conflict, and the resulting "ripple effect" as initial resource conflicts are resolved, reveals resources to be a bottleneck within

Project time units

	Resource	1	2	3	4	5	6	7	8	9	10	11	12	13	14	15	16	17	18	19	20	21	22	23	24	25	26	27	28	29	30	31	32	33	34	35	36	37	38	39	40	41	42	43	44	45	46	47	48
1	Desktop tech																																																
2	System engineer																																																
3	System engineer																																																
4	Purchasing rep																																																
5	Purchasing rep																																																
6	Purchasing rep																																																
7	Desktop tech																																																
8	Desktop tech																																																
9	Desktop tech																																																
10	Trainer																																																
11	Trainer																																																
12	System engineer																																																

Figure 5.37 The ripple effect of resource conflict resolution

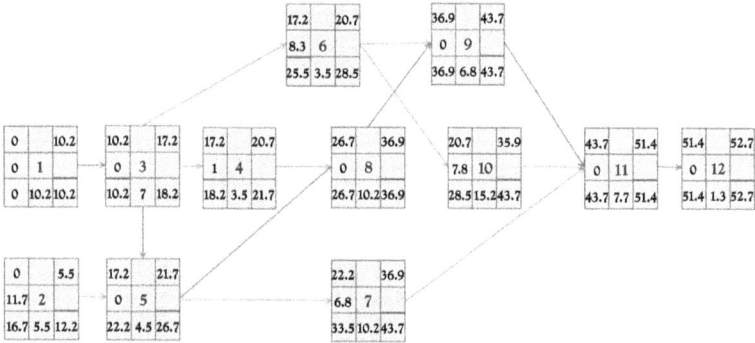

Figure 5.38 The revised critical path

the process of project schedule development. The term "bottleneck" suggests the applicability of the Theory of Constraints in project management schedule development. The theory of constraints, in general terms, observes that the system can never proceed faster than the speed of its slowest element. Said in another way, systems are governed by their constraints—and in project management—resources are often the most impactful constraint. Applying the theory of constraints requires that bottlenecks first be identified, and then exploited or widened to increase the overall capacity of the bottleneck—thereby increasing the capacity of the overall system. In the case of constrained resources in project scheduling, it has already been determined that additional resources are not available. Because of this, the bottleneck is resolved by pushing out activities so that the resource is not overloaded. As observed, this in turn creates new bottlenecks. This is expected in theory of constraints system optimization. Opening-up one bottleneck—for example—increasing the capacity of a workstation in a factory assembly line—creates new bottlenecks. The manager then proceeds to resolve these one by one until the overall system is performing in an optimal way. Likewise, in a project schedule, resolving one resource bottleneck inevitably leads to another. This situation should come as no surprise to the project manager. As one resource conflict (or bottleneck) is resolved, the project manager and team should step through remaining conflicts one by one until a schedule is produced that balances available resources with project activities.

Project time units

Resource		1	2	3	4	5	6	7	8	9	10	11	12	13	14	15	16	17	18	19	20	21	22	23	24	25	26	27	28	29	30	31	32	33	34	35	36	37	38	39	40	41	42	43	44	45	46	47	48
1	Desktop tech																																																
2	System engineer																																																
3	System engineer																																																
4	Purchasing rep																																																
5	Purchasing rep																																																
6	Purchasing rep																																																
7	Desktop tech																																																
8	Desktop tech																																																
9	Desktop tech																																																
10	Trainer																																																
11	Trainer																																																
12	System engineer																																																

Figure 5.39 Schedule delay due to resource conflict resolution

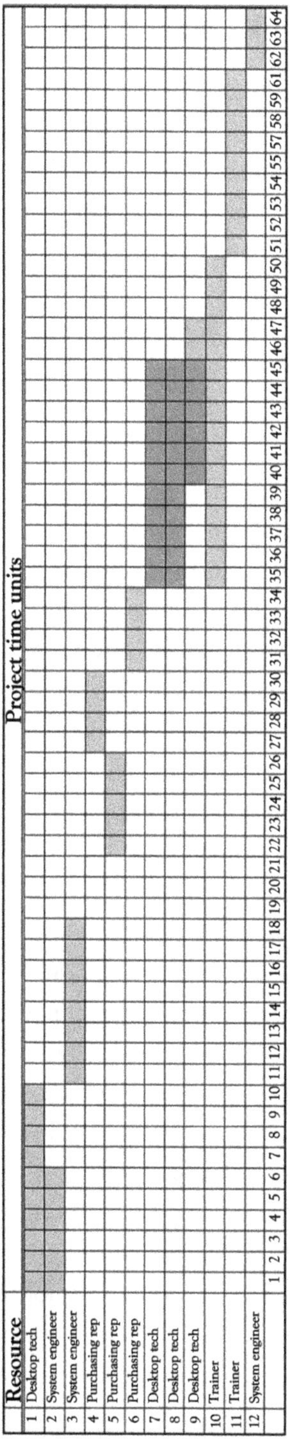

Figure 5.40 Adjusting schedule to maintain predecessor relationships

Further Conflicts and Additional Delays

At this stage of the resource conflict resolution process, the critical path remains the same—however, the schedule is delayed to 52.7 units of time. However, since conflicts continue to exist in the purchasing representative resource, Activities 4 and 6 must be resourced. Once again, the project manager must decide which activity to apply resources to first. Neither Activities 4 nor 6 is on the project critical path. However, Activity 4 has much less room to maneuver (i.e., slack), and as well, is a predecessor to Activity 8 which is located on the project critical path. The best approach to resourcing these activities therefore is to move Activity 4 to the end of Activity 5, followed by moving Activity 6 to the end of Activity 4 (Figure 5.39).

Although the conflict in the purchasing representative resource is now resolved, the desktop technician resource continues to be in conflict across Activities 7, 8, and 9. Further, Activities 7, 8, and 9 have not been adjusted so that the activity predecessors are maintained. This is an additional complexity for which project managers must be aware. When activities begin to move, predecessor and successor relationships must be maintained. Activities 4 and 5 are predecessors for Activities 7 and 8, and Activity 8 is a predecessor for Activity 9. Prior to resolving the desktop technician conflict, the activities are adjusted to reflect their predecessor activities. Further, Activities 10, 11, and 12 are also moved to reflect their respective predecessor relationships (Figure 5.40).

Although the predecessor relationships are now reflected in the resources over units of project time diagram, the desktop technician resources remain in conflict. It is observed by reference to the network diagram that Activity 8 is on the critical path (Figure 5.41).

Activity 9 is a successor to Activity 8 and is also on the critical path. Activity 7 is not only the critical path, but it is, along with Activity 9, a predecessor to Activity 11. Since both must be completed, and Activity 9 is shorter in duration as well as being on the critical path, Activity 9 is moved so that it begins once Activity 8 is completed. Activity 7 is likewise moved to begin after Activity 9 thereby resolving the conflict. The resources over units of time chart are updated to reflect the correct predecessor relationships for Activities 11 and 12 (Figure 5.42).

17.2		20.7
8.3	6	
25.5	3.5	28.5

36.9		43.7
0	9	
36.9	6.8	43.7

0		10.2
0	1	
0	10.2	10.2

10.2		17.2
0	3	
10.2	7	18.2

17.2		20.7
1	4	
18.2	3.5	21.7

26.7		36.9
0	8	
26.7	10.2	36.9

20.7		35.9
7.8	10	
28.5	15.2	43.7

43.7		51.4
0	11	
43.7	7.7	51.4

51.4		52.7
0	12	
51.4	1.3	52.7

0		5.5
11.7	2	
16.7	5.5	12.2

17.2		21.7
0	5	
22.2	4.5	26.7

22.2		36.9
6.8	7	
33.5	10.2	43.7

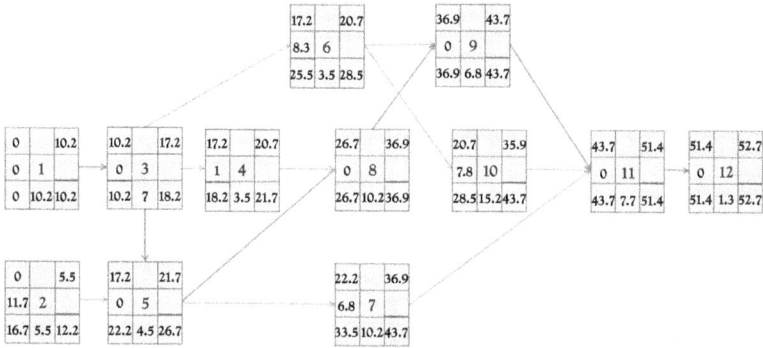

Figure 5.41 Critical path revised due to resource conflict resolution

Impact of Conflict Resolution

No resource conflicts now exist in the project schedule. However, the project has increased in duration from about 48 to 75 time units. This dramatic increase in the overall schedule duration is a testament to the impact of resource constraints on a project. This is also why the theory of constraints view on project management—known as "Critical Chain Project Management" (or CCPM) suggests that resources be considered at the earliest stage of or project schedule development—rather than after the creation of the network diagram. There is merit in this view in that it has the potential to foresee resource bottlenecks prior to the apparent collapse of an otherwise desirable schedule duration. On the other hand, since the resources applied to a project schedule are assigned based upon the activities that are required to produce the project deliverables, it is unclear how resources could be assigned to the project schedule prior to identifying and sequencing the project activities. CCPM therefore remains an important principle to consider when assigning resources to a project schedule; but, its full application to project management remains to be further operationalized.

Schedule Optimization

The project manager would naturally seek to optimize and compress the resulting schedule where possible without violating resource

Project time units

	Resource	1	2	3	4	5	6	7	8	9	10	...	75
1	Desktop tech												
2	System engineer												
3	System engineer												
4	Purchasing rep												
5	Purchasing rep												
6	Purchasing rep												
7	Desktop tech												
8	Desktop tech												
9	Desktop tech												
10	Trainer												
11	Trainer												
12	System engineer												

Figure 5.42 Revised resources over units of time chart

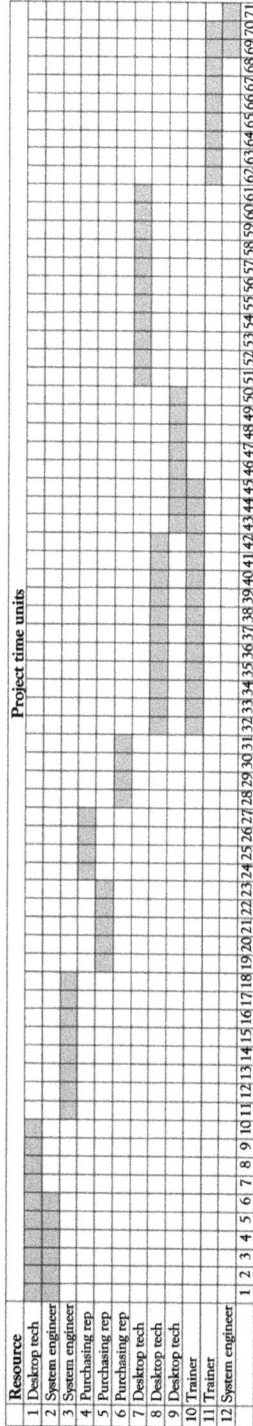

Figure 5.43 Schedule optimized to remove gaps due to conflict resolution

constraints or predecessor relationships. One such opportunity appears in the activities associated with the purchasing representative resource. When Activities 4 and 6 were moved beyond Activity 5 to preserve the critical path, a gap of 3 time units was created in the schedule. Although Activities 4 and 6 cannot be carried out until Activity 5 is completed, Activity 5 may be started immediately following Activity 3. The schedule is adjusted to eliminate the time gap—resulting in a 71-day schedule (Figure 5.43).

Although this series of measures does improve the schedule, it does not improve it significantly. Because of this, it is at this point that the project team will likely face significant scrutiny from the project sponsor and the client alike to further optimize the schedule. What other options are possible? Although schedule reduction techniques such as adding resources, fast-tracking, and scope reduction have been evaluated—and presumably discarded at this point—often, schedule negotiations will return to the application of a combination of these techniques.

Sponsors and clients also have a way of forcing the issue and pressing for schedule reduction by increasing the funding for and addition of resources to critical project activities. This schedule optimization discussion is referred to as "project crashing." The term "crashing" is an appropriate one since adding resources to activities—especially late in the project—can be a complicated and messy prospect. Although project crashing seeks to reduce the schedule by applying additional funding for resources, funding is never unlimited. For this reason, project managers proceed to apply funding and resources to the least expensive activities that, by the increase of resources, will result in the reduction of the overall schedule duration. Also, even though additional resources add cost to the project, the reduction of the project schedule has the potential to reduce some costs—for example, equipment rental and facility occupancy.

As the project team applies resources to least expensive to most expensive activities and the schedule duration is observed to improve, the team eventually arrives at a project "crash point" which is the optimal mix of additional resource funding per unit of schedule duration reduction. This point is the recommended additional investment that is presented to project stakeholders. Recall however that adding resources and using advanced management techniques such as fast-tracking increase project risk. The "improved" schedule should therefore be considered a proposed solution for schedule reduction. The benefits of the additional costs and resources may or may not be forthcoming in the actual project execution.

Schedule Precedence Impact

The rearrangement of the activities due to resource constraints has implications for the remaining activities as well as the overall schedule. This is illustrated by revising the network diagram to include the activities that have been moved. The new start and finish times are indicated, and the revised critical path is calculated using the forward and backward pass (Figure 5.44).

It is of interest to note the important results:

- The project critical path has changed.
- The critical path is no longer the path with "zero slack." Rather, it is the path with the least overall slack in each activity. This is because the start of Activities 4, 6, 7, 8, and 9 is fixed as highlighted in red due to the resource constraints.

What Just Happened?

The original project schedule as created using CPM and PERT changed significantly both in duration as well as logical sequence once resources were added to the schedule. This illustrates that a schedule is not a true schedule until resources are applied. It is therefore important that project managers avoid committing to a project schedule until resources are applied

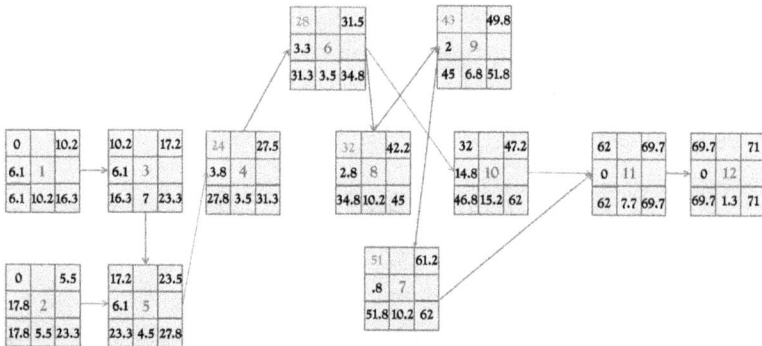

Figure 5.44 Revise network diagram with resource conflicts removed

and the conflicts are resolved. The good news is that most project management software tools will detect and correct resource conflicts automatically or with no more than a few clicks. Software tools use the same principles as the manual steps by seeking to minimize delays where possible by assigning resources to activities with the least slack first. However, schedule days are inevitable when resources are constrained. As soon as project manager software is directed to resolve resource conflicts—the schedule will move out depending upon the severity of the resource constraints.

Cost: What Funding Will Be Required to Complete the Project?

Although projects are estimated early in the schedule development process, costs are not known with certainty until resources are applied to the project activities. One way of thinking of the cost of a project is to visualize costs as being attached to the resources. When resources are added to the project, the costs of the resources follow. This can be visualized by imagining walking through a freshly painted hallway and occasionally brushing against the wall or touching the wall along the way. Every time the wall is touched or brushed against, by way of analogy, the more that wet paint gets absorbed by the person walking down the hall. Also, the more extensive the duration of the contact with the wet paint, the more that the individual is increasingly covered with paint.

Costs in project management follow a similar pattern. Every time a project "touches" or utilizes a resource—be it a team member or a piece of equipment—the more that cost is absorbed by the project. Also, the greater the length of time that a resource is employed in a project, the higher the resulting cost that is absorbed. This leads in turn to a higher resulting budget. The utilization of resources over the length of the project corresponds to the flow of cash associated with the cost of the assigned resources as they are used.

Categorizing Costs

Direct and Variable Costs

The cost that is of primary importance to the project manager is the direct cost of the project that varies with the level of the resource used—or "direct and variable" costs. For example, assigning an individual to the project brings direct cost to the project budget. This cost is also variable because it increases according to the use of the resource and by the number of resources added. For example, when two individuals are assigned instead of one, the cost is doubled (assuming that the rate for both individuals is the same). Variable costs also increase according to the length of the project. Direct and variable costs are directly under the control and management of the project manager. Direct and variable costs may also be incurred by the project when the project employs capital equipment in the project. Recall that a resource may be people—but, it also may involve equipment, funding, or anything used for the purpose of completing project deliverables.

Project Absorption of Capital Costs

Determining the cost associated with using capital equipment is slightly more complicated than calculating the cost of employed human resources. If the capital equipment is rented or leased by the project team during the period of the project, then the project is assigned the rental or lease expense of the equipment. Cash flows associated with rental or lease payments are then included in the overall project budget. If, on the other hand, the capital equipment is owned by the company, then the project is typically charged a cost associated with the amount of use during the project. This charge is calculated by taking the portion of the equipment monthly depreciation cost for the period of time that the equipment is used in the project. To illustrate this point, assume that the project uses test equipment for 10 days during a month of project work.

Assume further that the company originally paid $10,000 for the capital purchase, and that the company uses three-year straight-line depreciation. Depreciation is the charge that a company takes against its income statement to recognize the expense of the capital equipment, and to build a fund for its eventual replacement. A three-year straight-line depreciation would charge $3,333.33 per year, or $277.78 per month when assessed monthly. Assuming that the project used the equipment for 10 working days (roughly 2 weeks out of a 4-week month), then the expense incurred by the project by using the capital equipment for 10 days would be $138.89. This figure equates to V> of one month's depreciation charge for use of the capital equipment.

Direct Fixed Costs

A fixed cost by definition does not change. One common category of fixed cost that is absorbed directly by the project is known as NRE or "Nonrecurring Engineering." NRE fees are often paid to companies who design custom hardware, software, or intellectual property components for a project. After the project produces its deliverables, and ongoing licensing or royalty fee may be incurred by the company—but, the project fixed costs are linked only to the one-time charge. Any one-time expense paid by the project would be categorized as fixed cost.

Indirect Costs

Indirect cost includes costs such as the facility in which the project is carried out as well as the expenses associated with the facility. Indirect cost may also include an allocation of the management overhead of the company. Some companies automatically allocate a portion of indirect costs to resources. Such "fully absorbed" costing will automatically push indirect costs into the overall project budget as resources are added. In other accounting systems, the indirect costs are managed separately. In either case, the longer that it takes to complete the project, the greater the amount of indirect costs will be absorbed by the project (Table 5.12).

How Does the Schedule Become a Budget?

Upon resolving all resource conflicts in the project, what results is a sequence of activities that are linked to the resources assigned to perform each activity. Given that the project absorbs the cost of each resource used, the cost of resources for each period of project time can be captured using the resource versus project units of time chart that was created for allocating

Table 5.12 Cost categories

	Fixed	Variable
Direct	NRE	Human Resources
	Consultant fee	Capital Equipment
	License fee	
Indirect		Facilities
		Management Overhead

resources and analyzing resource conflict. The combined costs from the use of all resources for any given project unit of time are summed, and then the cumulative cost is captured. The budget creation process begins with assigning the cost of the resources used in the project (Table 5.13).

Table 5.13 Costs associated with project resources

Resource	Salary	O/H	Total
Desktop tech	$50	$15	$65
System engineer	$75	$20	$95
Purchasing rep	$65	$20	$85
Trainer	$85	$20	$105

The costs are then accrued for each unit of time that they are utilized. Then, the accrued unit of time costs for all resources used during each period is combined to produce a cumulative total. The call center project is broken into blocks of 10 units of time for the sake of simplicity and to enable an at a glance view of the relationship between resource assignments, resource costs per unit of time, and finally, cumulative costs (Figures 5.45 to 5.51).

	Resource	Project time units									
1	Desktop tech										
2	System engineer										
3	System engineer										
4	Purchasing rep										
5	Purchasing rep										
6	Purchasing rep										
7	Desktop tech										
8	Desktop tech										
9	Desktop tech										
10	Trainer										
11	Trainer										
12	System engineer										
		1	2	3	4	5	6	7	8	9	10
	Total	$160	$160	$160	$160	$160	$160	$65	$65	$65	$65
	Cumulative	$160	$320	$480	$640	$800	$960	$1,025	$1,090	$1,155	$1,220

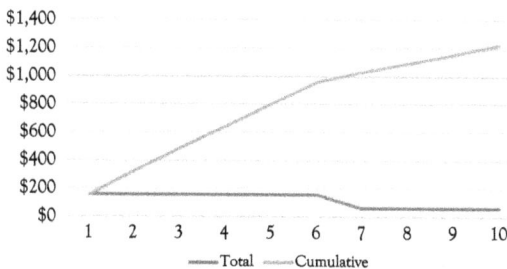

Figure 5.45 Time units 1–10

	Resource	Project time units									
1	Desktop tech										
2	System engineer										
3	System engineer										
4	Purchasing rep										
5	Purchasing rep										
6	Purchasing rep										
7	Desktop tech										
8	Desktop tech										
9	Desktop tech										
10	Trainer										
11	Trainer										
12	System engineer	11	12	13	14	15	16	17	18	19	20
	Total	$95	$95	$95	$95	$95	$95	$95	$95	$85	$85
	Cumulative	$1,315	$1,410	$1,505	$1,600	$1,695	$1,790	$1,885	$1,980	$2,065	$2,150

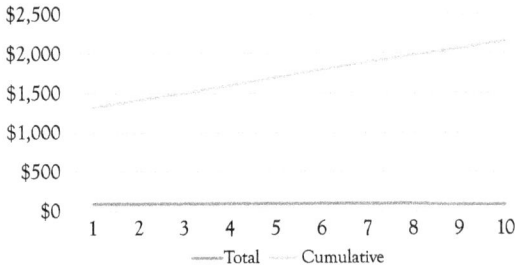

Figure 5.46 Time units 11–20

	Resource	Project time units									
1	Desktop tech										
2	System engineer										
3	System engineer										
4	Purchasing rep										
5	Purchasing rep										
6	Purchasing rep										
7	Desktop tech										
8	Desktop tech										
9	Desktop tech										
10	Trainer										
11	Trainer										
12	System engineer	21	22	23	24	25	26	27	28	29	30
	Total	$85	$85	$85	$85	$85	$85	$85	$85	$85	$85
	Cumulative	$2,235	$2,320	$2,405	$2,490	$2,575	$2,660	$2,745	$2,830	$2,915	$3,000

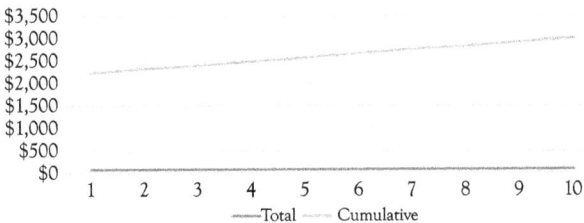

Figure 5.47 Time units 21–30

	Resource	Project time units									
1	Desktop tech										
2	System engineer										
3	System engineer										
4	Purchasing rep										
5	Purchasing rep										
6	Purchasing rep	▓									
7	Desktop tech										
8	Desktop tech		▓	▓							
9	Desktop tech										
10	Trainer		▓	▓							
11	Trainer										
12	System engineer										
		31	32	33	34	35	36	37	38	39	40
	Total	$85	$170	$65	$65	$65	$65	$65	$65	$65	$65
	Cumulative	$3,085	$3,255	$3,320	$3,385	$3,450	$3,515	$3,580	$3,645	$3,710	$3,775

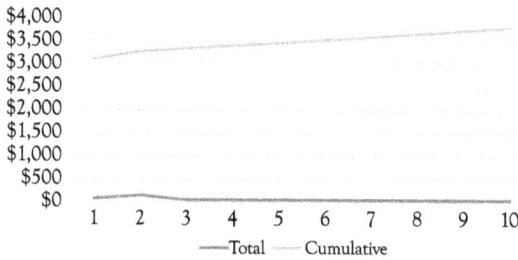

Figure 5.48 Time units 31–40

	Resource	Project time units									
1	Desktop tech										
2	System engineer										
3	System engineer										
4	Purchasing rep										
5	Purchasing rep										
6	Purchasing rep										
7	Desktop tech										
8	Desktop tech	▓	▓								
9	Desktop tech			▓	▓	▓					▓
10	Trainer	▓	▓	▓	▓						
11	Trainer										
12	System engineer										
		41	42	43	44	45	46	47	48	49	50
	Total	$65	$65	$170	$65	$65	$65	$65	$65	$65	$65
	Cumulative	$3,840	$3,905	$4,075	$4,140	$4,205	$4,270	$4,335	$4,440	$4,465	$4,530

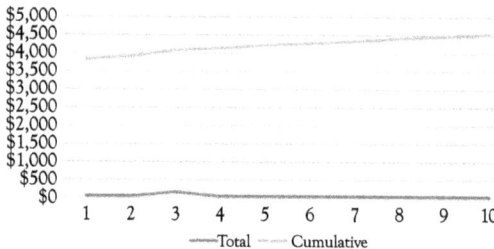

Figure 5.49 Time units 41–50

	Resource	Project time units									
1	Desktop tech										
2	System engineer										
3	System engineer										
4	Purchasing rep										
5	Purchasing rep										
6	Purchasing rep										
7	Desktop tech										
8	Desktop tech										
9	Desktop tech										
10	Trainer										
11	Trainer										
12	System engineer										
		51	52	53	54	55	56	57	58	59	60
	Total	$65	$65	$65	$65	$65	$65	$65	$65	$65	$65
	Cumulative	$4,595	$4,660	$4,725	$4,790	$4,855	$4,920	$4,985	$5,050	$5,115	$5,180

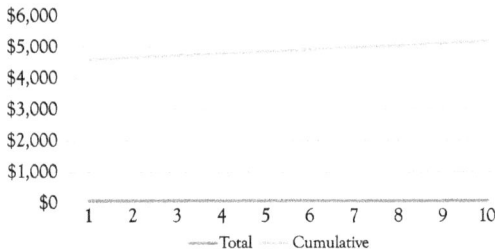

Figure 5.50 Time units 51–60

	Resource	Project time units									
1	Desktop tech										
2	System engineer										
3	System engineer										
4	Purchasing rep										
5	Purchasing rep										
6	Purchasing rep										
7	Desktop tech										
8	Desktop tech										
9	Desktop tech										
10	Trainer										
11	Trainer										
12	System engineer										
		61	62	63	64	65	66	67	68	69	70	71
	Total	$65	$105	$105	$105	$105	$105	$105	$105	$200	$105	$95
	Cumulative	$5,245	$5,350	$5,455	$5,560	$5,665	$5,770	$5,875	$5,980	$6,180	$6,285	$6,380

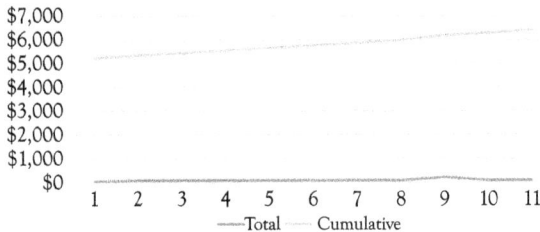

Figure 5.51 Time units 61–71

Budget Plot ("S Curve" or PV)

The cumulative cost of resources used throughout all time periods may be plotted to view the spending pattern over the life of the project. This plot is often referred to as an "S" curve. This is because project costs (and resulting spending patterns) tend to start small, then increase, and finally trail off at the end—resulting in an "S" pattern. Although the project budget line is referred to as an S curve, this does not mean that all projects necessarily follow this pattern. The project budget is also referred to as the "PV" or planned value. This is because the planned value is the amount that the project intends to spend over the life of the project while developing and completing project deliverables. The planned value is also a term used in the EVM (Earned Value Management) system used for monitoring and controlling project progress. In this system, the actual spending as well as the monetary value of the work completed are plotted together with the project PV curve to provide a realistic view of project progress (Figure 5.52).

From Budget to Gannt

Many project managers are readily familiar with the Gantt chart. The Gantt chart provides a list of project activities in order, and these are accompanied by activity durations and critical project milestones. Unlike the network diagram, the Gantt chart functions primarily as a communications tool. The important project dates may be observed at a glance. The "project resources over time" (Figure 5.53) chart has an appearance that is very similar to a Gantt chart.

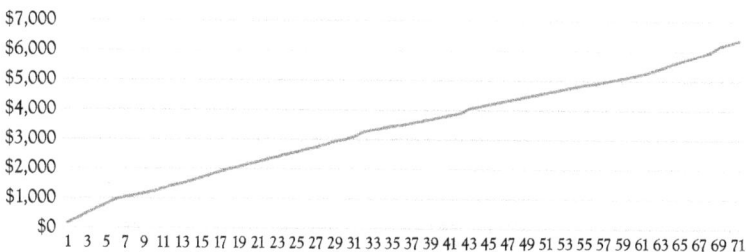

Figure 5.52 Overall project budget "S-Curve"

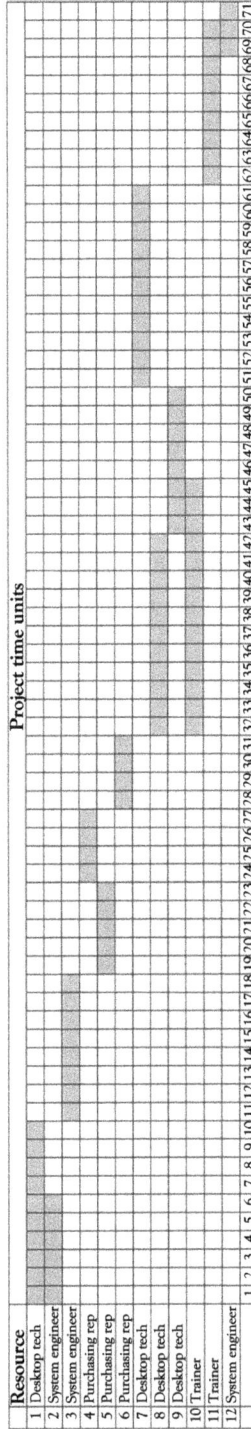

Figure 5.53 Project resources over time chart

The difference is that project resources are plotted over time instead of project activities. The Gantt chart is in effect a "project activities" over time chart. The Gantt chart may be developed easily from inspection of the network diagram and while using the framework of the project resources over timetable. Referring again to the final network diagram (Figure 5.54), the Gantt chart is developed using the following steps (Figure 5.54):

1. Refer to the table populated with dates created for the "project resources over time" chart (Figure 5.53).
2. List each activity in order of appearance in the network diagram and use these activities to populate the table.
3. In the same manner as the "project resources over time" table, darken in each date that is occupied by an activity.
4. Highlight each date that corresponds to a critical path element.
5. Connect predecessor and successor activities according to the relationships observed in the network diagram.
6. Identify critical milestones with a triangular marker (Figure 5.55).

With the creation of the Gantt chart project duration and milestone communication tool, the project manager now has a complete schedule that includes activities, the logical order of precedence in the form of a network diagram, PERT analysis with probability estimation, resource assignments, and project budget. The project team now has enough schedule information in place to either begin the project, or, to use the schedule that is developed to seek executive approval and funding.

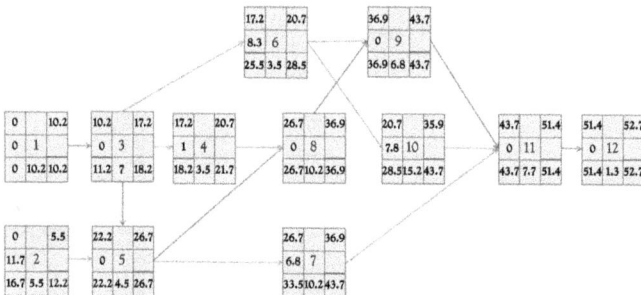

Figure 5.54 Final network diagram

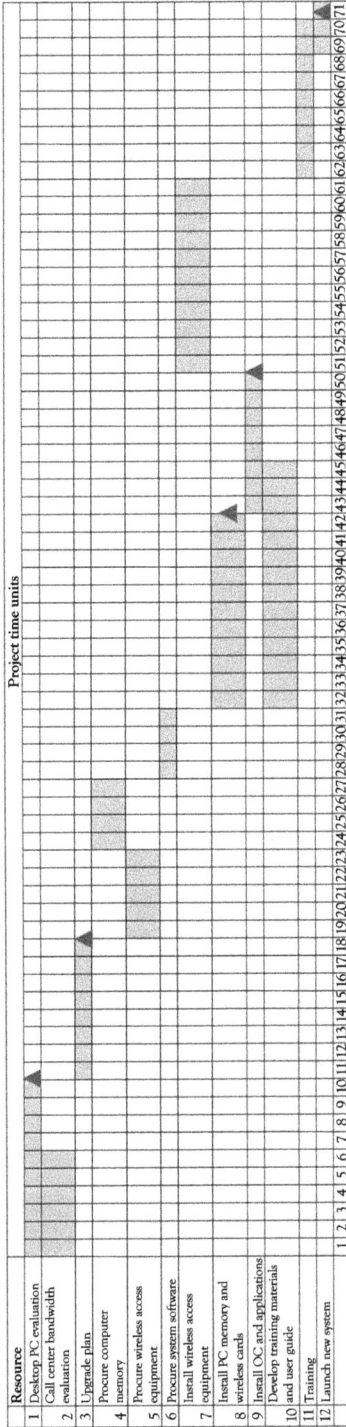

Figure 5.55 *Simple Gantt chart*

But Wait! The Schedule Is Not a Plan

It is not uncommon to think of a project schedule as a plan. After all, a schedule outlines what needs to be done, when the work will get done, how much the project will cost, and what resources will be assigned to the work. This sounds very much like a plan. The project schedule however focuses specifically on the "iron triangle" or, said another way, the intended trade-off between scope, cost, and schedule using the priority derived from the strategy of the company. Is the plan sufficient for the purpose of producing project deliverables? There is some appeal for the project manager in approaching the project in this manner.

Given that the schedule would appear to fill the most pressing needs of a project manager—what then would a project manager lack if the project moved forward with only a schedule rather than a complete plan? Here are five missing pieces that a novice project manager may want to consider:

1. Something unexpected happens! Unfortunately, something unexpected happens in every project. If it were expected, then it would be part of the schedule. The "something unexpected" is defined as risk. A project schedule, unlike a plan, does not include the risk analysis along with supporting processes for identifying, assessing, and responding to those unexpected matters that pop up.

2. The project team? A project schedule includes resource assignments, but says nothing about from where the resources originate, how they are selected, and how they are led and managed. It pays to remember that the project manager does not execute the schedule in isolation. Projects are executed by people—typically, a team of people. A project schedule does not include the holistic guidelines for team acquisition and management that a complete plan offers.

3. Who gets informed and how? A schedule may be communicated with a Gantt chart. A Gantt chart provides schedule activities, milestones, durations, and resource assignments. A schedule and a Gantt chart however do not provide ongoing progress reports tailored to specific stakeholders using specific information and delivered with custom media. Further, the schedule does not include forward look-

ing consideration for what specifically needs to be reported, when and to whom. The resource assignments in the project schedule typically are focused on project deliverables rather than communication and report generation assignments. The lack of detailed communication planning therefore will require the project manager to proceed using ad hoc reporting methods.

4. What if we need to outsource? Few companies that commission projects intend to do everything in-house. Project typically procure hardware and software components, systems and subsystems, labor, and support services. A schedule may provide some indication of outsourced resources, but no support is included for significant management issues such as vendor selection and contact negotiation. Additionally, outsourced work is often similar to in-house developed work—with the exception that communication is much more formal and intensive. Change control is an essential aspect of communication to suppliers. Finally, the level of required performance along with testing and acceptance criteria for supplier deliverables will need to be documented in a structured and legally binding manner. In short, a project will likely involve some amount of outsourcing— and this is something that is best not left to chance. In a project schedule—it is. A project plan, however, will include this supporting guidance, information, and documentation.

5. What level of performance is sufficient? A project schedule implicitly contains the quality level of the project deliverables within the description of what will be delivered and when. What is less clear in a project schedule is the means for deriving the requirements that drive project deliverables, the means for ensuring that the deliverables meet the specifications, and finally, the means for ensuring that the specifications for the project deliverables match what the client requires. What should be explicitly documented remains either implicitly stated, or not stated at all. A project schedule may therefore be carried out on time, on budget, and with the stated scope. However, whether the deliverables meet an acceptable level of quality, as well as how this is assessed by the client, is missing.

Answering the Unanswered Questions

A project schedule can be viewed as an incomplete plan that appears on the face of it—especially for novice project managers in a hurry—sufficient. Close inspection of what is clearly missing from a project schedule has revealed why planning is so comprehensive, and why project managers should take the trouble to complete a full project plan rather than jump into the execution of a project schedule. There is the old saying that "an ounce of prevention is worth a pound of cure." The truth of this statement is revealed in the inspection of the project life cycle. At the very beginning of the life cycle, the uncertainty is highest, but the expense of making course corrections is lowest. The reverse is true at the end of the project. The more forethought that is put into a complete project plan to create a solid beginning, the better the chances of a successful project ending.

Important "Takeaways" for the Project Manager

- Activities required to produce the WBS deliverables are identified as the first step in the schedule development sequence.
- Activities are placed in order of logical sequence to determine the overall project duration.
- The network diagram is the analysis tool used to analyze activity sequence and determine the longest path in the project.
- The longest path of activities in a project is known as the project critical path. This is the longest sequence of activities in the project, and the shortest possible time in which the overall project can be completed.
- The critical path is located by using the forward and backward pass algorithm. The forward and backward pass algorithm identifies all activities that have no slack.
- Activities within the critical path cannot be delayed without delaying the overall project.
- A project that has a critical path that is similar in duration to other paths within the network is said to be sensitive.

- CPM is the term used for network diagram project critical path analysis.
- PERT is like CPM except for the fact that PERT assumes that activity durations are not known with certainty.
- PERT analysis makes probabilistic predictions of project schedule achievement by durations are estimated using weighted averages along with the project mean and project standard deviation.
- Resources are assigned to project activities to execute the work of the project.
- Project resources are limited. Because of this, resource conflicts often arise in project scheduling.
- When resource conflicts are resolved in project schedules, this often results in the delay of a project.
- Costs are associated with resources. When resources are assigned to activities, the project absorbs the cost of the resources.
- The cumulative costs of the resources applied over units of project time become the project budget.
- Project activities plotted over units of project time, along with important milestones, are observed in the Gantt chart.
- The Gantt chart is an important tool for communicating project activity durations and important milestones.

CHAPTER 6

Project Work Performance Domain

The work of a project does not end with the carrying out of the plan. The project plan is completed by a project manager, a project team, and often an extended team. This means that work is assigned to others—and the project manager must therefore follow up to ensure that the assigned work gets done and is on-target with respect to plan. "Staying on top of things" is therefore the work of the project work performance domain.

A Plan Is Not a Plan Until ....

There is an old saying that "a plan is not a plan until it is fully resourced." The reason for this is simple: Resources are scarce. However, when a project schedule is developed, resources are often not initially considered. The developer of the project schedule at first considers only the activities that must be completed to produce the project deliverables as well as the logical sequence of events. The implicit assumption in building the schedule is that infinite resources exist, and, because of this, it is assumed that the activities outlined in the project schedule may be executed in the desired sequence and timeframe. The addition of resources to the project schedule adds a level of realism to the project. As resources are added to the schedule, it becomes clear that some activities rely on the same resources at the same time. For example, there may be two different pieces of software that need to be developed at the same time—and the specific know-how required to do this is available only in a single individual. Since no resource—be it human resources or equipment—can be in two places at once, something must give. That "something" is the schedule as previously proposed completion dates are pushed out and delayed due to resource constraints.

Planning Resources—What Do I Need?

The most obvious initial question to consider when planning resources is: "What resource do I need to complete a given activity?" In many cases, the resource is an individual who has a unique skill set. A system design activity within a project may, for example, require an individual who is highly experienced in system development, has systems engineering skills, or has experience in working in different technical domains. Not every available resource will have this skill. If multiple activities require this skill, then the project team will need to acquire more of this resource, outsource some (or all) of the activity, or delay the activity (or set of activities) so that the activity utilizes no more resources than that which are available to the project. It should be noted that resources are not always people. The term "resource" is a broad category that includes equipment, services, funding—or anything associated with project task completion. As an example, a project activity may require specific test or diagnostic equipment. This type of resource must be identified and planned for in the same way as a human resource. Determining what resources are needed is therefore an analytical exercise that focuses on the unique skills or capabilities required to complete project activities.

Planning Resources—How Many Do I Need?

At first glance, the question of how many resources are needed for a given activity is deceptively simple. To begin with, there is a clear relationship between the number of resources applied and the time it takes to get the job done. Consider, for example, a lawnmowing project. Assigning two people (and two lawnmowers) to mow a yard will generally take less time than if only a single resource is used. However, the possibility exists for resources to "get in the way" of each other and cause management challenges (Figure 6.1). In the lawnmowing example, an addition of a single resource may well reduce the time by 50 percent. However, if 10 resources are added, the activity may well take longer than what one might think. This is because time will be needed to coordinate the overall mowing activity so that no mower will mow the same patch twice, nor approach

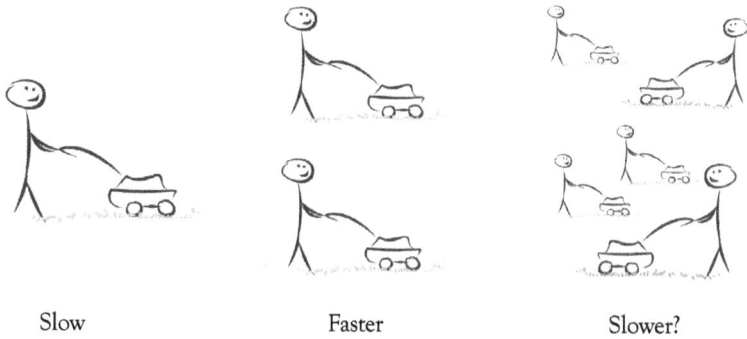

Slow   Faster   Slower?

Figure 6.1 Lawnmowing and adding resources

too close to another mower. Real projects however rarely involve mowing lawns. More commonly, projects today involve complex systems and are software intensive of the system under development and the development environment, tools, and processes and procedures.

The need for resources to learn or become integrated into the project infers that any resource added to a project cannot be expected to produce results immediately. In fact, given that existing project team members and managers may need to be assigned to bring the new resource "up to speed," productivity in the project may well drop in the period immediately following the addition of the resource. Also, as in the case of the "lawnmowing" example, even if it is assumed that additional resources added to the project are fully knowledgeable and may begin contributing to the development of deliverables immediately, the management and coordination effort may effectively limit the immediate output. In the case of nonhuman resources such as test equipment, development tools, or machines, programming or a setup (rather than learning) may be required. Increasing the output of deliverables by adding machines, tools, or workstations therefore may not immediately, nor ever, produce the desired result. Further, the later in the project that the resources are added, the more that the resource needs to learn, and the more time required to be effective. There may not be such time remaining as the project approaches completion. This is one reason why there is rarely a direct correspondence between additional resources and output. The determination of how many resources are needed to complete given activities ultimately depends upon many factors involving answering questions such as:

1. What is the target duration of the activity being resourced?
2. How many resources would be required to complete the activity within the target duration?
3. Is there a realistic, executable plan for dividing up the work so that it may be completed with the number of assigned resources?
4. Is the number of assigned resources manageable?
5. Does the complexity of the work associated with the deliverables lend itself completion by multiple resources?
6. Will resources assigned to the project be able to produce deliverables immediately? Or, will delays associated with learning and familiarity with systems and tools be expected?
7. Does the project activity require nonhuman resources that will need setup, programming, or other time-consuming preparation?

Peak Resources

It is reasonable to conclude that project task completion is constrained not only by the available resources, but also by the complexity of the work itself and the management burden of managing the assigned resources. These are not the only constraints. Once resources are assigned to all project activities, it is important for the project team to step back, "look at the big picture," and acquire an overall understanding of the peak project resource requirements (Figure 6.2).

This is because it is advantageous from both a cost and management perspective to minimize the peak number of resources required. A lower peak resource level translates to fewer people and equipment that need to be acquired and kept "on the books" adding cost to the project.

Although a lower level of peak resources is desirable, it is given that resources are linked to tasks that need to be completed to produce project deliverables.

How then are peak resource requirements minimized? Recall that the process of producing the project schedule identifies activities that include "slack" or "float." Activities that have slack are not on the schedule critical

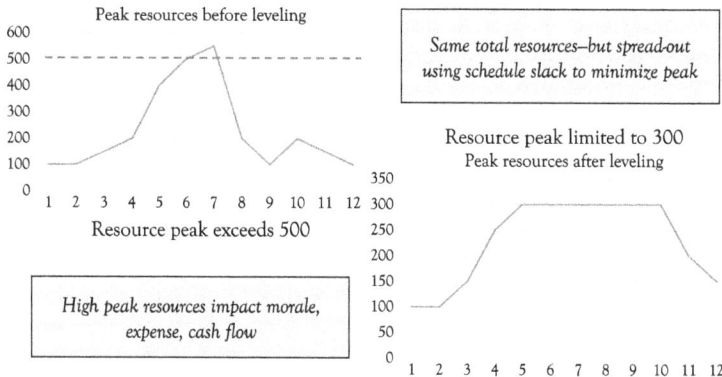

Figure 6.2 Reducing peak resources

path but instead are in parallel with activities on the critical path. Such activities may be delayed by the amount of slack associated with the schedule duration. The slack in each noncritical path activity may be used to reduce the overall level of peak resources. If an activity is delayed by its associated amount of slack, then resources may be applied to this activity late rather than immediately following a predecessor activity. This delay in activities with slack pushes out the associated resource requirements and contributes to lowering the overall peak resource requirement.

The decision for the project team therefore involves balancing and trading-off the peak resource demand with the overall duration of the project. Additionally, it is important to recognize that utilizing slack to maneuver around resource constraints leads to a project that includes little to no slack. A project with no slack means that all paths in the project are critical and that a delay in any activity will lead to a delay in the overall project. Reducing peak resources using slack may well involve trading budget and resource risk for schedule risk.

Resource Leveling

Available slack in project activities is used not only for minimizing peak resource requirements, but as well for smoothing out or leveling project resources. When project resources are leveled, each resource assigned to complete project activities is utilized in a balanced manner. This means that resources are applied evenly rather than assigned to tasks in an "on-again, off-again" manner. Using an example of human resources who are assigned to complete project activities, it is understood that it would be a poor practice to assign an individual 60 hours of work one week, followed by 10 hours in the following week, followed by another 60-hour week. This uneven scheduling is not ideal for many reasons. First, the morale of any employee who faces a week of significant overtime followed by relative inactivity is likely to be negatively impacted. Further, the employee assigned in such a manner may be forced to start work, then stop and do something else, and then start again. This form of multitasking, and its associated multiple startup and ramp-down sequences, is likely to reduce productivity.

Similar observations may be made regarding the use of machines and equipment to conduct project work. The productivity of capital equipment employed within a project is maximized under conditions of high utilization. Idle equipment incurs cost without producing output. Further, equipment that is used, set aside, and used again wastes time. Leveling resources—whether human or otherwise— serves to minimize waste and maximize productivity of project resources that would otherwise be due to human factors such as morale, or through the natural waste associated with stopping and starting work activities. Once again, resource leveling is carried out primarily by shifting activities based upon the available slack in the project.

Resource assignment may be more balanced when resources are leveled, but balance comes at the expense of schedule risk due to the limited amount of slack remaining after resource-leveling adjustments. An alternative to using up project slack is to simply push out activities and thereby delay the schedule. Neither of these solutions are ideal, so the project team must balance morale and productivity, schedule management risk, and schedule delay.

Planning Resources—Where Do I Acquire Them?

The project charter authorizes the project team to acquire resources. This is necessary because the project team operates outside the ongoing functional operation. While the functional organizational structure is managed and governed by budgets and long-term goals, project teams are created and disbanded according to the need to produce specific deliverables. The project team effectively "borrows" resources from the organization and then returns them once the work of the project is done. Exactly how this works within an organization depends upon the type of organization that is in place. In some organizations, the project is highly structured and, in others, the resources are acquired in a less formal basis. Regardless of the maturity of the resource acquisition process, the identification of required skill sets as well as the selection of project resources typically involves negotiation between the project manager and the functional manager.

Project Procurement

Few companies today are 100 percent vertically integrated. Vertically integrated companies, in addition to producing the final project, also make their own components. Because of complexity and specialization involved in modern highly technical projects, most companies rely on others to supply skills, know-how, and hardware and software components. Because of this, project managers will need to apply focused attention on developing a plan for managing outsourced components and labor. Some companies and projects alike experience varying degrees of success when outsourcing. One of the reasons for this is that, although companies may follow processes inside the company, the day-to-day nature of internal interfaces between functional groups can lead to an informal style of management.

Requests for work products or resource assignments may be carried out with simple verbal requests and limited documentation. This style of management does not lend itself to working with outsource partners. An outsourcing partner is an entity outside of the internal organizational framework in which the project team resides. Such entities are likely to have a different culture, perhaps a different language, and may follow different processes and procedures. These differences require that all interaction must be formal and explicit rather than informal and implicit. All communications, requests, and orders within the outsourcing environment must be well documented so that nothing is left to chance. Project teams are supported by the PMBOK framework because they operate outside the well-defined structure of the functional organization. Likewise, outsourcing to a team that operates outside the scope of both, the company and its associated project team and functional hierarchy, requires the highest degree of process discipline.

Make or Buy?

The first step in project procurement is making the procurement decision. This decision is based on "make or buy" analysis. Make or buy is a determination whether it makes more sense to produce internally something needed for the project, or to pay for third-party execution. Whether something makes sense or not depends upon many factors including the strategy of the company. Strategic management informs companies that strategically important work should be retained in-house whereas work not associated with the core competence of the company should be outsourced. Further, attention will be paid to the cost of the development—including the opportunity costs—as well as the overall capability of the project team. There are two questions associated with make or buy, and these are stated simply as:

1. "Can we do this?"
2. "Should we do this?"

Can We Do This?

This first consideration in make or buy is one of feasibility as in "Can we do this?" It may make sense to produce hardware and software components in-house, but this really depends on the capability of the company. Capability may refer to resources, skills, time, specialized equipment, and funding. As a word of caution, project teams should observe caution the first time a feasibility study is conducted for an activity or component development. It may be tempting to compare in-house know-how with existing firms who have a lengthy track record of working with a given technology. Is it reasonable to expect that, even though in-house talent exists, a project team can match outside competence the first time that it is attempted? Chances are that the first attempt to produce a technology in-house will face more difficulty, consume more schedule, and cost more money than expected (Figure 6.3).

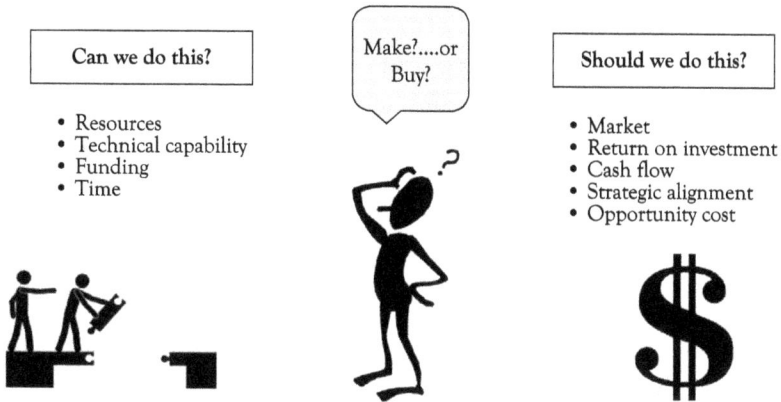

Figure 6.3 Make or buy analysis

Should We Do This?

If it is determined that the team can produce a component or technology in-house, it is still important to consider if the team "should" attempt it internally. Regardless of cost or level of difficulty, strategic reasons at times will drive make or buy decision making. For example, if a piece of work or component is in alignment with the company's core competence and is a source of strategic advantage, it may be prudent to keep the work in-house. Conversely, if an element of project work is deemed to not be of strategic advantage to the company, the work may automatically be considered a candidate for outsourcing.

Another critical determining factor of outsourcing is the cost of internal development as compared to outsourcing. There are many pitfalls associated with the cost analysis of the "make versus buy" equation. These include the following important considerations:

1. *First time*: The first time a technology or component is developed internally, it will likely cost more than expected. A first-time make versus buy decision may understate the cost. Project management texts often refer to the learning curve in this respect. Although the principle of the learning curve applies, the mathematics behind

it usually does not within the context of a project. In manufacturing, the learning curve assumes that the cost of a product or component decreases according to a specific formula as the output doubles. The doubling of output is rarely, if ever, a factor in the project context. Instead, the general principle that the "second time around" (or the "second time something is done is easier than the first") applies.

2. *Outsourcing quote*: An initial quote from a potential outsourcing vendor may be appealing. However, it pays to examine the quotation closely. Often, the quoted cost makes overall favorable assumptions. These assumptions may include the availability of well-documented requirements as well as the project team experience in managing outsourced partners. Further, it may be assumed that requirements and specifications will not change. Each of these assumptions is unlikely—leading to surprises in the actual cost experienced in the outsourcing engagement. Recall that informal communication and changes are likely to take place between the project team and functional groups inside the organization. If this informal ad hoc approach typical of the internal environment is undertaken with an outsource partner, expect costs to rise quickly.

3. *Lifecycle costs:* It is one thing to develop a hardware or software component and estimate the expense of the development from conception to launch. It is quite another matter to support the developed component long after it is delivered. The ongoing support of the system or component after it is delivered is something that is often missed in the "make versus buy" example. For example, the use of open-source software provides an example of lifecycle costs that often get missed. Open-source software may be appealing as a basis for development. The license itself is free—but development using such software will often assume that an in-house staff is available to update and repair defects. It is also possible that the ability to maintain such software may exceed the capability of the project team in the long term. If so, then outsource service providers will be required to assist. The failure to consider total lifecycle costs tends to understate the internal costs in a make versus buy analysis.

A common thread throughout these examples is the tendency to understate costs. The fact that internal costs are often understated should be a caution to avoid making an outsourcing decision too quickly.

Vendor Selection

Once it is determined that project activities or deliverables will be outsourced, the project team will need to select an outsource partner. There are many facets to this decision, and this may require taking steps to understand what outsourcing players exist in the market, and what they offer in terms of skills, know-how, or intellectual property. Often, the process involves reaching out to the vendor community using formal inquiry and solicitation documents.

The Request for Information

In many cases, a project team may lack sufficient expertise to determine an appropriate outsource partner. The project team may need a better understanding of the options that exist in the market, the architectures that are employed (in the case of components employed in complex system development projects), and the level of expertise and experience that exists. In this situation, the project may issue a RFI or Request for Information. Although the RFI is used to reduce the unknowns in a procurement setting, the RFI should provide sufficient context for vendors regarding the nature of the problem that, through outsourcing, they will attempt to solve. Further, the RFI should seek answers to specific questions. Finally, RFIs are then evaluated and used as a means for educating the project team so that may properly frame further solicitations for potential outsource partners (Figure 6.4).

The Request for Quote

When the project team has decided to outsource a relatively simple component—or labor to produce project deliverables—the project team may issue a Request for Quotation or RFQ. An RFQ could also be

RFI outline

1. Background
2. Requirements
   a. Technical
   b. Commercial
   c. Legal
   d. Timing
3. Supplier questionnaire

The primary goal of the RFI is to ask specific questions of suppliers after first providing information regarding the context of the project.

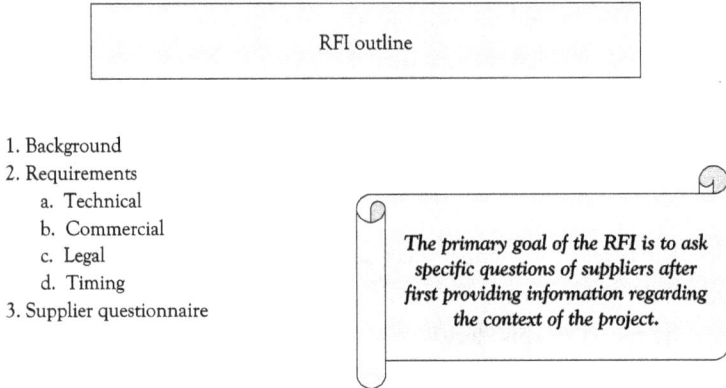

Figure 6.4 Elements of the RFI

issued in the case of a complex outsource engagement but is typically only employed if the solution is already defined. The RFQ may follow the issuing of an RFI and be based upon the information supplied from vendors. On the other hand, the RFQ may succinctly state the need, possibly the desired terms and conditions, and request a pricing quotation. Finally, it is also not uncommon for a project team to work regularly with different vendors. In this case, a formal RFQ is not always issued. However, in some cases an RFQ may be issued simply to avoid a biased decision and to ensure that competition is fostered between vendors (Figure 6.5).

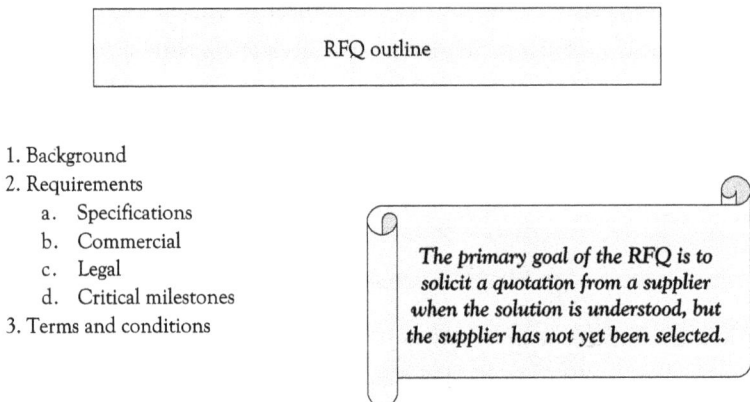

RFQ outline

1. Background
2. Requirements
   a. Specifications
   b. Commercial
   c. Legal
   d. Critical milestones
3. Terms and conditions

The primary goal of the RFQ is to solicit a quotation from a supplier when the solution is understood, but the supplier has not yet been selected.

Figure 6.5 Elements of the RFQ

The Request for Proposal

A complex procurement involving a major subsystem, or significant hardware or software component, may require a detailed proposal from a supplier. Such a proposal may be nearly as complex as the overall project as it may involve multiple deliverables, milestones, technical details, and payment schedules. When the project team has decided to outsource work or deliverables at a significant scale, a request for proposal or RFP is an appropriate vehicle for inviting suppliers to submit plans and compensation requirements for supporting the needs of the project team. The RFP will involve considerably more details than an RFQ and will follow the RFI in sequence if an RFI is used. The RFP therefore requests vendors to propose a solution to a problem or set of problems. In the RFP, neither the supplier nor the exact solution has been chosen. It should be noted that some project teams do not make a distinction between the terms "RFQ" and "RFP." In some cases, a project manager or supplier may find that the terms are used interchangeably regardless of the degree to which the solution has already been defined (Figure 6.6).

Vendor Quality Management

The quality management processes of the supplier are of key concern to the project team prior to initiating an outsourcing agreement. Having a

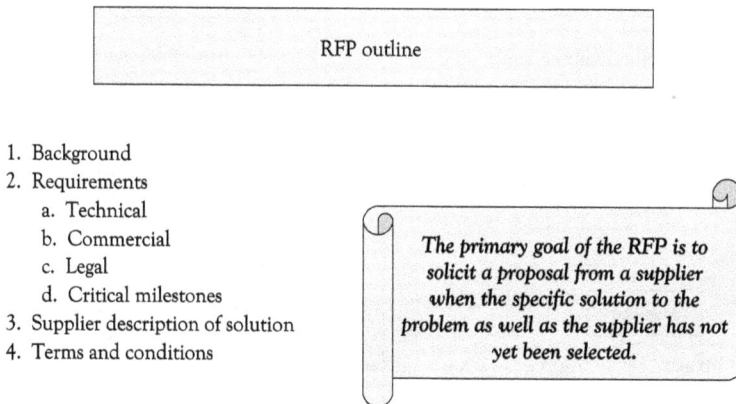

RFP outline

1. Background
2. Requirements
   a. Technical
   b. Commercial
   c. Legal
   d. Critical milestones
3. Supplier description of solution
4. Terms and conditions

The primary goal of the RFP is to solicit a proposal from a supplier when the specific solution to the problem as well as the supplier has not yet been selected.

Figure 6.6 Elements of the RFP

certification such as the ISO 9000 family of certification is no guarantee of quality. Certifications require that a quality process be documented and followed—but, it is not normative in the sense that it does not specify what quality process is to be followed. It is up to the project team to visit the candidate supplier, evaluate the processes, and audit the supplier to confirm that the processes it follows are sufficiently robust to support the requirements of the project team. It pays to consider normative quality management systems such as project management and software development maturity models. These are the Organizational Project Management Maturity Model (OPM3) and the Capability Maturity Model (CMM). Maturity models relate to quality in that they not only require that a company document and follow process but that the organization follow a specific set of processes (Figure 6.7).

Maturity models suggest process steps that, if followed, are recognized to produce superior outcomes. Another concern of maturity models is "process maturity." A company is said to be mature in terms of process if it follows documented processes without fail and has initiatives in place to improve processes over time. Mature organizations reject the use of informal ad hoc action. Regardless of quality management system or maturity model said to be followed by the candidate vendor, there is no substitute for face-to-face engagement and evaluation by the project team.

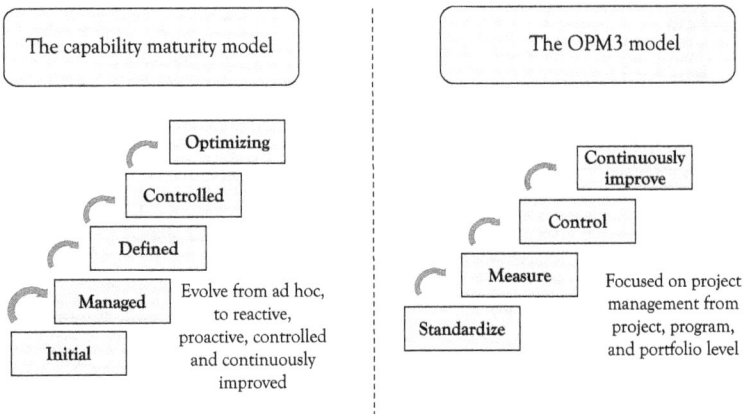

Figure 6.7 Maturity models

Performance Track Record

It is no secret that candidate suppliers have the tendency to "put their best foot forward" when making proposals. Vendor proposals will almost always appear to be very appealing. Project teams should be aware of this and seek to go beyond proposal responses and conduct due diligence on the historical performance of the supplier. One important means for accomplishing this is to reach out to previous customers of the supplier. A project team would be well advised to seek out these contacts without assistance from the candidate supplier to avoid bias in the process. As an additional suggestion, if the vendor customer base is relatively large, performance data may be collected via an electronic survey instrument. Regardless of how the data is collected or from where it originates, historical performance is a good indicator of the performance that may be expected in the future.

Supplier Financial Health

Although the project team will seek to minimize outsourcing costs, it is important to recognize that a supplier, just as in the case of the sponsoring project team, must be profitable to achieve long-term health and success. The project team must include in its procurement planning an evaluation of the financial situation of the supplier. The worst-case scenario is to design in a component or hire rare skills—only to have the vendor go out of business. Although outsourcing may appear on the face of it to be a short-term engagement, the project deliverables as well as the support of the deliverables are likely to be of concern for the long term. In addition to tangible requirements such as cost, performance, and delivery schedule, it is essential that support after the launch be considered in the quote and the cost of the quote. In keeping with this sentiment, recall the old saying that "If something appears to be too good to be true—it probably is." It is there is a good idea to scrutinize and possibly avoid the lowest outsourcing offer—particularly, if long-term support is required.

In addition to scrutinizing the offer itself, the project team can collect financial information on the company. If the company is publicly traded, the project team may easily acquire the supplier financial reports for the past several years and, in addition, download current financial status from the supplier's investor relations website. Further, investors who follow the company may periodically report their views on the long-term financial prospects of the company. This is another important source of information.

Contract Negotiation

When the project team selects a supplier for an outsourcing engagement, the details of the outsourcing are spelled out in detail using contracts. The terms of the supplier contract make a significant difference in the outcome of the project and may make the difference between profit and loss. The vehicle for achieving the right contract terms is negotiation. Supplier negotiation, like all project activities, is planned prior to execution. Because of this, the approach to negotiation to be used by the project team should be outlined in the project plan. Project managers may well ask "What is it about project negotiation that can be planned?" This question is likely spawned by the presumption that negotiation is all about argumentation and meeting tactics.

Contrary to popular belief, project contract negotiation is not something best carried out by "pounding the table," but rather by clearly identifying what the project team needs as well as what the project team is willing to exchange for something else. Additionally, project teams include in their preparation an assessment of what the supplier is likely to need as well as what the supplier may be willing to exchange. The goal of a successful supplier negotiation is to achieve a result in which the project team exchanges what to them is less important for something that, to the project team, is more important. The possible scenarios for exchange should be carefully considered and rehearsed prior to the negotiation engagement. The results of the preparation should result in a spreadsheet that anticipates possible exchanges so that the meeting may be steered to a desired conclusion.

When the negotiation begins, recognize that negotiation usually proceeds in phases—so, do not expect to walk away with exactly what is needed for a project right away. In fact, a quick resolution to contract terms is not always desirable. One reason for this is that multiple

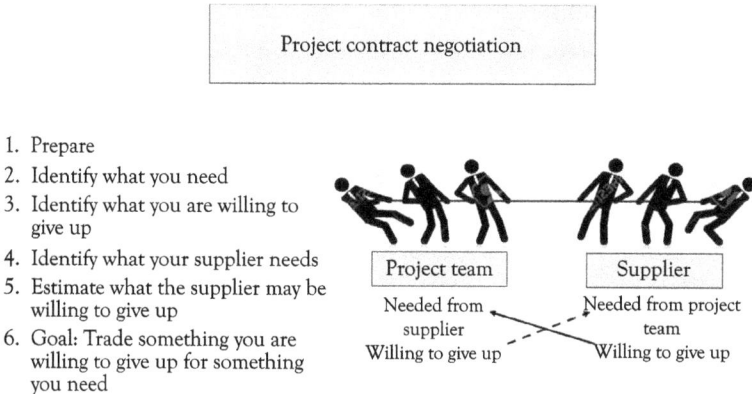

1. Prepare
2. Identify what you need
3. Identify what you are willing to give up
4. Identify what your supplier needs
5. Estimate what the supplier may be willing to give up
6. Goal: Trade something you are willing to give up for something you need

Figure 6.8 Project contract negotiations

vendors may be in the running for the project team contract. The longer that multiple vendors are competing, the better the opportunity for the project team to receive favorable terms. Delays based on commercial considerations must be balanced however with the logistics of producing the producing the project deliverables. Keep in mind that commercial considerations are only one part of the supplier engagement. Technical professionals on the project team will seek to complete contractual terms quickly so that work on technical solutions may proceed as soon as possible. When developing the plan for supplier engagement and negotiation, recognize up front the conflict that is likely to arise between the technical and commercial arm of the organization (Figure 6.8).

Contract Scope and Acceptance Criteria

Contracts elaborate the responsibilities and assumptions of each party to the agreement. Contracts are also a means for distributing risk among the parties. For example, contracts typically outline a schedule for both deliverables as well as payments. The contract includes any required up-front payment amounts. Up-front payments reduce the risk of the contracted—but not necessarily the contractor. Further, the contract will describe any alternative risk-sharing arrangements such as making resources available to aid in completing the work—either on the side of the outsource party or the project team. Just as importantly, a good contract describes not only the scope and specifications of the contracted deliverables but also the acceptance criteria for the deliverables. The acceptance criteria include the acceptance testing process, set expectations for quality, and describe the order of events required for final payment. A contract without a clear set of acceptance criteria expectations is one that will likely lead to conflict with the supplier as the end of the project approaches. For example, it is possible that the supplier will declare that the work is finished—only to have the project team formally announce that it isn't. Acceptance criteria solve this problem long before it emerges in the project as a problem.

Contracts and Risk

The type of contract issued by the project team determines the level of risk sharing between the parties including which party bears a greater measure of risk. The ideal contract type for a project team is a fixed-price contract. In this type of contract, the supplier agrees to an overall amount for the work and deliverable thereby locking in the price for the project team. Such a contract is of high risk to the supplier given that cost over-runs are not covered by the contract. Accepting a fixed-price contract therefore requires significant skill at project estimating. Although a fixed-price contract limits the risk of the project team, fixed-price contracts are not without risks. It is possible for a supplier to underbid for project work and end up in a position where the supplier is not able to complete the work. Worse still, if the project is a significant one, the supplier could go out of business due to losses associated with underbidding.

The financial analysis of the supplier by the project team becomes even more important in the context of a fixed-price contract. Another way to attempt to reduce the risk of a fixed-price contract when multiple suppliers are bidding for the contract is to avoid accepting the lowest bid. One approach is to make it known that the project will accept the "second lowest bid." This encourages suppliers to bid low—but not so low that they put their business in danger. Finally, the project team is advised to carry out its own cost analysis of the work for comparison and bench-marking to ensure that the quotation received is reasonable (Figure 6.9).

At the opposite end of the risk spectrum lies the "cost-plus" contract. In the cost-plus contract, the project team agrees to cover the cost of the

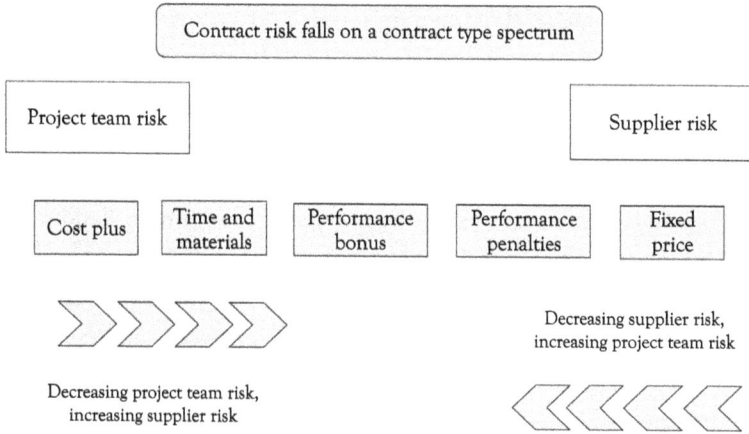

Figure 6.9 Contracts and risk

supplier and, in addition, pays a percentage of the overall amount as profit. Such an arrangement takes the risk burden off the supplier and places it with the project team. The project team lacks in this contract a clear way to control the cost and will naturally lack visibility in the final cost of the deliverables. While the cost is a disadvantage, the cost-plus contract may be necessary in some circumstances depending upon the financial health of the supplier. In addition, taking such an approach, although increasing the cost risk, may reduce other risks such as the lack of suppliers for an element of project work. A cost-plus arrangement is one method of "locking in" a supplier during a period when such resources are scarce. Between the two extremes of contractual arrangements, many others exist that may be employed depending upon the project circumstances. The choice of contract ultimately depends upon the context and which risk category is most desirable on the part of the project team to reduce.

Closing Procurements

Closing procurement engagements are particularly important because they involve considerable expense. For example, outsource labor and equipment rentals will likely involve ongoing monthly payments. If the contracts of these resources are not terminated, then the invoices for service will continue to be billed to the project. It is often the case, however, that some level of ongoing support for supplied components or other project deliverables will be required. This type of support will typically involve a contract addendum or an additional contract. Further, when a project terminates, there must be a formal methodology in place to manage the ongoing support. If the ongoing vendor support is continuous in nature, it may be prudent to formally hand over the long-term support of the deliverables to the ongoing operation of the company. On the other hand, if the support is likely to consist of a series of releases, it may make sense to charter a maintenance project team to work with the supplier after the initial procurement is terminated.

Communication and the Project Plan

Project deliverables and project goals are produced and achieved through people. This includes people within the project team, people outside the project team but within the company, the client, and finally people within the community at large. Such people can be a great support to the project—or, at minimum, avoid presenting barriers to project success. The secret to maximizing support of those impacted by the project is to keep all informed. Why does communication hold the possibility of improving stakeholder support? One reason is that information tends to reduce uncertainty among stakeholders. Uncertainty may lead to fear or concern, and in turn fear and concern may lead to resistance. Communication therefore breaks the negative spiral at the beginning by removing or at least minimizing uncertainty.

Communication, however, is by no means a simple task and it requires quite a bit of work on the part of the project team. In much the same way that journalists think about informing the public of news, project communication considers the "5 W's" (who, what, when, where, how, and why) (Figure 6.10). The "Who" of project communications involves stakeholders. The "Who" therefore will be addressed in the project stakeholder management portion of the overall project plan.

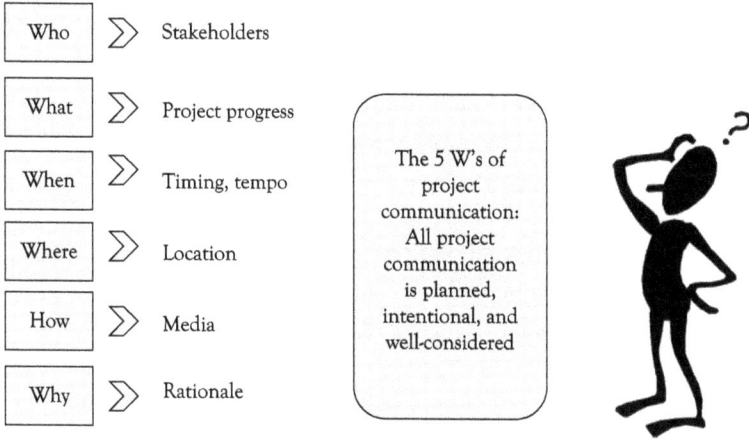

Figure 6.10 The communications plan and the five "W's"

The "What" of Project Communication

The project triple constraint is a significant generator of project information. Those who have an interest in the project and its outcomes will want to know if the project will be on time, if it will be within its budget targets, and finally if it will meet the requirements of the client and the sponsor. The updates on the status of the triple constraint are essential project progress reporting information. This information would appear to be straightforward to communicate since it is at the heart of what a project does. The difficulty is that this information is likely to change every day. Progress reporting is therefore a moving target. In addition, it is not always the case that this information is generated automatically. It takes work to produce progress updates. Also, the progress of the entire project depends upon the progress of the underlying work packages of which it is composed. This infers that multiple individuals within the project team will likely be involved in generating and collecting information—as well as putting it into a format that is relatively easy for stakeholders to consume.

The effort required to develop and report information could be considered a "tax" upon the project team. The irony is that the further the project progresses, the more progress information is needed. The more the information required, the more significant is the effort to produce it. It is possible that so many team members could be tied up in collecting and reporting information that the project progress begins to fall behind. What does this mean for the project manager? Simply that the communication plan must identify in advance:

1. What information will be communicated?
2. How the information will be generated, collected, and formatted?
3. What resources will be assigned to do it?

It pays to notify parties of interest up front of the project policies on reporting information so that the burden to project resources may be minimized. It also pays to consider up front the degree to which information may be generated automatically. The rule of thumb is to try to "enter information only once" and avoid spending resources on manual data collection and re-entry for further reporting. Finally, an ideal way to determine "what" is to be reported is to set up an application to collect information from a project management information system (PMIS) and report it automatically without the need to tie up project resources. This is an ideal that few project teams can achieve and may be limited to such teams that work within a large enough organization so that a high-capability PMIS is affordable.

The "When" of Project Communication

The pace of project activity can be modeled on the project budget or "S-Curve." A project tends to begin small—and slow at first—but then the activity increases. The project activity tends to peak as it moves beyond planning and into executing—and then gradually declines as the project moves toward closure. Project communication tends to follow the project activity with on serious exception: *project communication rarely decreases as the project inches toward project completion.* Instead, the demand for project communication from stakeholders tends to increase. Why should this be? Human psychology may play a role with respect to the pace of project communication. At the beginning of the project, team members and stakeholders often perceive that time is endlessly available. This is especially true within lengthy projects. Because of this, stakeholders may be less demanding in terms of frequency of information.

Project status meeting monthly tempo
(as launch approaches)

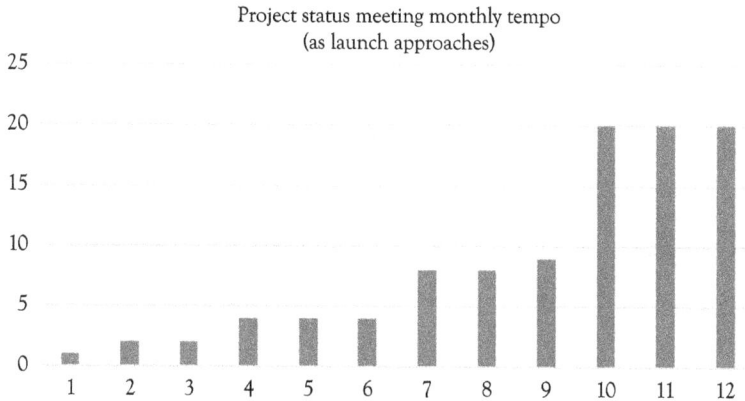

Figure 6.11 Project communications plan tempo

Project reports submitted every two to three weeks may be considered adequate at the beginning. After all, the project activity is just beginning. As the activity in the project picks up, time itself will seem to speed up. The information that was presented biweekly may soon be requested weekly. As the project gets closer to the end, all who have an interest in the outcome of the project will want to understand what is happening. The weekly reports may become reports that are delivered twice a week. Soon, the reporting cycle may well shift to a daily report—and perhaps twice daily. It is easy for a project team to get caught up in this negative cycle of increased communication frequency (Figure 6.11). It is for this reason that the project communication plan should establish from the beginning of the project the frequency of the project communication as well as the degree to which the frequency of reporting will be permitted to change as the project progresses. Keep in mind the phrase "inquiring minds want to know" and be prepared for those demands for increased communication frequency.

Planning the "When" of Communications

In the spirit of "Plan first, then do," develop and clearly state policy on communication frequency up front to set stakeholder expectation. Finally, the category of information communicated plays a role in "When" the information is communicated. There is an old saying in project management that project managers should communicate "Bad news early, and good news late." The key is to ensure that apparent good news is actual good news so that the credibility of the project team is maintained. Further, bad news hidden from interested parties has a way of "backfiring." Be assured that bad news will eventually leak from the project team and find its way to sponsors and clients.

Reporting bad news early demonstrates both that the project management is aware of all serious issues and more importantly that the project manager may be relied upon to tell the truth (even when it hurts!). Finally, it is recommended to establish a weekly communication cycle in the minds of stakeholders that captures the flow of work, evaluation of status, review meetings, and reports. In this way, it will become clearer that information demanded prior to the completion of the weekly information gathering cycle will likely be incomplete—or perhaps even erroneous.

The "Where" of Project Communication

The resource impact of project communication is also an issue when the location or the "where" of project communication is considered. Will, for example, reports be delivered face-to-face in formal meetings? If so, where will these meetings take place? Who will arrange such meetings? Also, if the client is distant from the project location, traveling to such meetings can consume considerable time. Further, in addition to regular project progress reports, to what extent will project and design reviews take place—and where will these be held? If at a different location, will the venue alternate between meetings? Finally, if conference calls or videoconferences are used for virtual meetings, will this be sufficient in all cases? Or, will it be supplemented by physical face-to-face meetings? The location—rather physical or virtual—requires thought, planning, and specification up front. It is because of these questions—to identify only a few—that "Where?" is an essential element of the project communications plan.

The "How" of Project Communication

When project managers consider "How" to communicate information to a wide audience, inevitably the overlap between "How" and "Where"

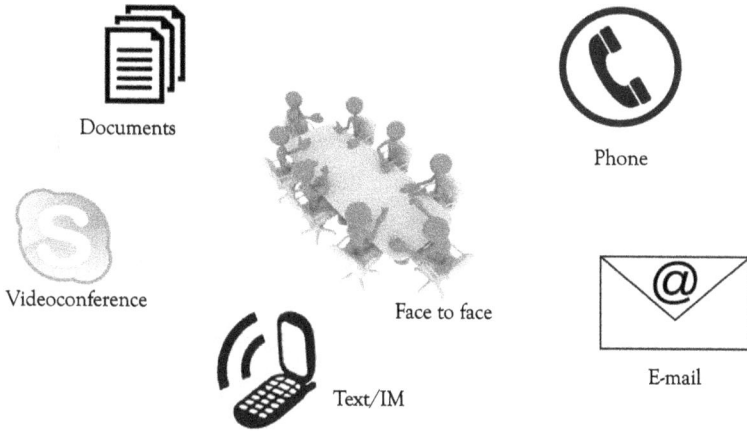

Figure 6.12 *Project communications media*

becomes obvious. "Where" communication takes place refers to location—be it physical or virtual. Also, a face-to-face or virtual meeting can describe a communication methodology or media type. A project communication plan outlines the communication methodology—or media employed—for different types of reporting (Figure 6.12). For example, when communicating project progress data, an ideal method for reporting would be to automatically populate an Intranet dashboard using information extracted from the PMIS. This saves considerable effort in extracting and formatting information for stakeholders. Caution should be applied with respect to what information is automatically extracted and reported. This is because project status tends to change daily—and putting too much raw data on an Intranet too soon may lead to a "roller-coaster" ride of sorts for stakeholders with reported daily ups and downs. In this situation, a certain amount of information control may be healthy.

The Audience Determines "How"

An additional consideration is the nature of the audience receiving the communicated information. For example, some audiences may benefit from a presentation using slide presentation packages such as Microsoft PowerPoint. Others may find documents more useful—and spreadsheets may be appropriate for stakeholders who require more data-intensive information. A range of media possibilities exists depending upon the context. However, some communication media require more preparation than others. Project managers when developing the communication plan should therefore consider the nature of the information, the preferences of the audience, the context in which the information is delivered, and finally the effort required to produce it. In general, the greater the level of preparation, the more the project team can distill the information and put the status of the project in its best light. Less preparation infers that the information presented will be more in the form of raw data than information—leading to the possibility of misinterpretation on the part of stakeholders. Communication media planning and preparation is therefore often a delicate balance between "too much" or "too little"—in terms of both effort and information distillation.

The "Why" of Project Communication

It is reasonable to expect that those who have an interest in the status and outcome of the project will request information. Some interested parties may be comfortable with regular, standard reports. Others such as the client, the project sponsor, or functional groups associated with the project may demand ad hoc reports that address specific areas of concern. Preparing this type of information requires time, and resources—both personnel and funding. It is incumbent upon the project team to ask "Why?" specific information is required as well as how it is expected to be used. Ideally, special requests may be addressed by referring to elements of existing standard reports—including presented data of which the interested party may not be aware. The minimization of effort produced by pointing stakeholders to existing information may only be done if the question of "Why?" is first posed.

There are situations where asking "Why?" may be difficult. As an example, it is common to respond immediately without thinking to a client request for information. However, the client may well appreciate hearing this question as it suggests that the project team is carefully thinking through all demands placed upon the project so that scope, schedule, and cost are minimized. Although the client will be a frequent requestor of information, the client also tends to prioritize project deliverables over administrative tasks. Asking "Why?" when it comes to communications planning is important, not only important for the utility of the project team. Asking tough questions is also likely to foster an environment of mutual respect.

Another factor influencing "Why" is associated with the communication of low-level technical or financial details. Some information of this nature may go beyond the ability of the audience to understand. This is especially true when reporting information to executive sponsors or clients. When a presentation is being prepared, it is reasonable to review each element of the report and to ask, "Why are we communicating this information to this audience?" Asking "Why" in this context has the potential to match the information delivered with the audience capacity to receive and process it.

The Elements of the Communication Plan

What elements should be included in the resource plan? The project communication plan for a project should answer the following questions for the purposes of developing project communication policies and guidelines:

1. Who are the interested parties that require project information?
2. What categories and specific details of information are required?
3. How often will information need to be communicated?
4. Who will be assigned to collect, prepare, and deliver the information?
5. Where will communication take place?
6. What preferred media will be required for transmitting project communication?
7. Why is the information being requested? Why is it being communicated?

CHAPTER 7

Delivery Performance Domain

When a project manager begins a project, it is assumed that the purpose of the project and the underlying rationale for the effort are clear. Unfortunately, this is not always the case—especially in companies that routinely commission projects to produce deliverables such as new products and services for the marketplace. With so many different project options from which to choose, how does a company select the best one? Making this decision is rarely easy—and therefore project selection is approached in a systematic way. Project selection is often visualized as a "funnel." A funnel is very wide at one end, and very narrow at the other as is observed in Figure 7.1.

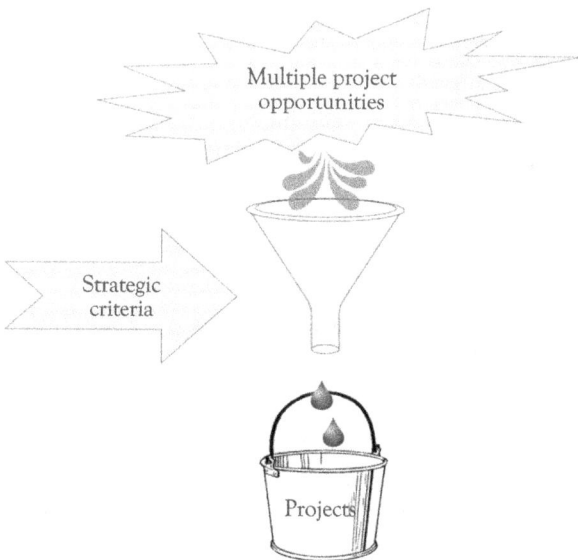

Multiple project
opportunities

Strategic
criteria

Projects

Figure 7.1 Project opportunity screening

Likewise, the set of all possible projects that a company could undertake is potentially very large. However, the funding available to pay for projects is limited. The limited funding is what makes the funnel narrow rather than wide. The objective of an organization therefore is to vet the large population of potential projects so that only a very few projects are chartered. The projects that survive the vetting process are those that are most likely to be successful. Selecting projects does not end at the project charter. As the project progresses through its life cycle, it is vetted at each phase to ensure that the original assumptions about the project and its likelihood of success remain sound.

Strategy: Knowing "Why" Comes Before What

Projects produce deliverables—and companies that commission projects to produce these deliverables do so to contribute in some way, no matter how small, to the overall mission and objectives of the company. A project is considered an investment in time, effort, and money. When a company invests money, it does so in pursuit of its mission to achieve and maintain a competitive advantage within the markets it serves. The term "competitive advantage" is a reference to competitive positioning. A company is better able to succeed when it is well positioned compared with those against whom it competes. A company is well positioned when it can set the price level for its products and maintain it—while at the same time—minimizing its costs.

Michael Porter (2008), a well-known strategist from the Harvard Business School, informs us that companies that are best able to do things such as minimize competition and rivalry, minimize the threat of substitutes, and keep new entrants out of the marketplace have the power to set their prices and minimize their costs. They do so because they are said to be well positioned in terms of Porter's strategic model. To use an analogy drawn from the military, imagine a platoon preparing to engage with the enemy. The platoon leader will survey the surrounding environment to find the best position within the field of battle. A hill is a position that is likely to be preferred over a valley. A mediocre platoon may still have a strong chance of winning the battle if it fights from the hill rather than the valley. Fighting from a hill provides an almost "unfair advantage" that may be exploited. This is graphically illustrated in Figure 7.2.

Figure 7.2 Strong and weak strategic positions

Returning to the business arena and using an analogous example, during the housing crisis of 2007, a home buyer would be far better positioned strategically than a home seller. The individual trying to sell the home may well have an excellent product that includes many different upgrades. However, since the seller is poorly positioned, the seller has little power to obtain the desired price. The difference in power between buyer and seller seems unfair—in the same way that "fighting from a hill" is. However, this is simply a result of strategic positioning. A similar situation exists between consumer electronics manufacturers and electronics distributors. A large nationwide retailer has the choice of many electronics manufacturers from which to choose. Because of this, the retailer has more power to set prices than the manufacturer.

Every company therefore has a fundamental approach that it employs to seek the optimal position within its competitive landscape. All operations, products produced, and projects in which the company carries out plays a role in achieving the company's competitive positioning strategy. The first rule therefore for selecting the optimal project for which to invest is to deeply understand the strategy of the company both in terms of what it is as well as how it works. Managers involved in project selection must therefore be able to readily answer the question of "Just what is it exactly are we trying to do here, and why?" If this question cannot be answered, it is not possible to choose an optimal project from a range of possibilities.

Strategic Alignment

The term alignment suggests that elements put "in alignment" must be ordered so that they are all facing in, or pointing to, the same direction. Strategic alignment uses this concept—but in terms of activities carried out by the organization. All initiatives, tasks to be carried out, deliverables to be produced—as well as projects—must "point in the same direction" as that indicated by the strategy of the company. It follows then that when a company selects an optimal project for execution, it will be a project that is in alignment with the company mission. It further follows that the degree of alignment of a project with the mission of the company is obvious. This is not always the case—which is why tools are applied to make the degree of alignment clear.

How to Narrow Down Project Choices

The concept of alignment provides the project manager with only a starting point for deciding upon which projects to fund and execute, and which to discard. It is only a starting point because the degree of strategic alignment of each project proposal must be determined. There are many ways to do this including the application of judgment using qualitative tools, as well as analytical techniques that apply quantitative measures to assess the degree to which the project fits the goals spelled out in the strategy of the company. Often, the process begins with a qualitative approach by quickly weeding out projects that obviously do not fit well with the company mission. Eventually, the vetting process leads to a small number of projects that on the face of it, all seem to satisfy company strategic requirements. It is at this point where the application of tools becomes more advantageous by making small but important differences clear for the purpose of decision making.

Qualitative Selection Tools

An experienced project manager with a long career within a particular company is usually very familiar with the company strategy and culture. In this case, the application of judgment may be all that is needed to select projects that make sense to pursue, and which do not. Not all project managers have this skill or background. As a result, the collective expertise and judgment of the company may be gathered in the form of a strategic checklist. Often, a checklist used for this purpose is developed over a long period of time by successive project managers and executives who have selected and delivered successful projects. The checklist then forms part of the vetting process, and as such, becomes organizational policies, and once mature, organizational governance. Further, how the checklist is used, who uses it, and when it is used may become part of the culture of the company.

The purpose of the strategic checklist is to compare the goals of the project and its proposed results with the strategic goals of the company. When the checklist method is used, the more elements in the checklist that the project satisfies, the more that the project is said to be in alignment with company strategy. An example of a strategic project selection checklist is provided below:

1. Does this project meet the company objectives for financial return?
2. Does this project address markets that the company deems to be important?
3. Does this project make strategic use of company resources?
4. Is our company capable of developing and delivering this project?
5. Does the company have adequate funding to deliver this project?
6. Is this project consistent with the company mission, vision, and values?

One problem with using a strategic project selection checklist is that it weights all elements of the checklist equally. It is not often the case that all elements within a checklist would be equally important. A weighted checklist provides the project manager with the means for putting greater emphasis on some elements versus others. Instead of simply indicating the presence or absence of an important strategic factor, the project manager—and perhaps the project team and executive sponsors—may apply weights to each strategic factor. The weighting of each category is derived from the emphasis each category is given in the strategy of the company. Each score is then multiplied by the weight of each element and total. Multiple projects are then compared against each other based upon the total weighted score for each. An example of a weighted project selection checklist is provided in Table 7.1.

Table 7.1 Weighted project selection checklist

Project (A, B, C)	Weight	Score	Total
Financial returns	0.3		
Markets	0.1		
Strategic resources	0.2		
Capabilities	0.2		
Funding	0.1		
Mission consistency	0.1		
Total	1		

Although the weighted selection checklist uses numbers—this does not necessarily mean that the method is a quantitative method. This is because the numbers used for scoring and weighting are based upon the collective subjective judgment of the management team. The numbers are therefore interpreted as relative measures of emphasis—rather than absolute quantitative measures.

Quantitative Selection Tools

Selecting a project that aligns with the strategy of the company is important—but, it may be only a beginning. For example, companies often have multiple possible choices of projects from which to choose that each align with the strategy of the company. What should a project manager do if (and likely when) this happens? The next level of consideration usually involves determining if the project will result in financial rewards. There are several techniques that may be applied to make this determination—and different companies will likely use different methods. Each of the analysis techniques are designed to answer questions that lead to project selection decisions.

Project Selection Questions and Analysis Techniques

The first question of interest from a project manager seeking to understand the viability of a possible project selection is:

If we do this project, how much money will we make?

The amount of money made is simply the total revenues generated by the project deliverables less the cost of the project (including overhead) as well as the costs of the deliverables. This may be easily expressed in the form of a formula:

Total project revenues – (Total cost of project + Total cost of project deliverables) = Money made

While it is true the project managers seek to make money, it is also true that they want to avoid losing money—and they seek to recover the initial project investment as soon as possible. This leads to the next important project evaluation question, which is:

When can we expect to recover the investment we made in this project?

Answering when (and possibly if) the project investment will be recovered is answered by means of the standard formula for the payback period. At a high level, the payback period formula is given as:

Project payback period = Total project cost ^ (Project deliverable revenues—Cost of project deliverables per period)

Although this is a rather simple formula, calculating the payback period may be complicated in practice. This is because the exact revenues and the cost of project deliverables may be difficult to project or even calculate depending upon the nature of the deliverables and the accounting system of the company.

The simple payback period is intended to be simple and because of this, it ignores the complexity of the time value of money (TVM). In projects with relatively low up-front costs and high sales and gross margins—the TVM may prove to have negligible impact since the recovery period of the investment will as a result be rather short. Longer-term projections that include a great deal of uncertainty of cash flows and gross margins may benefit from the use of TVM in the payback period calculation to obtain a more realistic picture.

The TVM: What Does It Mean?

Understanding TVM in the project selection process is simple, if you start from a familiar financial scenario. For example:

$100 in your pocket today will be worth more tomorrow if you put it in the bank and it earns interest.

How much more? If we assume 5 percent interest, then $100 in your pocket today (and put in the bank) will be worth, in one year:

$$\$100 * 1.05 = \$105.00$$

The difficulty of incorporating the time TVM in project selection scenarios is the understanding of this simple financial scenario in the reverse sense. For example:

What if you didn't have $100.00 today, but someone promised to give you $100.00 one year from now? The question now becomes:

How much is "$100.00 promised in one year actually effectively worth today?"

If we could have earned 5 percent interest by putting it in the bank for a year, then the value of $100.00 promised one year from now is effectively worth:

$$\$100.00 - 1.05 = \$95.24$$

Said another way,

If I put $95.24 in the bank today earning 5 percent, in one year it would equal $100.00.

As can be observed in the formula for "discounting" future cash to the present, the formula is reversed from that of banking $100 and calculating the one-year interest. This simple scenario however ignores the fact that cash flows from projects typically continue beyond one or more years. Multiyear cash flows from project deliverables complicate the TVM calculation, but once the algorithm is understood, it is a simple process to discount multiple future cash flows to the present.

To begin with understanding multiyear TVM, we can start at the beginning and assume that we are putting $100 in the bank at 5 percent interest for several years. In this case, we have the following:

*One year: $100 * 1.05 = $105.00*
*Two years: $100 * 1.05 *1.05 = $110.25*
*Three years: $100 * 1.05 * 1.05* 1.05= $115.75*

In multiyear TVM, the principle that is invested, plus the interest it accrues, feeds the next period. Interest is therefore earned not only on principle, but on the interest of previous periods. This is the principle of "compounding" that naturally leads to significant growth of an initial monetary stake over time. In mathematical shorthand, these equations tell us that the money in your pocket today, multiplied by the discount rate raised to the power of the number of periods, equals the final value of your deposit. Expressing this mathematically leads to the following formula:

Money · Rate^ Period n

For example, using the previous example for three years but employing the simpler formula, we have:

*Three years: $100 * 1.05 ^ 3 = $115.75*

To reverse the process, it could be asked, "What is the value today of $100 promised three years from now?" The answer comes from reversing the process of calculating the value of a deposit within three years and "discounting to the present." This is done as follows:

$100.00 – (1.05) ^ 3 = $100 – 1.16 = $86.38

What if the going rate of interest was not 5 percent—but instead—it was 10 percent? In this case, we would have:

$100.00 – (1.10) ^ 3 = $100 – 1.33 = $75.13

There are some observations that can be made by comparing the value of $100 promised three years from today versus one year from today, as follows:

1. The longer the waiting period for the promised money, the less it is worth today.
2. The higher the discount rate, the less the money is effectively worth today.
3. The higher the discount (or "hurdle") rate, the more money the project will need to generate to compensate for the higher rate.

From these simple observations, regardless of the project scenario being considered, "Early money is better than late money," meaning, that it is preferred for projects to return money sooner rather than later—regardless of the TVM. Also, we observe that in times of high discount rates—or in times when the project is assigned a high discount rate due to its relative high risk—the project must "work harder" to prove its worthiness as an investment.

How Is TVM Applied to the Payback Period Calculation?

If TVM is considered when using the payback analysis, then the cash from project deliverables (less the cost of project deliverables) is simply discounted to the present. Again, this is useful for presenting a more accurate assessment of the payback when future cash flows are less certain, and the initial investment is high. In simpler cases, TVM may be dispensed with when calculating TVM. What would constitute a "simpler case?" An example would be a project whose payback timeframe is short compared to its project life cycle. A project that produces deliverables that lead to profits that pay back the initial investment within one to two years need not be overly concerned with the TVM. However, projects that are not expected to pay back within 5 to 10 years and include widely spaced and inconsistent cash flows would likely benefit from the incorporation of TVM within payback analysis.

Risk and Reward in Project Selection

An important question that is asked in the project selection goes beyond the payback period to consider if the project is worth doing considering the risk. The question asked is:

Are the forthcoming rewards consistent with the risk undertaken?

Risk and reward in project selection are considered using TVM techniques with a specific emphasis on the discount or hurdle rate. This is simply another way of expressing the fact that a project that has more risk must produce more return. In life, we see the discount rate difference when we examine the cost of a mortgage loan (which guarantees the payback of the loan via the collateral of the house) versus a credit card charge that has no collateral backing. The default risk of the credit card loan is higher than the default risk of a mortgage loan. As a result, the interest rate charged in a credit card loan is much higher—often, several times higher than a mortgage loan.

The same principle applies to project selection which is in effect a decision regarding the determination of which project to invest. A high-risk project must be judged using a higher return on investment (ROI) than a low-risk project. What rate of return then should a project manager seek and how is this rate determined? This is a question that the company Chief Financial Officer (CFO) can play a role in answering. The CFO knows the rate that the company pays for its funding. This rate is derived from the weighted average of the mix of debt and equity financing used by the company. This rate, known as the Weighted Average Cost of Capital (WACC), will likely not be the same as the hurdle rate or return rate required for the project. The reason is that the project is likely to exhibit more risk than the company. Therefore, the required return rate for the project would necessarily need to be higher. Again, the specifics of this rate are derived from a consideration of the strategy of the company as communicated by senior management.

One of the most important questions to be asked in selecting projects is:

What is the return on the money invested in this project and how does it compare with the return on secure financial instruments?

There is both a simple as well as a complex answer to this question. The simple answer is to compare the total profit of the project deliverables to the expense of creating the deliverables. For example, if the project cost is $100,000.00 and the resulting profits are $110,000.00, then the ROI is 10 percent. Why does ROI matter? It matters because the more capital that is at stake, the greater the resulting return that is expected. This goes hand in hand with risk versus reward.

There is a more complex answer to this question, and it involves considering TVM, and the comparison of the overall project return to the return offered by a similar, but more secure, financial instrument. To put it in simple terms, the Net Present Value (or NPV) method not only considers the project return based on TVM, but it also answers the question:

Should I invest in this project, or should I just put my money in the bank?

The NPV project selection and evaluation procedure is a step-by-step process and works as follows:

1. Estimate the project cash outlays required to produce the project deliverables.
2. Estimate the future cash flows associated with the profits from the project deliverables.
3. Discount the future cash flows to the present (the Present Value (PV) portion of the NPV process).
4. Combine the present value of future cash flows with the estimate project outlay of the present (the N or Net portion of the NPV process).
5. Assess whether the result is positive, zero, or negative.
   a. Positive: This means that the present value of future cash flows associated with project profit cash flows—discounted to the present—is greater than the amount invested. Also, it can be said to exceed the project's discount rate. A positive NPV is therefore money well spent.
   b. Zero: A zero NPV means that the present value of future cash flows associated with project profit cash flows—discounted to the

present—is the same as the amount invested. Also, the returns can be said to equal the returns consistent with the project's discount rate. A zero NPV infers that the project returns no more than the required discount rate. The implication of a zero NPV is that the return of the project is no more than that which could be earned in a secure financial instrument—for example—"putting it in the bank" to use the vernacular.

c. Negative: This means that the present value of future cash flows associated with project profit cash flows—discounted to the present—is less than the amount invested. Also, it can be said to produce returns less than the project's discount rate. A negative NPV is therefore money not very well spent. The implication is that funds intended to be invested in this project would be better utilized in other projects.

What does it all mean? When a project manager selects from several projects—the optimal choice from a purely risk and reward perspective would be the project with the highest NPV. In simple terms, positive NPVs result from projects that produce returns above the required project discount rate. The higher the NPV, the greater the return exceeds the project discount rate. An NPV of zero indicates that the project returned profits sufficient to equal the required project discount rate. Although zero is considered acceptable—it may be a question mark for project selection. Because the project result is only an estimate—it is not difficult to imagine a scenario when the future expected cash flows are less than expected. In this case, the zero NPV could shift to a negative value depending on events and circumstances. Finally, a negative NPV is an indicator that the project returns less than the return targeted by the discount rate. In most cases, this is an indicator that the project should be rejected. However, negative NPV projects might be selected if some higher-level strategic reason exists for pursuing the project. A project that is commissioned simply to produce a placeholder product in the market or to maintain market share may be one example of a strategic reason to pursue a project with a negative NPV.

Table 7.2 An NPV example

Cash outlay		Year 1	Year 2	Year 3	Year 4	Year 5
$100,000	CF	$15,000	$25,000	$40,000	$45,000	$50,000
Net	Discount	1.05	1.1025	1.1576	1.2155	1.2763
$47,712.87	PV	$14,285.71	$22,675.74	$34,553.50	$37,021.61	$39,176.31

An NPV Example ....

Assume a project that cost $100,000.00, but returns $15,000, $25,000, $40,000, $45,000, and $50,000 in Years 1 to 5. What is the NPV given a 5 percent discount rate? Is the project "worth it?" An inspection of the NPV table shows that the project is very much "worth it." The project returns $47,712.87 more than its discount or hurdle rate of 5 percent (Table 7.2).

What if, however, the project projected the same cash flows—however—the case flows would occur later in Years 1 to 5. Should a project manager continue to select this project?

An inspection of Table 7.3 illustrates that, although the NPV is lower, it remains very high. Project managers would take note that as a principle, the longer that project sponsors must wait for cash flows—the lower the NPV will be. This is because the longer investors must wait for promises of cash in the future—the less that the money is valued today due to the exponential property of discounting.

Finally, what if the sponsors of the project are concerned about the lack of cash flows in Years 1 and 2, and as a result, request a higher discount rate? In Table 7.4, the rate of 15 percent is suggested given the risk concerns. By inspection, the NPV has gone marginally negative—thereby making the new series of cash flows and higher discount rate a question mark in terms of project selection.

Table 7.3 Impact of delayed cash flows on the NPV

Cash outlay		Year 1	Year 2	Year 3	Year 4	Year 5
$100,000	CF			$55,000	$55,000	$65,000
Net	Discount	1.05	1.1025	1.1576	1.2155	1.2763
$43,688.90	PV			$34,553.50	$37,021.61	$39,176.31

Table 7.4 Higher risk reflected in the NPV discount rate

Cash outlay		Year 1	Year 2	Year 3	Year 4	Year 5
$100,000	CF			$55,000	$55,000	$65,000
Net	Discount	1.15	1.3225	1.5209	1.749	2.0114
–$73.69	PV			$34,553.50	$37,021.61	$39,176.31

Another View of Return—The Internal Rate of Return

The NPV returns three possible results—positive, zero, and negative. The NPV therefore is a comparative measure that examines how the project performs by comparison to a given target discount or hurdle rate. Another way to evaluate a project however is to determine its effective return rate known as the Internal Rate of Return (IRR). The formula for the IRR is rather complex—although the formula is embedded within Microsoft Excel and does produce the correct result when used correctly. However, a project manager who first performs and NPV may easily determine the IRR in a spreadsheet by adjusting the discount rate until the NPV becomes exactly (or at least very close to) zero. The discount rate at an NPV of zero is the IRR. Revisiting Table 7.4 shows a slightly negative NPV. This infers that the discount rate applied was in fact very close to the IRR rate since it is close to zero. Adjusting the discount rate to 14 percent returns a positive NPV of $3,446.81. This informs the project manager that the IRR is between 14 and 15 percent—and likely very close to 15 percent. Granted, this is a ballpark IRR figure—but—project selections involve estimates and judgment including the estimation of the investment level, timing of cash flows, and choice of discount rate. Finding the IRR in this way makes it a simple process to work hand in hand with the NPV calculation in project selection.

Returning to the Original Question ....

After carefully evaluating several possible projects using both quali-tative and quantitative selection remains, "Which project should be selected?" Although the final answer may be difficult to answer with perfect clarity—the fact that the question is being asked is an important first step. In all things project management—anything to be done must be first planned. One of the objectives of the project selection process is to ensure that projects are not commissioned by the organization in an ad hoc manner. Instead, possible projects should be evaluated in terms of their alignment with company strategy and in terms of the potential for rewards consistent with the risk undertaken. Project selection techniques provide the means to make this assessment.

Numbers Do Not Ensure Unbiased Results

The use of financial techniques in project selection often gives the impression that the selection of the project is without bias, and it is wholly scientific in its methodology. Nothing could be further from the truth. The project manager should be aware of the shortcomings associated with the use of financial selection methods. The shortcomings relate to the underlying assumptions made in the analysis. For example, it is easy to create a financial analysis that causes a poor project to be selected. This can be done by selecting an abnormally low discount rate. Recall that the higher the discount rate, the harder that the project must work (in terms of future cash flow generation) to demonstrate its merit. The reverse is also true. Set too low—the discount rate can make a bad idea look better than it is. Also, beware of a financial analysis that rejects a promising project due to the selection of a discount rate that is too high. An abnormally high discount rate effectively forces a project to work harder than it needs to justify its existence. The lesson for project managers is that project selection is a time for asking questions. When financial selection techniques are used, the first question to be asked is: "Where did that discount rate come from—and how was it derived?" Finally, regardless of the chosen discount rate—it pays to challenge future cash flow assumptions. The future is always uncertain—so, the project selection process would benefit from the use of conservative future cash flow estimates.

Integration, the Plan, and the Project Manager

The term "integration" implies "summing up" or "tying things together." This is exactly what a project manager does. The project manager creates a holistic picture of the work that needs to be done and communicates this to project stakeholders via the development of a comprehensive project plan. The charter is the foundation for a project manager as it provides the authority to the project to do work, acquire resources, and spend money—but more importantly, it communicates this authorization to stakeholders. When stakeholders are aware that such an authority has been provided, the project charter (Figure 7.3) becomes a hub that links together the resources and support from internal and external stakeholders.

Integration as "Tying Together"

While there is no doubt that the bringing together of all elements of the project creates an integration of the pieces of the project, making the transition from the project schedule—the project scope, schedule, and cost—to the complete project plan, it pays to keep in mind that the overall project plan as identified that integration is an "umbrella" necessary to develop and execute a complete project. Prior to getting lost in the details of the PMBOK, consider that a key role of project manager is one of integration. Beginning with the project schedule as the foundation or bedrock of the project, the next step in integrating the project "big picture" is to layer each of the additional subcomponents of the plan onto the project schedule (i.e., scope, schedule, cost). At the end of development of the project plan, the project team will have at its disposal a "layer cake" of sorts with the essential supporting project subplans layered on top and integrated with the project schedule (Figure 7.4).

Simple project charter

Project Name:
Date:
Project manager signature: _____
Project sponsor signature: _____

Project purpose & description:		Project role	Team members
		Position	Name
Key milestones:		...	...
		...	...
High-level budget:		...	...
		..	...
Constraints:			

Figure 7.3 Simple project charter

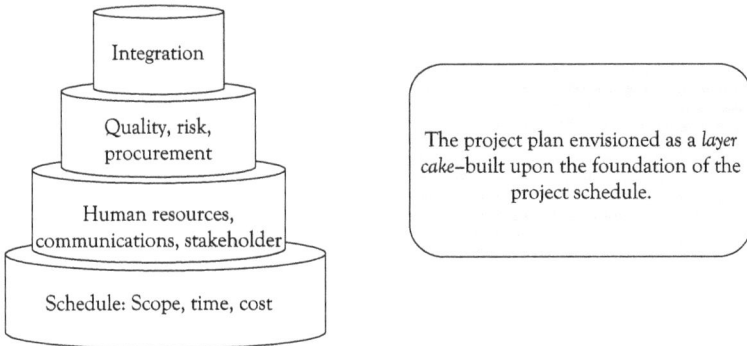

Figure 7.4 The project plan "layer cake"

Quality Management: The First Step Beyond Scope, Schedule, and Budget

Project quality management is an integration activity of the project charter, and the planning activities that include the development of the project scope, schedule, and budget. Project quality is closely linked to project scope. This is because a clearly defined project scope will articulate the specific performance levels of the project deliverables—and performance is one attribute of quality. There are, however, many facets to managing quality within projects that go beyond the focus on the performance of project deliverables. Further, the significant differences between managing quality in the temporary environment of a project versus the continuous environment of an ongoing operation require that project managers think carefully about how to approach the development of project quality management.

Quality Management in Projects

The underlying principle in the "management of quality" is to manage the system (i.e., control the process) rather than the product. It is said that, if the system is under control, the product (output of the process) will be of good quality. It is upon this underlying principle that statistical process control in quality management has evolved. This idea of managing a process with upper and lower control limits over the long run however is difficult to apply within an environment that has no "long run." According to the definition, a project is a temporary endeavor that produces unique deliverables. This begs the question, "What process (or processes) within the context of project management should be controlled to produce quality deliverables?" Further, the fact that projects are temporary and unique and often produce singular deliverables such as systems, or construction artifacts such as homes and buildings, would appear to question the degree to which many of the traditional quality management systems even apply within the project management context. It may also be observed that the role of projects that develop products for mass production is to produce a prototype design for which the manufacturing operation produces thousands and perhaps millions of copies. The significant difference between these roles would naturally suggest that some differences in the approach to quality management are warranted. This has significant implications to the development of the project quality plan including what processes should be applied as well as what project quality management tools should be employed.

Quality Management Tools

Quality management tools are typically studied in the context of operations management and are therefore borrowed from the context of the ongoing operation and suggested to be applied within the project context. More appropriately, quality management in project management is used to support the development of project requirements and standards used to guide the development of the project deliverables. In this way, it outlines how the project will comply with such requirements by planning the overall strategy that the project team will use to manage quality.

Project managers can benefit from understanding the "Seven Quality Control Tools." The project manager uses these tools for solving quality problems within the project. In the plan quality management group, the project manager would determine which of these tools would be applied in managing project quality through each of the project phases. Project teams are advised to carefully consider which of these seven tools are appropriate to use for each phase of the project as many of the tools have more apparent applicability to ongoing operations rather than temporary project activity.

Seven Quality Control Tools

The Cause-and-Effect Diagram: This diagram, pioneered by Ishikawa, is a generic tool that could be used in virtually any setting. It is particularly appropriate for simplifying troubleshooting and problem solving. The project environment is known to face time constraints. Troubleshooting problems with deliverables and interim deliverables are likely to be a significant component of achieving the goals of the project. The cause-and-effect diagram therefore appears to be a tool that fits well within the project environment. Cause-and-effect analysis is also useful within the ongoing operation. In addition to its use in problem solving, it is of interest however to consider how this tool might be used in the context of project quality planning. Ultimately, project deliverables could be viewed as an exercise in meeting needs or solving specific problems faced by the client. The cause-and-effect diagram could therefore aid in visualizing the client problem or need so that planned project deliverables adequately address them.

Flowchart: Projects are often complex. It is not easy to readily understand how the inputs to the project fit together to ultimately become deliverables. Further, the process for completing deliverables may not be well understood. Given the time constraints under which a project operates, a flowchart would likely be useful in providing a guide for understanding the systems under construction as well as the processes used to deliver them. The flowchart therefore could play a role in project planning—as is the case in its use within ongoing operations. The flowchart could also be used to document or clarify the behavior of the underlying project deliverables. The flowchart therefore is consistent with troubleshooting and correcting problems and with mapping out processes associated with the creating of project deliverables as well. Is the flowchart a quality planning tool, or is it more related to project execution? The versatility of the flowchart indicates that it is both.

Check sheets: Projects are often organized according to a series of lifecycle phases. Project lifecycle governance therefore typically proceeds to manage projects on a phase-by-phase basis. The checklist plays the role of ensuring that all targeted goals for each phase are completed. Further, the check sheet provides a means for confirming that the project deliverables satisfy the project specifications. Also, the checklist could be used to confirm that the specifications for the project deliverables are consistent with the original requirements as communicated by the client. A successfully completed check sheet could be used as evidence that the project has met the exit criteria for a given project lifecycle phase. Although checklists are routinely applied in operations, the check sheet tool does not assume a perpetual ongoing process or activity. This makes the check sheet a good fit for use in managing project quality to the degree that project quality is associated with the confirmation of the achievement and validation of requirements.

Pareto Diagrams: Pareto diagrams, emphasized by **Juran**, focus the attention of the manager on those issues that are creating the most problems. The general principle of the "80/20" rule would likely be applicable to any management context regardless of whether it was permanent or temporary. The Pareto chart, however, does tend to have more impact when there are volumes of issues to deal with. In highly complex projects, or in software-intensive projects where defects are analyzed and prioritized, the Pareto chart may be a good fit. However, the long-run application of the Pareto, such as in the case of a manufacturing or service setting and its associated data volumes, appears to be generally more applicable to an ongoing operation rather than a project. It is in the context of ongoing operations that the use of the Pareto chart in quality management originated. For this reason, the project team will need to consider if the Pareto analysis tool belongs in the project plan.

Histograms: The histogram aids the manager in seeing patterns in data—typically, large volumes of data. Because the usefulness of the histogram increases with the volume of data under analysis, the histogram would appear to be very useful for data collected as the result of long-running ongoing operations rather than short-term projects. However, the histogram may have a place in project management whenever significant data points may be generated over a short period of time. Such circumstances include software defect analysis and data collection from highly complex systems. The histogram therefore also appears to be moderately applicable to the project management context. As in the case of the Pareto chart, the histogram may or may not be applicable for inclusion in the project plan.

Control Charts: Control charts, as advocated by Shewhart, are the foundation of statistical process control. The control chart samples data over the long run, to determine if the overall system is in control. A system is said to be out of control if successive long-run data points skew in a particular direction and exceed a given control limit. Given the temporary nature of project management, long-run data is rarely available. The control chart would therefore appear to be highly applicable to a high-volume manufacturing setting rather than within the project management context. High-volume manufacturing is said to be the birthplace of the control chart; so, it follows that the control chart would appear to be out of place within project management—particularly with respect to the planning of quality management. On the other hand, the use of the control chart may well depend upon what process is being controlled. If the process under control is the overall project life cycle, then control charts may be useful in tracking project progress. An example of this is using control charts to monitor earned value indexes so that action is triggered should the project appear to be drifting out of control. Again, the decision to use control charts in this manner is made when creating the project quality management plan.

Scatter Diagrams: The scatter diagram assists managers in seeing relationships between different variables represented by collected data. Like the Pareto chart and the histogram, the scatter diagram would appear to be a tool that is a better fit within a context where a large amount of data was collected. An ongoing operation such as manufacturing, or a project that produces software-intensive or otherwise complex deliverables that involve detailed testing, analysis, and troubleshooting, might implement this tool. The scatter diagram would therefore appear to be only moderately applicable to the project management environment. Its place in the project quality plan would depend upon the nature of the project and the amount of data that the project would reasonably be expected to produce.

Quality Tool Applicability Summary

The purpose of each of the seven quality tools as well as their applicability to the project management context is provided in Table 7.5. Each tool is categorized as "High," "Low," or "Moderate" applicability to project

Table 7.5 Seven quality tools

Tool	Purpose	Applicability to Project Management	Applicability to Operations Management
Cause and effect	Troubleshooting	High	High
Flowchart	Analysis	High	High
Check sheet	Audit	High	High
Pareto chart	Analysis	Moderate	High
Histogram	Analysis	Moderate	High
Control chart	Process control	Low	High
Scatter diagram	Analysis	Moderate	High

management based on the degree to which it is useful within the context of a short-term endeavor versus an ongoing operation. A summary table outlining quality management tools may be used to stimulate project team discussion and brainstorming regarding which tools would be employed in managing quality throughout the project life cycle.

Project Quality Assurance

Quality assurance in project management puts in place systems that are designed to produce the desired level of quality in a project. In project management, such systems are audited to ensure that the correct standards are being used. However, the plan for managing quality is intended to establish the basic approach or system for managing quality. It is the system in the quality plan that assures quality in the project.

The Affinity Diagram: A structured method of brainstorming that groups together similar ideas. Given that projects are led by project teams, and such teams are tasked with producing solutions constrained by schedule, budget, and cost, the affinity diagram would appear to be a very useful tool. It is conceivable that this tool could be employed by the project team in putting together the overall quality plan.

The Process Decision Program Chart (PDPC): This tool is a technique for identifying the source of potential problems in a system. In the planning phase of the project, the PDPC tool appears to be ideal for managing risks and safeguarding against potential defects in deliverables.

In these respects, the tools appear to be useful in developing a quality management strategy. Further, this tool could also likely be employed in risk management planning. The PDPC would appear to be more applicable to quality planning rather than quality assurance. However, the plan once developed does become the management system that assures quality.

The Interrelationship Diagraph: A method of analysis that identifies the relationships between components in a system. Projects often develop and deliver complex systems. Systems are best understood when the relationships between the components are made clear. The interrelationship diagram serves this purpose. This tool appears to be a natural fit for the project quality assurance context. This tool could be employed directly in the quality management plan to illustrate the quality management processes to be used and upon what deliverables and activities the processes will interact.

Tree Diagrams: An analysis tool that breaks down a high-level goal, problem, system, or process for use in detailed analysis. The tree diagram decomposes problems in much the same way that the project work breakdown structure decomposes deliverables. Decomposition of larger goals or problems so that they may be acted upon is essential in the management of projects. The tree diagram therefore appears to fit the context of project management and would appear to be a good fit within the project quality plan.

Prioritization Matrices: The prioritization matrix is a weighted matrix used as a decision-making tool. Project execution is said to involve extensive decision making as well as information processing. The development of quality deliverables therefore involves decisions of priority. The prioritization matrix would appear to aid in such project decision making—perhaps even more so than in the context of operations management.

Network Diagrams: The network diagram is a tool for mapping out activities into a logical sequence. The network diagram is an inherent part of developing a schedule. It is a tool in which project managers will already be familiar. The network diagram would appear to be a natural choice for analyzing sequence and flow of events, activities, or deliverables for the purposes of assuring quality. Network diagrams and the associated critical path method are also cited as being useful for the context of mapping out the process flow for ongoing operations. However, this application is a secondary use for this tool.

Matrix Diagrams: The matrix diagram is an analysis tool for illustrating relationships between groups. The matrix diagram is commonly used to capture and trace project requirements. This tool is therefore useful in assuring that the deliverables required by the client are the ones that are produced. Such a tool is likely to be applied regularly within the context of project quality management as meeting the client requirements is an essential element of managing project quality.

Quality Assurance Tool Summary

Tools provided for project quality assurance are outlined in Table 7.6. Once again, each tool is categorized as "High," "Low," or "Moderate" applicability to project management based on the degree to which it is useful within the context of a short-term endeavor versus an ongoing operation. Further, the choice of tools employed in the quality management plan is tailored according to the context of the project.

How Do Project Managers Manage Project Quality?

Where does the limited applicability of some project quality management toolsets mean for project managers? If project quality is generally defined as meeting the requirements of the client, and projects are considered

Table 7.6 Quality assurance tools

Tool	Purpose	Applicability to Project Management	Applicability to Operations Management
Affinity diagram	Brainstorming	High	Moderate
PDPC	Planning	High	High
Interrelationship graph	Analysis	High	High
Tree diagrams	Analysis	High	High
Prioritization matrices	Decision making	High	High
Network diagrams	Analysis	High	Moderate
Matrix diagrams	Analysis	High	High

successful when they meet such requirements, then it could be said that project quality must be a primary goal for all project managers. It seems reasonable then that the overall project quality and assurance plan should emphasize the control of a process (or processes) that results in met requirements and satisfied clients. Project quality planning therefore involves deciding upon what standards need to be met to satisfy the client as well as how the project will assure that such standards are met. This is fundamentally an exercise in requirements collection and implementation.

Project Management as Problem Solving

The client holds a central position within and throughout the project as an ongoing source of requirements information and progress confirmation. A project therefore could be viewed as the development of a solution to a problem that is delivered to the client as an output of a process in which the client participates. The process of developing requirements is that of requirements elicitation and vetting. Once the solution is delivered, the project is said to be successful to the degree that the requirements were met or, in other words, to the degree that the problem was solved. Viewing project management as a problem-solving process would appear to allow for the use of additional toolset for planning and assuring project quality. Such tools could be included in the project quality management plan.

Problem-Solving Process

The field of problem solving acknowledges that a structured process is essential for identifying the right problem, implementing a solution, and then following through to confirm that the solution is successful. The project life cycle proposed by the Project Management Institute (PMI) is offered as a means of governing the overall project management process so that the delivery of correct solution is assured. As such, the project management life cycle itself may be viewed through the lens of problem-solving process. The PMI life cycle includes the following steps:

1. Feasibility: Can we do it?
2. Design: What does the client need?

3. Build: Who, how, and when will we do it? Building the solution
4. Test: Verifying and validating the solution
5. Deploy: Delivering the solution
6. Close: Archive and lessons learned

The project lifecycle process flow appears by inspection to have much in common with quality processes such as DMAIC (define, measure, analyze, improve, control), PDCA (plan, do, check, act), and the PMBOK 6 IPECC (initiate, plan, execute, control, close) sequence. The emphasis of each is on determining the requirements and the feasibility before taking action to implement, course-correct, or improve. The comparison of processes is given as follows in Table 7.7.

It is interesting to note that the project life cycle and its associated phases framework is the process used to produce quality deliverables. It is therefore reasonable to assume that quality assurance is an activity performed and managed within the project lifecycle phase. What then within the life cycle could be audited so that quality is assured? As the project life cycle is the process that ensures quality, it is essential that each phase of the process be carried out completely. The audit function therefore would be performed at the entrance and exit of each project lifecycle phase. This type of audit function is outlined in stage-gate models of product or system development. The challenge of achieving quality in a project is successfully completing all lifecycle phase entrance and exit criteria. Characteristic of the auditing function, complete assurance of quality requires an objective, neutral observer that can judge and make "Go/No-Go" decisions for each phase to ensure the integrity of each gate. Project lifecycle governance models such as the Product and Lifecycle Excellence (PACE) process as championed by the Product Development

Table 7.7 Quality and the project life cycle

Project life cycle and problem-solving process flow comparison						
Feasibility		Design	Build	Test	Deploy	Close
Define	Measure	Analyze	Improve		Control	
		Plan	Do	Do	Check	Act
Initiate		Plan				

Management Association (PDMA) in fact propose that a committee of management act as a product approval committee (PAC) to carry out this function. The passing of quality audits and quality reviews employed as project phase exit criteria is an example of quality assurance measures that could be included in the project quality plan.

Planning for a Quality Project

To plan for a quality project, the project manager should collect and vet the client's requirements. Further, to formalize a "quality plan" will explain how the project team will ensure that the deliverables produced not only meet documented specifications but as well match the requirements communicated by the client. The quality plan will also document the quality management processes that will be employed as well as the approaches that will be applied.

What is most important is that the quality plan be documented that what is executed within the project follows the quality plan, and finally that the plan is tailored for the project environment and for the specific nature of the project deliverables. Finally, it bears remembering the dictum that "quality is free." The implication of this statement is that the cost of quality management is small compared to the cost of repairing and addressing problems with deliverables after launch when they are in the field and being used by the client. Since quality is related to performance, quality could be said to increase scope as well as project effort. However, project managers are encouraged to consider the overall lifecycle costs to observe the balancing out of resulting quality costs.

The Elements of the Quality Plan

What elements should be included in the quality plan? In much the same way as a quality plan for an ongoing operation, the quality plan for a project should answer the following questions:

1. Who are the key players in project quality management?
2. What are the roles and responsibilities of the key players?
3. What is the overall strategy or approach for managing quality in this specific project?

4. What lifecycle methodology will be employed and how will it be linked to project quality?
5. How will both quality assurance and quality control be incorporated into the project?
6. What quality management tools will be employed in managing project quality?
7. How will quality process improvements from previous projects be incorporated into this project?

Important Takeaways for the Project Manager

- Understanding company strategy is an essential element of project selection.
- Project opportunities are many, but strategically aligned projects that are likely to be successful are few.
- Project selection involves both qualitative as well as quantitative methods.
- The checklist selection method compares projects against a list of strategic criteria.
- A weighted scoring model mirrors the project selection checklist method—but weights some strategic criteria higher than others.
- Multiple financial methods exist for selecting projects. These include, but are not limited to the ROI, the payback period, the NPV, and the IRR.
- Financial methods generally weigh the expense of the project compared to the promise of future cash flows.
- The discount rate is an important component of financial selection methods.
- High discount rates generally reflect project risk and force the project to produce higher returns to justify selection.
- Lower discount rates are a general indicator of lower project risks.
- The choice of discount rate highly influences the project selection result and should therefore be closely inspected to ensure the right balance of risk and reward is being applied.

CHAPTER 8

Measurement Performance Domain

The Overall Project: A Practical Example

The difference between a project schedule and a complete project plan is easier to understand with the use of an example of a simple project that is likely to be encountered within the workplace. The project used to demonstrate the elements of a complete project plan is an office relocation project illustrated in an outline form. Further, the plan is elaborated by successively progressing through the project phases. Let's look at a detailed example.

Office Relocation Project Plan Example: Before We Measure, We Have to Understand How We Got Here

Project charter. An office relocation project usually begins with an assignment from a sponsoring executive. The sponsoring executive will typically appoint a project manager to lead the effort. In some cases, the project may be assigned informally. However, following good practice requires the formalization of the project by means of issuing a project charter. The project charter will likely include some high-level direction regarding scope and key constraints. On the other hand, the development and management of the project scope will likely be carried out by the project team (Figure 8.1).

Budget Estimates and the Project Charter

One of the constraints typically provided in the project charter is the budget estimate. This is an early estimate and likely to be inaccurate. The project team will at this early stage consider this estimate as an indication

Office relocation project
charter

Project name: Office relocation
Date: 1/1/2018
Project manager signature: John Smith
Project sponsor signature: Ed Jones

Project purpose & description : Identify a new office location, acquire it, and prepare it for occupation. Pack and move existing furniture and equipment and close the legacy facility

Project role	Team members
Position	Name
Project manager:......	John Smith
IT lead:	Noah Weyers
Facility lead: ...	Bree Kause
HR lead:	Ben Effits
..	...

Key Milestones: Select new location : + 30 days. Location move-in Ready: +60 days pack and move from existing building: +75 days. Close project: +90 days
High-level budget: $25,000 target total budget

Constraints: Operations must not be interrupted by move. Maximize use of existing equipment. New facility must be within 25 mile radius of existing facility

Figure 8.1 Office relocation plan project charter

of the scale of the project as well as the financial statement of intent from senior management. The project manager should accept this as a top-down budget guide and proceed to develop a bottom-up cost estimate after collecting detailed financial information associated with each activity in the office relocation.

Project stakeholder identification: At this critical juncture, it is essential to think holistically in terms of who may have an interest in the outcome of the office relocation project. The project team would likely identify the following roles and individuals as candidates for project stakeholders (Figure 8.2).

Office Relocation Project Plan: Design Phase

It is in the Design Phase where the work of developing the project plan for the office relocation project unfolds.

Project scope: A project that touches upon so many different stakeholders can easily grow in scope. Clear identification of what is in scope and out of scope is an essential step to prevent the runaway growth of scope. This begins with stating the basic strategy for managing scope to direct the project team to outline the basic approach for identifying, planning, and controlling scope. This need not be a complex plan—rather, it must serve as a useful guide to direct the management of scope from the beginning to the end of the project. Since this is focused on

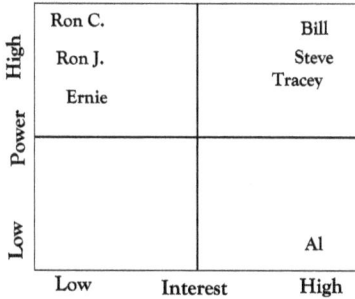

Power		Low Interest	High
High	Ron C. Ron J. Ernie		Bill Steve Tracey
Low			Al

| Low | Interest | High |

Name	Title	Project role	Contact info	Notes	Power	Interest	Ranking
Al Wilson	Prop. manager-old	Supplier	123@456.com	Final inspection	L	H	3
Steve Shen	Prop. manager-new	Supplier	456@789.com	Move-in support	H	H	1
Ron Jones	Local newspaper	Communications	abc@def.com	Inform community	H	L	2
Ernie Smith	Local radio	Communications	ghi@jkl.com	Inform community	H	L	2
Ron Cabernet	Local TV	Communications	ghi@jkl.com	Inform community	H	L	2
Bill Edwards	City mayor	Support	ghi@jkl.com	Inform community	H	H	1
Tracey John	Chamber of commerce	Support	ghi@jkl.com	Networking	H	H	1

Figure 8.2 Office relocation project stakeholders

documenting the approach the project team will use to manage scope, it may require no more than a simple checklist or "fill in the blank" checklist (Figure 8.3).

Scope statement: The scope of the project is fully elaborated within the work breakdown structure (WBS). The WBS follows the simple and succinct statement of what is and what is not included in the project. The scope statement for the office relocation is stated as follows:

We will assess our current needs as well as growth needs for the next three years. We will identify, select, lease, and create an office layout in a new building and move our company. We will seek to use as much existing infrastructure as possible. Modifying our existing building will NOT be considered as an option.

Simple scope management plan outline

#	Scope category	Management strategy
1	Scope statement development	Team brainstorming
2	WBS development	Facilitated team planning meeting
3	WBS dictionary development	Assigned to project core team members and reviewed by team
4	Scope baseline management	Client and sponsor sign-off followed by change control process
5	Requirements tracing and confirmation	Requirements database and client validation
6	Deliverables acceptance criteria	Document for each deliverable with client sign-off

Figure 8.3 Scope management plan

Work breakdown structure: The project WBS provides a hierarchical and categorical structured outline of what the project will deliver. It is hierarchical in that it consists of multiple levels. It is categorical in that it includes all categories of project scope. The WBS outlines 100 percent of what the project will deliver. The WBS for the office relocation project is as follows (Figure 8.4).

Scope baseline: A project plan includes a baseline of project scope. The baseline is the agreed upon scope that is fixed as part of the plan. Any change to project scope after the baseline has been established is governed by the project change control process. The scope baseline includes the scope statement, the WBS, and the WBS dictionary. The WBS dictionary in the project plan includes, in addition to the WBS elements, a succinct definition of each WBS element (Figure 8.5).

Project schedule management: The first step in schedule management is to describe the basic approach or strategy for managing the overall project schedule. This strategy will outline how activities will be defined and associated with deliverables, how the logical sequence of events will be determined, and what methods will be used to determine the overall project duration. Schedule management could also describe the methodology

A **high-level WBS** for the office
relocation

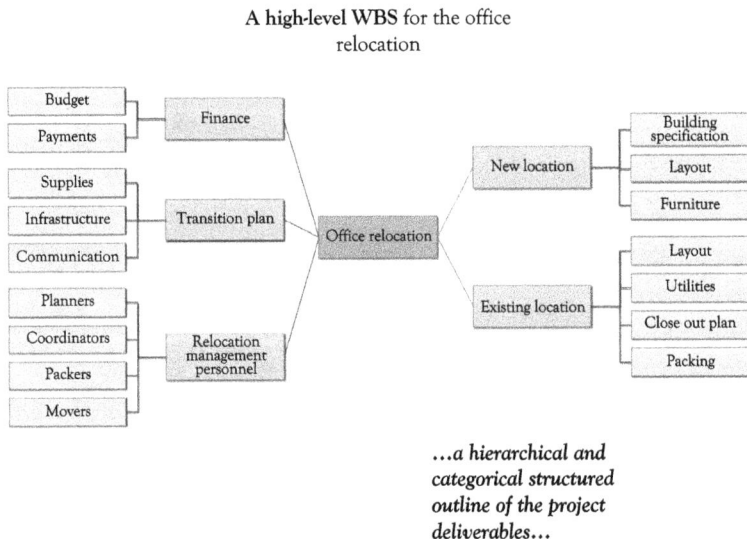

...*a hierarchical and categorical structured outline of the project deliverables...*

Figure 8.4 WBS for the office relocation project

	Office relocation	Description
1.00	Finance	Funding and cash flow for move
1.10	Budget	Spending plan for move
1.20	Payments	Compensation for outside contractors
2.00	Transition plan	Plan for move and uninterrupted operations
2.10	Supplies	Materials required for move
2.20	Infrastructure	Physical facility requirements
2.30	Communication	Information delivered to stakeholders
3.00	Relocation management person	Team members assigned to relocation project
3.10	Planners	Project team members assigned to develop plan
3.20	Coordinators	Project team members interacting with functional groups
3.30	Packers	Outside contractors responsible for packing
3.40	Movers	Outside contractors responsible for moving
4.00	Existing location	Plans for transition from and shutdown of office
4.10	Layout	Documentation of existing layout
4.20	Utilities	Documentation of utility requirements
4.30	Close-out plan	Plan to shut down existing office
4.40	Packing	Preparing and packaging furniture and equipment
5.00	New location	Plan for identifying, selecting.,and occupying new facility
5.10	Building specifications	Documented specifications of new building
5.20	Layout	Design of layout for new facility
5.30	Furniture	Plan for furniture in new facility

Figure 8.5 The WBS dictionary

used to analyze and predict project completion including tools such as PERT, Monte Carlo, and Bayesian analysis. The high-level schedule management plan for the office relocation project is outlined in Figure 8.6.

Identify project activities: The WBS is created by considering all deliverables that will be produced by the project. Once the deliverables are defined, the project team next considers what activities will be required to produce the deliverables. The only activities that are used to develop the project schedule must be linked to specific deliverables. Activities are often identified by the project team using a brainstorming methodology,

**Simple schedule management plan
outline: Office relocation project**

#	Schedule category	Management strategy
1	Methods	Facilitated team schedule development workshop
2	Tools	Network diagrams, PERT analysis, Gantt charts
3	Time units	Weekly time units given relatively short overall duration
4	Reporting	Weekly updates on schedule progress to plan: Executives and stakeholders
5	Control	Tracking Gantt chart and change control process with executive sign-off

A small-scale project requires only brief description of the basic strategy for developing and managing the project schedule

Figure 8.6 Schedule management plan

1	New location requirements
2	New location search
3	Select location
4	Inventory current location
5	New location layout
6	Select moving company
7	Order utilities
8	Purchase network and servers
9	Negotiate lease
10	Pack furniture
11	Pack computer equipment
12	Transport moved items
13	Unpack
14	Cutover to new network
15	Close existing building

Figure 8.7 *Office relocation activities*

by the application of expert judgment, or historical project experience. The specific method used is identified by the schedule management plan. The activities required to support the deliverables of the office relocation project are identified in Figure 8.7.

Sequence Project Activities

The office relocation project team next arranges the project activities in a logical order. To clarify the order of activities and prepare for the determination of the overall project duration, the project activities are sequenced using a network diagram. The office relocation project critical path is tentatively identified using initial duration estimates for each activity (Figure 8.8).

Project duration: The project activity nodes given in the office relocation network diagram are then expanded to provide three-point estimates for each activity. The three-point estimates are then combined using the PERT-weighted average method. The critical path duration that results

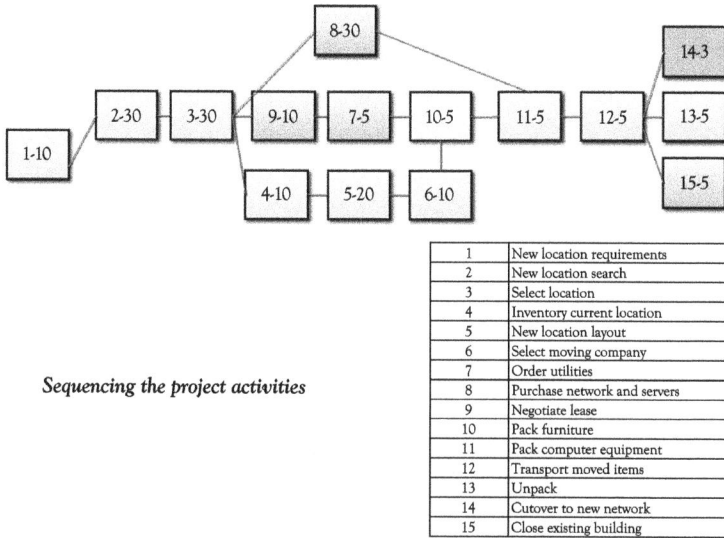

Figure 8.8 Sequencing office relocation activities

from the PERT analysis includes variances in project activities so that the result further supports the development of schedule completion predictions (Figure 8.9).

Project cost management: The cost of human resources assigned to project activities is typically the most significant source of cost within

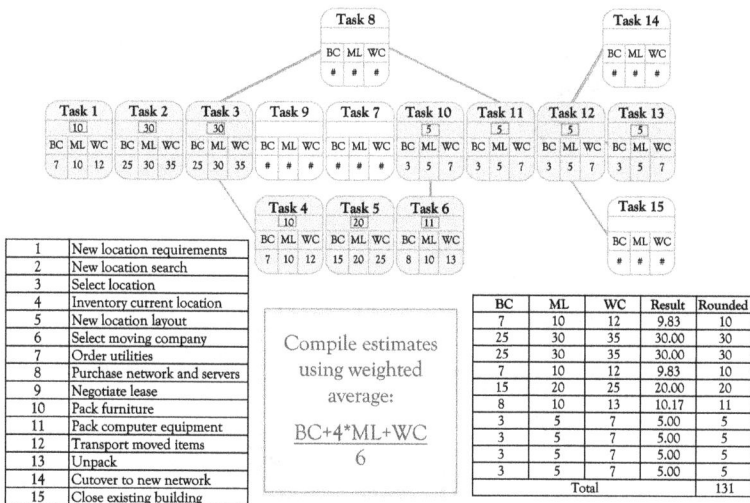

Figure 8.9 Identifying project critical path

a project. However, many of the resources assigned to the office relocation project are internal resources who remain on the payroll regardless of assignment to the project or when working within an assigned functional group. However, the average "fully-loaded" costs (salary, benefits, plus overhead allocation) for each internal employee are captured in the project cost plan as they are assigned to the project. Such costs are not indicative of an additional cash outlay but could be viewed as opportunity costs. Further, the costs of external resources used for packing, moving, new facility setup, and so on are captured in the budget as the resources are employed in the schedule. The project will track internal resource costs as opportunity costs, and actual cash outlays to outside vendors in separate accounts. The simple high-level project relocation cost plan is provided in Figure 8.10.

Project quality management: The focus of quality management within the office relocation project includes the meeting of requirements for the new facility, achieving the target budget and schedule, and minimizing disruption to the company during the transfer and relocation. In addition, the project team has the additional requirement of ensuring a smooth cutover of office networks and utilities as well as leaving the existing office in pristine condition. The project quality management plan for the office relocation project outlines the tools, techniques, and specific actions that the project team will take to ensure that the relocation project aligns with goals and requirements as the project unfolds (Figure 8.11). Quality in this project is defined as "meeting the requirements of the project stakeholders."

Project resource management: The office relocation project will draw upon internal as well as external resources throughout the project. It is

Simple quality management plan outline

#	Quality category	Management strategy
1	Control	Checklist verifying deliverable specifications
2	Assurance	Quality system audits, lifecycle milestone quality reporting
3	Process improvement	Documentation of defects and solutions reviewed and used to update processes
4	Reporting	Weekly updates on schedule progress to plan: Executive and stakeholders

> Since office relocation projects are relatively rare, the process improvement may take the form of an office relocation manual to be used in future projects.

Figure 8.10 Office relocation cost plan

Simple quality management plan outline

#	Quality category	Management strategy
1	Control	Checklist verifying deliverable specifications
2	Assurance	Quality system audits, lifecycle milestone quality reporting
3	Process improvement	Documentation of defects and solutions reviewed and used to update processes
4	Reporting	Weekly updates on schedule progress to plan: Executive and stakeholders

Since office relocation projects are relatively rare, the process improvement may take the form of an office relocation manual to be used in future projects.

Figure 8.11 Simple quality management plan outline

anticipated that some overtime will be required during the critical period of the move. In addition, the move will occur during a holiday weekend to minimize operational downtime. The resources assigned to the project will be informed of the extended calendar for the move dates. Finally, the resource management will direct functional groups and departments to form teams to inventory equipment and organize desk and personal items for packing and transfer. Of key concern of a project of this type is the clarification of responsibilities of team members assigned to carry out project activities. The tool used for this purpose is the responsibility assignment matrix (RAM) (Figure 8.12). A common approach to populating a RAM is to assign responsibility to specific activities that produce WBS deliverables, and in addition identify the nature of the responsibility held by each stakeholder. Some stakeholders may be involved with the development of a deliverable as a *participant*. The team lead for a specific deliverable may be ultimately *accountable* for that deliverable. Other stakeholders may be asked to *review* the work or to provide *input*. Finally, a stakeholder may be assigned to provide the final *sign-off* on the completed work. These responsibilities may be abbreviated as *PARIS*. Each responsibility category for each key stakeholder and deliverable is labeled as P, A, R, I, or S in the responsibility assignment matrix.

Project communication management: Of central importance to an office relocation plan is the reduction of employee uncertainty as well as helping stakeholders within the old and new building and community to feel comfortable with the relocation. The office relocation plan emphasizes communication to these important stakeholder groups and, in addition, describes the media to be employed as well as the frequency

PARIS	Sponsor	Project manager	HR lead	Facility lead	IT lead
New location requirements	S	A	I	P	P
New location search		I	A	I	
Select location	S	A	P	P	I
Inventory current location		I	P	A	P
New location layout		S	P	A	P
Select moving company		A	P	I	I
Order utilities		S		A	P
Purchase network and servers		S		I	A
Negotiate lease	S	A	I	I	I
Pack furniture		A	I	P	I
Pack computer equipment		S	I	P	A
Transport moved items		A			
Unpack		P	P	A	I
Cutover to new network		S		P	A
Close existing building	S	P	P	A	P

Participant-accountable-review-input required-sign-off

Figure 8.12 Office relocation project responsibility assignment matrix/PARIS chart

of communication. One of the key elements of the communications plan will be kickoff meetings to announce the project, a farewell event at the existing facility, as well as a ribbon-cutting event in the new facility (Figure 8.13).

Project uncertainty/risk management: An office relocation project has the potential to negatively impact the business in many ways. Employees who do not favor the new location or the commute may be tempted to look for alternative employment. System and operational downtime

Simple communications plan

Name	Title	Project role	Contact info	Person responsible	Information	Media
Al Wilson	Prop. manager-old	Supplier	123@456.com	Facility lead	Schedule, progress	Document, powerpoint
Steve Shen	Prop. manager-new	Supplier	456@789.com	Facility lead	Schedule, progress	Document, powerpoint
Ron Jones	Local newspaper	Communications	abc@def.com	Project manager	Milestones	Powerpoint
Ernie Smith	Local radio	Communications	ghi@jkl.com	HR lead	Company updates	Phone
Ron Cabernet	Local TV	Communications	ghi@jkl.com	HR lead	Company updates	Face to face
Bill Edwards	City mayor	Support	ghi@jkl.com	HR lead	Company updates	Face to face
Tracey John	Chamber of commerce	Support	ghi@jkl.com	HR lead	Company updates	Face to face

Use the stakeholder register as the foundation, then add assignments, information, and media

Figure 8.13 Office relocation communications plan

may damage the reputation of the company and cause customers to seek other options. These risks are linked to many causal factors such as poor communication to stakeholders and the community, to external suppliers failing to meet timely transition targets. The risk management plan for the office relocation project will therefore employ multiple brainstorming sessions as well as scenario planning so that risk and causal factors are identified, and risk response mechanisms are planned. The high-level office relocation project risk plan is shown in Figure 8.14.

Project procurement management: Of primary importance to the office relocation project is the selection of major vendors including the owners of the new building property, the moving company used to pack, move, unpack, and assist with the setup of the new operation, and finally the outside information systems support required for the shutdown of the existing office network operation and the cutover to the new. Minimizing problems with these key vendors will require clear documentation of requirements, significant communication, and negotiation, and finally a contract that rewards performance and possibly penalizes lack of compliance in areas that touch upon business operation fundamentals. Further, contractual arrangements will place emphasis on timing so that the transition is completed during a quiet period so that impact to customers and employees is minimized. The high-level office relocation procurement plan is shown in Figure 8.15.

Project stakeholder management: Stakeholders in an office relocation project are many—and they may go considerably beyond what project initially expects. Office relocations touch entire communities, families,

Simple high-level risk plan

Risk identifier	Risk description	Date	Assigned to	Response strategy	Probability	Impact	Ranking
4252018	Operation interruption	1/25/2018	IT lead	Avoid	0.25	$17,500	$4,375
2182018	Move delay	1/18/2018	PM	Accept	0.2	$15,000	$3,000
3202018	Equipment damage	1/20/2018	Facility lead	Mitigate	0.15	$10,000	$1,500
1152018	Employee resignation	1/15/2018	HR lead	Mitigate	0.05	$15,000	$750
1152018	Legacy building damage	1/15/2018	Facility lead	Transfer	0.1	$10,000	$1,000

Use the risk register tool as a basic risk-planning tool. Use it to identify risks, rank risks, assign risks, and identify risk response.

Figure 8.14 High-level office relocation project risk plan

Simple project procurement plan

Project name: Office relocation project

Date: 1/15/18

Moving company selection method: Weighted ranking method
Building selection method: Weighted ranking method with key stakeholder input
Contract negotiation: Moving company: PM with executive support Building lease: General manager Equipment and supplies: Project manager
Contract type: Moving company: Fixed price Building lease: Fixed term lease Equipment: Purchase </=$2,000, otherwise fixed term lease Supplies and materials: Bulk purchase
Miscellaneous: Insurance: Project manager review and recommendation, executive sign-off

Figure 8.15 Office relocation project procurement plan

customers, and the general public. Further, relocations are sources of uncertainty among stakeholder groups as new neighbors and new facilities are encountered. During the time of greatest uncertainty, it is highly desirable to work with supportive and cooperative stakeholders. The project team will conduct multiple brainstorming sessions to capture different categories of stakeholders and uncover the layers of stakeholders within the community that may not be obvious initially. Further, stakeholder engagement tactics are outlined in the high-level office relocation project stakeholder management plan as shown in Figure 8.16.

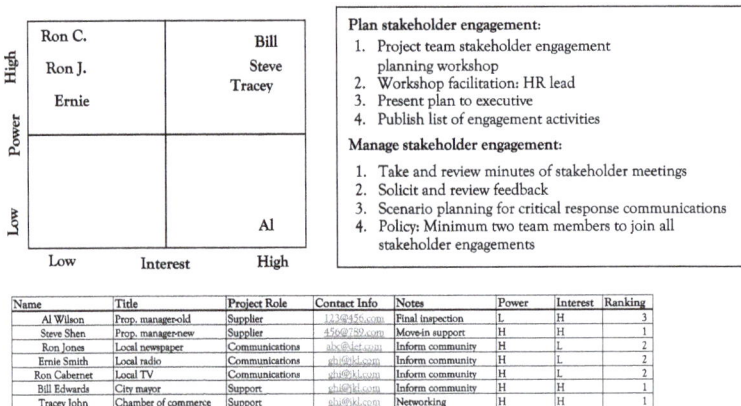

Name	Title	Project Role	Contact Info	Notes	Power	Interest	Ranking
Al Wilson	Prop. manager-old	Supplier	123@456.com	Final inspection	L	H	3
Steve Shen	Prop. manager-new	Supplier	456@789.com	Move-in support	H	H	1
Ron Jones	Local newspaper	Communications	abc@def.com	Inform community	H	L	2
Ernie Smith	Local radio	Communications	ghi@jkl.com	Inform community	H	L	2
Ron Cabernet	Local TV	Communications	ghi@jkl.com	Inform community	H	L	2
Bill Edwards	City mayor	Support	ghi@jkl.com	Inform community	H	H	1
Tracey John	Chamber of commerce	Support	ghi@jkl.com	Networking	H	H	1

Figure 8.16 Office relocation project stakeholder management plan

A Schedule Is Not a Plan-Revisited

The simple example of the office relocation project plan illustrates how extensive is a project plan compared to a project schedule. The schedule offers details about the project scope, the activities required to produce them, the duration of the schedule, and finally a limited estimate of the budget based on the resources assigned to the activities. By way of contrast, the complete project plan lays out the strategy for communicating with and managing stakeholders, to setting and achieving quality goals, to managing risks. A project schedule may be referred to as a plan, but a schedule is only a small subset of the many elements under the purview of the project team (Figure 8.17).

Carrying Out the Design: Understanding the Deployment Phase

What is it that project managers do when executing a project? According to the PMBOK 6, executing begins with "directing and managing project work." From the definitions of "direct" and "manage," this expression infers that the following activities will be carried out during the executing process group:

- Providing instructions
- Giving orders
- Administering
- Regulating

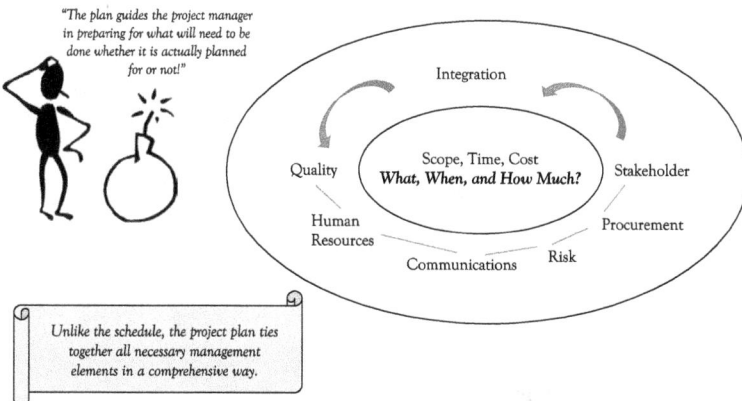

Figure 8.17 Project schedule versus project plan

How is this done in practice? Project managers and team members typically bundle related activities into documented work assignments not to exceed two weeks in duration. This device for administering project work is referred to as the work package. The work package contains deliverables from the lowest level of the WBS. It also includes a high-level description of the activities associated with the deliverables, critical milestones, budget constraints, and finally tracking and accounting information. It is important to note that the work package contains elements typically found in the WBS (deliverables) as well as information typically found in the project schedule (activities, milestones, budget constraints). Because of this, the work package is neither a WBS nor a schedule—but rather, a tool for assigning and managing work. It should be recognized however that "giving orders" in a manner that might be envisioned in the context of a military engagement rarely applies in the project management context. Work package instructions are rarely "thrown over the wall" to those who complete the work. Instead, what is included within the work package is a result of interaction, discussion, and negotiation between the project team and the individual who takes the lead role in managing the effort and activity as outlined within the work package (Figure 8.18).

Work package ID:			Account #:		
Description:			Assumptions and constraints :		
Important dates:			Quality:		
1			Technical:		
2			Contractual:		
3					
		Labor estimate			
Activity	Assigned to:	Hours	Rate	Total	
		Material estimate			
		Description	Cost	Total	
				Overall cost	
Testing criteria:					

Figure 8.18 Work package example

Managing Project "Tribal" Knowledge

Managing project "tribal" knowledge requires the project team to collect and refine data and information, and actively apply it so that it becomes knowledge. Further, "lessons learned" is viewed less as an event or set of activities—but rather, a way a life in which project process improvement is undertaken as each project is executed. Further, instead of filing away important lessons for future consideration, new learning is adapted into new processes and procedures, policies, and templates.

Manage quality: In the deployment phase, project teams take action to ensure that the project deliverables are of the desired quality level. This is done by communicating requirements, conducting team meetings, holding project reviews, and checking work in progress to confirm that the correct scope and specifications are being applied. Managing quality in project deployment involves constant comparison between progress to plan, between project specifications versus actual, and finally between client requirements versus project deliverables.

Project resource management: Project managers acquire resources to do the job. In most cases, the effort expended to acquire resources is far more than putting forward requests. Instead, it may require extensive negotiation—or in the case of acquiring rare resources such as exotic test equipment, extensive networking, and search. In many cases, acquiring resources is an ongoing battle—particularly when promised resources—currently assigned to other projects that had previously been expected to be complete—are not forthcoming. This usually requires the initiation of contingency plans involving outreach to other sources.

When resources do arrive, it may take time to make them productive. Equipment may require configuration and setup. Human resources will likely experience a learning curve as they seek to understand the context of the project and its associated technical details so that they can be productive and contribute to the project. This is especially true of resources who arrive late to the project and, as a result, not only require technical training, but also need to learn how to work together with existing team members. It could be argued that the real work of project execution involves the acquisition, development, and management of project resources. After all, it is not the project manager who completes the work of the project—but rather, the core project team as well as the resources associated with the extended team.

Project communications management: It is at this challenging time within the project where the project team discovers whether the communications plan developed earlier in the project was sufficient or not. Managing communication goes beyond "communicating" and involves assigning reports to be developed, information to be released, and meetings to be organized. Further, the role of managing communications as well as the associated workload tends to grow as the project progresses and the tempo of the project speeds up. The dictum "90 percent of project management is communication" becomes obvious to project managers when communication is managed during project execution. It should be remembered that the message to be communicated and the stakeholders receiving the message are not the only elements of key interest in managing project communications. The number of project communications paths in the overall project is also an important concern. The number of communications paths increases exponentially according to the number of stakeholder groups that require individual attention. The number of communication paths in the project is described by the following formula:

Number of communication paths = $(n\,\char`\^\,2 - n)/2$

Where "n" equals "number of project stakeholder groups"

Project uncertainty/risk management: If risk is defined as "anything that stands in the way of project success" and the job of the project manager is to navigate through barriers to success to successfully deliver a project, then the primary role of the project manager is that of risk management. In the project's deployment phase, project managers implement risk responses. Risk responses are often categorized according to the mnemonic device "MART" which stands for *mitigate, avoid, retain*, and *transfer*. The decision to retain or transfer risks is typically decided early in the design phase. Once the project is deployed, there will likely not be sufficient time to transfer risks once they have materialized as issues. Further, risks that the project team has decided to retain may only be minimized once they have arisen as issues. This leaves risk mitigation and avoidance as key measures likely to be taken during execution. Project execution therefore employs risk reduction activities such as planning ahead, developing a "plan B" for major activities, and risk avoidance when carrying out activities identified in the plan.

Manage stakeholder engagement: Recall that engagement implies much more than simple communication. Because of this, project team members in the deployment phase will, in addition to managing project work, be networking and seeking to understand and bond with stakeholders to maximize benefits of stakeholder relationships.

Keeping Things on Track: Measuring Performance

Measuring the performance of a project begins with the assumption that the project team has a baseline plan that the team and the stakeholders have agreed to and is under change control. The baseline is important because the control of a project may only be managed with respect to a standard of reference. The standard of reference is the project baseline. Monitoring therefore is an exercise associated with comparing the current project progress—or actuals against the scope, the schedule, and the budget of the original plan. Without a baseline, it is impossible to determine what was originally committed by the project team.

Measuring the performance of a project is possible when a project baseline is established—but, it is by no means easy to do. The project baseline lies at one side of the monitoring and controlling equation—but the progress of the project is the other. How does the project team determine the progress made by the project so that it may be compared to the baseline plan? For projects that produce tangible outcomes, progress measurement may be relatively simple. For example, a homebuilding project presents tangible measures of its progress as the lot is cleared, the foundation is put into place, and the frame is built. However, a complex software-intensive system development project may be a completely different matter. For example, suppose that a project was chartered to develop a system composed of multiple subsystems. The progress on each of the subsystems is determined to be good based upon the fact that the design and coding is complete and module testing is in progress. It is possible after hearing a progress report that the project could inform the senior management team of the excellent progress. Based upon the status of the subsystem development, it is estimated—and reported—that the project will complete ahead of schedule. Assume further that, in the following week, all subsystems are integrated in a scheduled project integration milestone. Upon linking together each of the subsystems, it is determined that the overall system is nonfunctional, and hundreds of defects are recorded. It is determined that it may take weeks to work through the integration issues to make the system functional. This is a major setback—and one week after reporting good progress, the project team now reports that the project will be at least two to three weeks late. Progress reporting in the context of complex systems clearly presents both progress measurement and progress-reporting dilemmas.

Another measuring performance dilemma faced by the project team involves the reporting of the project budget status. Assume, for example, that the project is at the halfway point of the schedule—but less than half of the project budget has been spent. Is the project team under budget? Should it be reported to senior management that the project is under budget? The answer is that "it depends." To begin with, it is important to recognize that it is rare for projects to be completed under budget. Project managers would be well advised to view claims of positive project budget news with skepticism. In fact, it is possible for a project to appear to be under budget at a given point in the project—but in fact be over budget. How is this possible?

Earned Value and Progress Reporting

The difficulty of reporting project budget status is observed when only two pieces of information are communicated. As in the example of a project that appears to be under budget at a given point in time in the project, there are two pieces of information: the amount spent to date and the planned spending at a given point in time in the project. When only two pieces of information are used in monitoring the project status—in this case, spending to date and planned spending—it is not clear whether the spending is less than planned because:

a. The project is being run by a financially savvy project manager who truly understands how to save money; or
b. The project has spent less than planned because the project is behind schedule and therefore has yet to spend money associated with completing the planned work.

In many cases, the reason for a project being apparently under budget is due to option "b" rather than "a." However, it is impossible to know for certain unless—in addition to reporting spending to date and planned spending—the progress made in completing the project work is also reported. As an example, assume that a project had planned to spend $1,000.00 each on four work packages within a month's time. At the end of the month, the project reports that only $3,000.00 was spent and was therefore apparently under budget by $1,000.00. However, it is learned that only two work packages were completed rather than the four planned for the month (Figure 8.19). This means that:

(a) The project is not under budget.
(b) The project is behind schedule.
(c) The project is in fact over budget.

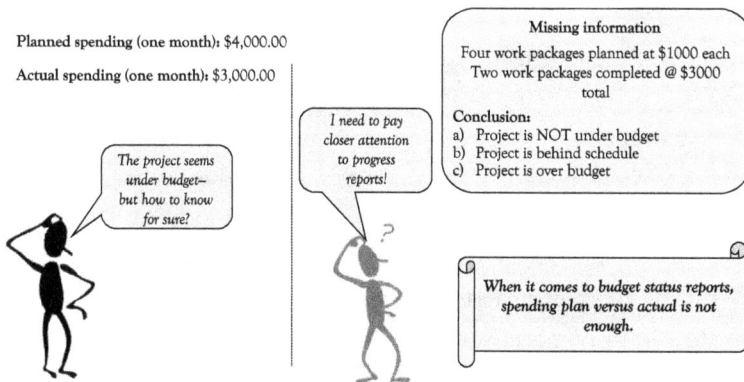

Figure 8.19 Work package budget reporting example

The earned value method of monitoring project progress includes the progress made toward the project deliverables in addition to actual and planned spending. This third piece of information—the work progress—clears up the ambiguity associated with project progress and budget. Although earned value is often thought to be confusing with its acronyms and many derived formulas, the essence of earned value is determined by only three metrics, as follows:

1. *PV* (planned value—or "Budget"): The amount of money planned to be spent by the project over time.
2. *AC* (actual cost): The amount of money spent in the project to date.
3. *EV* (earned value): The monetary value of the completed work. This figure is calculated using the formula:
   % Complete x budget

Note that the budget component of earned value is the total budget for the work being measured. Also, earned value can be calculated per period or per project stage. A "per stage" approach to earned value often simplifies the calculation of work progress. In the example of complex system development and subsystem integration—for example—the earned value would not be typically reported until the system reached a specific stage such as an integration milestone. Once the system reached such a milestone, progress is often easier to assess.

Earned Value Work Package Example

Earned value may be used to evaluate the exact status of the "four work packages" project example. The project had planned to spend $4,000 during the month on completing four work packages. Therefore, the PV (or planned value, or budget) for the month is $4,000. Recall that the project appeared to be under budget since only $3,000 was spent for the month. Since $3,000 was the amount that was spent, the AC or actual cost is $3,000. These figures are relatively simple to determine within any project. The challenging number to calculate is the EV or earned value amount. The monetary value of the work completed is "% complete × budget." Since only two work packages were completed out of four, the per cent complete is 50 percent. The PV or budget for the month is $4,000. Therefore, the earned value or EV is 50 percent of $4,000 or $2,000 (Figure 8.20).

Planned Spending (PV) = 4 x $1,000.00=$4,000.00

Planned spending (PV): $4,000.00

Actual spending (AC): $3,000.00

Earned value (EV): $2,000.00

| WP#1: $1,000 | WP#2: $1,000 |

| WP#3: $1,000 | WP#4: $1,000 |

Two out of the four work packages were completed or .5 (50%). 50% of the $4,000 budget is $2,000

Earned value (EV): .5 x budget =

2 x $1,000.00 =$2,000.00

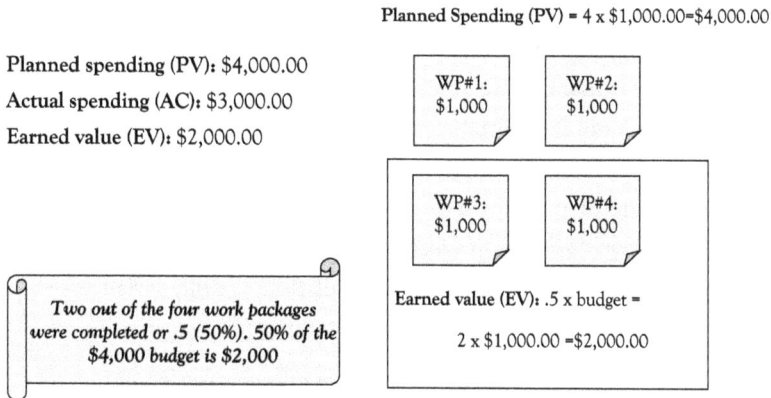

Figure 8.20 Work package earned value example

What Does Earned Value Really Mean?

The beauty of earned value is that the three metrics—once calculated—can provide clear information regarding project status. This is done in two ways by calculating earned value variances and earned value indexes. Each of the calculations begins with the earned value metric as follows:

Earned Value Variances

Cost variance (CV): EV – AC or $2,000 – $3,000 = –$1,000

Schedule variance (SV): EV – PV or $2,000 – $4,000 = –$2,000

The negative cost variance of –$1,000 illustrates that the project is over budget by $1,000. Recall that the project was initially understood to be under budget given its actual spending was less versus planned spending. However, once the additional earned value metric was included, it becomes clear that the project is over rather than under budget.

The negative schedule variance of –$2,000 indicates that the project, in addition to being over budget, is also behind schedule. The schedule variance in earned value management may be a source of confusion. This is because the schedule variance is described in the form of a monetary amount rather than a period. A monetary metric for schedule delay, though confusing at first, could be easily explained in terms of the value of work that should have been completed, but was not. In the case of the work package example, the schedule is behind by $2,000 worth of work.

Earned Value Indexes

Earned value variances are informative but since they generate absolute values the numbers produced make it difficult to compare progress between projects of different scales. Earned value indexes provide a consistent measure of progress regardless of project scale. Further, indexes may be employed to make projections regarding the final project schedule and budget. Earned value indexes calculations are like variances—but employ division instead of subtraction as follows:

Cost performance index (CPI): EV/AC or $2,000/$3,000 = .67
Schedule performance index (SPI): EV/PV or $2,000/$4,000 = .5

An inspection of the indexes illustrates that when an index is less than one, the project is over budget in the case of the CPI, and behind schedule in the case of the SPI. Note that a value of "1" occurs when the actual cost or planned value equals the earned value. Further, when the earned value is greater than the actual cost or planned value, the project is ahead of schedule or under budget. Since indexes are ratios, project progress may be compared regardless of the project scale.

Earned Value Curves

The numeric variances and indexes may be viewed and evaluated in a tabular form and presented in reports. However, it is useful to employ curves when communicating project progress using earned value. Recall that the budget or PV is displayed as a curve. The level of the curve changes over the duration of the project as it tracks the cumulative spending that is associated with the resources assigned to the project. This budget curve can be paired with curves that describe the actual project spending or AC as well as the monetary value of the work completed, or EV. Using this type of curve, the project status may be observed briefly by confirming if the EV or AC curve is greater than or less than the budget or PV (Figure 8.21).

"Reeling In" the Project

It is observed that the budget curve in an earned value reporting chart curves upward and then downward as the project ends. This curve is

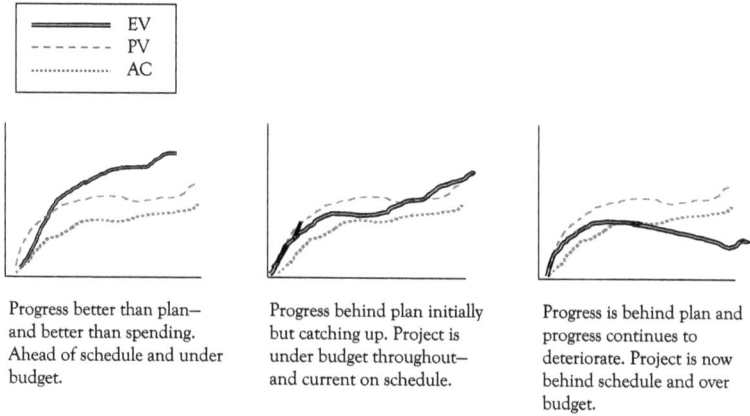

Progress better than plan— and better than spending. Ahead of schedule and under budget.	Progress behind plan initially but catching up. Project is under budget throughout— and current on schedule.	Progress is behind plan and progress continues to deteriorate. Project is now behind schedule and over budget.

Figure 8.21 Earned value curves

said to resemble the bend of a fishing pole. A fishing pole bends upward more steeply when the fisherman is reeling in the fish. Further, end of the pole bends inward toward the fisherman. Likewise, a PV or budget curve bends upward to the degree that planned project spending is planned to increase. Why increase the planned spending? Often, it is done as a means for improving the project schedule. When the target schedule improves, the end point of the project budget bends inward. The analogy to the bending of the fishing pole applies in this case as the end of the project, like a "big fish" is "reeled in (Figure 8.22)."

Making Projections With Indexes

An additional benefit of using earned value indexes is that they can be used to make predictions regarding how the project will end if the current work progress and spending patterns continue. For example, assume the following project details (Table 8.1).

Indexes applied to these project numbers can provide a simple "back of the envelope" calculation to predict final cost and schedule targets— assuming that the existing "run rate" of spending and progress continues. For example:

Simple project cost projection:

(Cost to date) + (Remaining budget/CPI) =
Simple project cost projection
$10,000 + ($17,500/.67) = $10,000 + $26,119 = $36,119

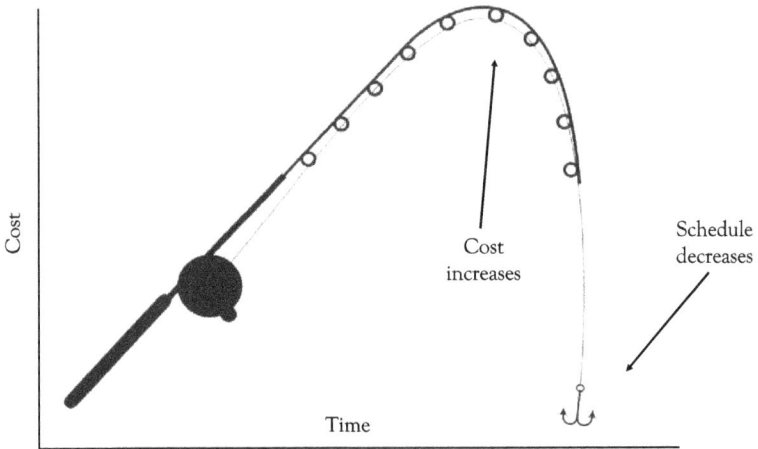

Figure 8.22 Reeling in the schedule

Table 8.1 Work package project data

Costs to date	Remaining budget	Duration to date	Remaining duration
$10,000	$17,500	9 weeks	12 weeks

This budget monitoring signal is very beneficial to the project manager as it suggests that intervention is needed to mitigate the significant projected cost overage. In the "work package" example, the original project budget would be no more than $27,500 (and likely much less given the assumption that the project is currently overspending).

Simple project schedule projection:

(Duration to date) + (Remaining duration/SPI) =
Simple project schedule projection
9 weeks + (12 weeks/.5) = 9 weeks + 24 weeks = 33 weeks

This simple schedule projection method provides an indication to the project manager that action is warranted to improve the schedule that is already currently delayed.

Additional Earned Value Metrics

The number of different derived earned value metrics is nearly endless, and the calculations may become quite complicated. Project managers are advised however to keep calculations as simple and intuitive as possible. Reporting earned value metrics are useful—but only if the project manager can explain the metrics to stakeholders. Also, keep in mind that not all reference texts use the PV, AC, and EV nomenclature. The principles are the same regardless. Also, no matter how complex the metrics become, the essentials of earned value are contained in the three fundamental metrics (Figure 8.23).

EV Is Measuring—But What Is Controlling?

Ideally, controlling a project involves the project taking action to prevent the project from deviating from the plan. Also, project controlling often refers to the returning of the project to the planned state after it has deviated from the plan. In practice, the project rarely tracks the project plan exactly. Controlling therefore requires constant attention and course correction on the part of the project team. Some steps that could be taken include adding resources, equipment, or funding to attempt to return the project to an ideal condition. In other cases, the project team may seek a different approach to one or more work packages to save time by increasing work efficiency. Finally, the project is likely to have fallen out of control due to risks becoming issues. In such a case, the project team could consider implementing risk mitigation plans as identified in the project risk management plan.

Should the project team seek to improve the schedule by adding resources or funding (as in "reeling in" the project), some caution should be observed. First, adding resources to a project after it is well underway

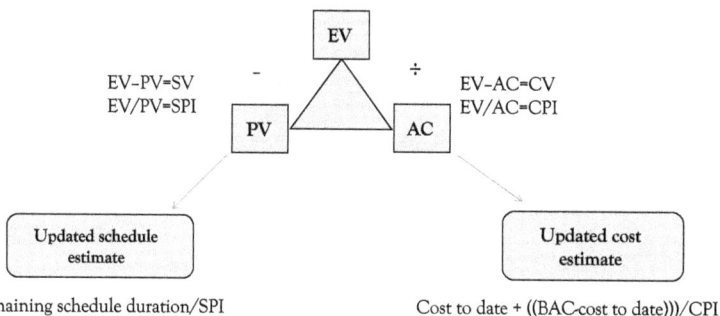

Figure 8.23 Earned value metrics

comes with an inherent risk. Further, adding resources and funding may not in the end improve the position of the project schedule. It is advisable, under circumstances when the project schedule cannot be brought fully back into control, to attempt to negotiate a reduction in scope. Often, this is a feasible option—particularly when software that may be later updated is involved. However, there may be circumstances when there is no other option but to attempt to reel in the project by adding resources and funding and accepting the risk. Schedule reduction done in this manner is referred to as "project crashing." The term is an appropriate one given the risk. When project crashing is attempted, it is approached by analyzing remaining project activities, determining those activities on the critical path that have the possibility of being reduced, and finally applying resources to the least costly activity first. The goal is to maximize schedule reduction while, at the same time, minimizing additional project cost and resource addition (Figure 8.24).

Controlling as "MBWA"

Controlling the project is not strictly limited to analyzing performance and evaluating metrics. It also involves talking to project team members and the larger project stakeholder community to perceive problems before they become problems. In this way, the project team members can anticipate problems likely to derail the project and thereby keep the project under constant control. One approach to accomplishing this is "management by walking around" or MBWA. Constant interaction with

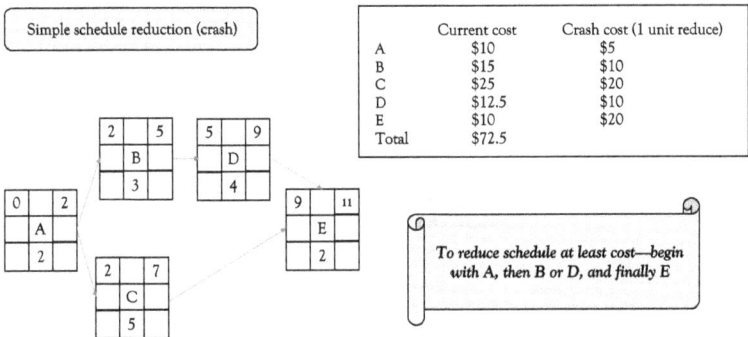

Figure 8.24 Crashing the project

those who are doing the work and those who have interest in the project can pay dividends.

While it is true that issues constantly arise in projects and those issues reveal themselves in project metrics, it is also true that the resolution of issues is accomplished by people. The agile approach to project management recognizes the importance of frequent communication along with careful management of scope. Scope is carefully managed by attempting only a small portion of the overall project scope at a time, proving it out, and then building on it. There is less opportunity for the project to shift significantly out of control using this method. Further, consistent with the strategy of MBWA, agile project management employs a stand-up meeting at the beginning of each day. The stand-up meeting—or scrum—is kept focused and simple and asks each team member the following questions:

1. What did you do yesterday?
2. What will you do today?
3. What is getting in your way?

Interaction through face-to-face communication is an excellent method for keeping the finger of the project team on the pulse of the project. Likewise, control is maintained by the very human activities of discussion, negotiation, and commitment—rather than a purely cybernetic response to indicator metrics.

Returning to the Office Relocation Project: The Closing Phase

The termination of the office relocation project provides a challenge to the project team. This is because of the combination of deliverables, stakeholder groups, and outside vendors employed in the move. Where should the team begin? Recall that project closure amounts to good housekeeping so it is recommended to conduct a bottom-up evaluation of each WBS element to confirm that it is satisfactorily completed. The WBS elements in the case of this project may be used as a checklist for confirmation of completed activity. The completion status is evaluated by answering questions triggered by the WBS elements as follows: *Finance*: The finance deliverables for the office relocation project include the budget, and the required payments. Final questions to be asked and confirmed:

1. Have all payments to outside contracts been completed?
2. Have all fees and final payments for the existing location been paid?
3. Have the initial fees and lease payments for the new location been paid?
4. Have all initial fees and payments for utilities and services for the new location been paid?
5. Have all outstanding payments been audited for completion, recorded in the budget, and reported in the final budget close-out report?

Transition plan: The transition plan deliverables for the office relocation project include the supplies, infrastructure, and communication. Final questions to be asked and confirmed at the closing of the project include:

1. Are the telecommunications and utilities in the new facility confirmed to be working?
2. Have the telecommunications and utilities in the legacy facility been shut down?
3. Have building services such as security and maintenance for the new facility been notified of opening dates and schedules?
4. Have building services in the legacy facility been terminated?
5. Have all remaining supplies acquired for the facility move been collected and stored or distributed to departments that could use them?
6. Have final details regarding shutdown and startup been communicated to all?
   (a) Managers
   (b) Employees
   (c) Suppliers
   (d) Facility managers
   (e) Members of the community

Relocation management personnel: The relocation management personnel deliverables for the office relocation project include the planners, coordinators, packers, and movers. Final questions to be asked and confirmed with all relocation management personnel include:

1. Have all internal personnel involved in planning and coordinating the move confirmed that their individual plans are complete?
2. Have all internal planning and coordinating personnel been returned to their respective functional groups?
3. Are all moving activities confirmed to be complete? Is any follow-up required to finish any outstanding move work?
4. Has the completion of the work been confirmed with the moving company and the contract closed?

Existing location: The existing location deliverables for the office relocation project include the layout, utilities, packing, and the close-out plan. The packing and utility deliverables overlap with the transition plan checklist. Therefore, final questions to be asked and confirmed regarding the existing (now legacy) location include:

1. Has the legacy facility been closed?
2. If the legacy location has not yet been closed, is there a plan in place to address this?
3. Have all furniture, cubicles, or other elements of the layout of the legacy facility been taken down?
4. Has the area of the layout of the legacy facility been cleaned?
5. Has a final walkthrough of the legacy facility been undertaken?

New location: The new location deliverables for the office relocation project include the building specifications, layout, and furniture. It can be safely assumed that the specifications for the new facility are complete given that the move itself is complete. However, the layout and the furniture of the new location remain to be confirmed as part of the project closure. Final questions to be asked and confirmed include:

1. Is the layout for the new facility working well and are any adjustments needed?
2. Is all furniture for the new location set up and occupied?

Looking Back and Looking Forward

The series of questions asked to confirm the completion of the project provide a glimpse of the detailed consideration required to ensure that everything that was intended to be completed was actually completed. The successful closure of a project leaves no remaining "loose ends." Project termination, as revealed in the series of confirmatory questions, is a matter of good housekeeping. In the example of the office relocation project, the questions are but a guide to the type of information required to confirm that the project is truly over. There is however one final aspect of closing the project—and that is to review the lessons gleaned from the successes as well as the mistakes made as the project was planned and executed. A good way to carry this out is to hold a final project review meeting including project team members and key stakeholders such as the building manager. The outcome of the meeting would be to not only formally bring the project to a close, but to document lessons from the project that could be used as a guide for the development of future project plans.

CHAPTER 9

Uncertainty Performance Domain

No project plan is complete without consideration of uncertainty and risk. What is uncertainty in the context of project management? Defined loosely, uncertainty is risk and risk is anything that can stand in the way of project success. Risks are events that have not yet occurred but could occur (once risks do occur, they become issues and are no longer risks). Although it is true that there is such a thing as a "positive risk," that is, the chance that something good could happen within a project, positive risks are the exception rather than the norm. "Murphy's Law" could be said to govern project risks given that "anything that could go wrong, will go wrong" within a project. When uncertainties are viewed as barriers to success, and project managers do their work so that barriers to success are minimized or eliminated, then project managers could be viewed as risk managers.

Risk and Reward

Viewing the project manager as a risk manager provides a lens for more clearly understanding the connection between risk and reward. It is often said that "without risk, there is no reward" and, as well, it is understood that the reward that is sought in any venture must be commensurate with the risk undertaken. Given that risks are defined in the project context as "anything that stands in the way of project success," in a project that had no such risk, the project results would just "happen" and would not require management. In this imaginary environment, there is no need for project managers. In the real world that projects and project managers inhabit, things do not just "happen." They require management under conditions of risk. The role of the project manager is therefore a necessity, and it is a role for which the project manager earns a reward in the form of a salary. Further, once the project manager successfully shepherds the project to completion and produces deliverables, the client and the sponsors earn the rewards from the deliverables produced regardless of the ongoing risk of failure. Without the presence of risk in project management therefore, there would be no opportunity to earn the reward.

Uncertainty and Risks—What Are They?

Project risks are insidious in that they are often elusive, difficult to imagine, and usually intangible early in the project. It is often the risk that no one has considered that ends up being the one risk that brings down the project. Also, risks have a way of cascading. Small, apparently nonrisky events may lead to other events that lead to yet others that snowball into a project catastrophe. A project team may be aware of a possible catastrophe as well as what that catastrophe might look like—but be completely unaware of the very small initial event that triggers the catastrophic chain reaction. Because of the elusive nature of risks, the risk plan begins with risk identification. Risk identification is an activity for which a project manager must get creative and "think out of the box."

Uncertainty and Risk Identification Methods

No one can accurately foresee the future. Most project teams have difficultly imagining what might be as the project unfolds. This is the reason why brainstorming is a fundamental and very important part of risk identification. Brainstorming takes many different forms, but at its essence is the emphasis of encouraging participants to think and speak freely unencumbered by constraints. Speaking freely opens the doors to ideas that on the face of it may seem highly unlikely. Yet, it is precisely these apparently unlikely risks that have a way of catching the project team off-guard. It is only after ideas are collected in brainstorming and discussion sessions that they are vetted for inclusion into the project risk plan. The risks that remain after vetting are those for which the project will keep within its sights and pay ongoing close attention. An additional tool for use in risk identification is the risk breakdown structure

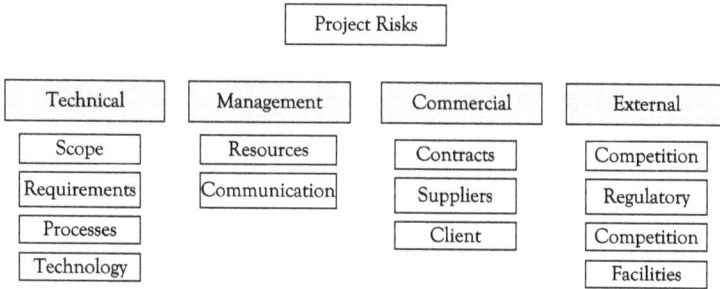

Figure 9.1 The risk breakdown structure

or "RBS" (Figure 9.1). The RBS provides a structured set of categories that seed the risk identification process by highlighting typical categories likely to be sources of project risk.

Risk—How Bad Is It?

An infinite array of risk events could appear in any given project to disrupt the possibility of project success. No project team or project manager could identify—much less manage—the total range of possible risks that the project might encounter. It is for this reason that the project team directs its attention to the most pressing risks. How are the most important risks identified? First, risks are evaluated in terms of the likelihood of occurrence. A risk that is more likely to happen is considered more important than a risk that appears only rarely. To consider an extreme example, a risk such as a component delivery being delayed is more likely to occur than a tsunami event or an eruption of the Yellowstone Super volcano. The likelihood of occurrence is expressed as a probability ranging from 0 to 1. A likelihood of zero will never occur whereas a likelihood of 1 is a certainty. The likelihood of a coinflip resulting in "heads" is .5.

Once the probability of a risk is established, the resulting impact of the risk is considered and captured in the form of a monetary value. In the case of a delayed component delivery, the impact of this risk would be analyzed in terms of the cost incurred to the project by the resulting delay. Costs are driven by the additional activity required to recover from the delay, costs or penalties associated with the late deliverable, and finally other costs such as overhead or expediting fees.

Finally, the severity of the risk, in terms of its importance, is quantified by multiplying the probability of the risk event by the impact of the risk should the risk occur. If, for instance, the cost of the component delivery delay was determined to be $1,000.00 and the probability of the risk occurring was .35 (or 35 percent), then the severity of the risk would be calculated as .35 × $1,000.00 = $350. The risks identified in project team brainstorming sessions are quantified by risk severity and ranked within a table known as a risk register (Figure 9.2).

The risk register includes ranked risks and associated details about each risk. The risk register is continually monitored and updated as necessary— but, the primary focus of the project team is on the highly ranked risks based on the risk severity calculation. Most commonly, the review and updating of the project risk register is a weekly project meeting agenda item. Risks in the risk register may also be plotted in a matrix format for ease of visibility (Figure 9.3). The probability-impact matrix presents risks briefly and as well uses colors to identify the most severe risks.

Keep in mind that the primary focus of the risk register and especially the probability-impact matrix is risk visibility. Again, this is because of the tendency of risks to be intangible and difficult to perceive. For this reason, the probability-impact matrix is usually color-coded so that the most severe risks stand out. The colors used follow that of a traffic light with red meaning "alert," green meaning "OK," and yellow meaning "caution."

Qualitative Versus Quantitative Risk Analysis

When numbers are employed within risk analysis, it is tempting to draw the conclusion that the analysis is quantitative. However, it is important to be aware that the presence of numbers does not automatically involve

Simplified high-level risk register

Risk identifier	Risk description	Date	Assigned to	Response strategy	Probability	Impact	Ranking
4252018	Supplier delay	1/25/2018	Jan	Avoid	0.25	$17,500	$4,375
2182018	Contract delay	1/18/2018	Jaclyn	Mitigate	0.2	$15,000	$3,000
3202018	Design flaw	1/20/2018	Jamie	Mitigate	0.1	$10,000	$1,000
1152018	Server failure	1/15/2018	Levi	Transfer	0.01	$10,000	$100

Figure 9.2 The risk register

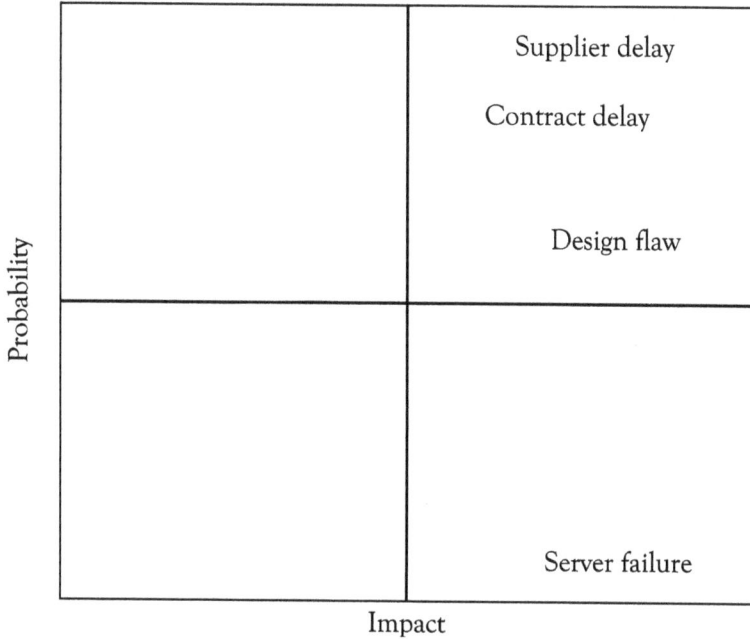

	Supplier delay
	Contract delay
	Design flaw
	Server failure

Figure 9.3 The probability-impact matrix

quantitative risk analysis. As an example, when the severity of the risk is determined, both the probability and the impact are provided by numeric values. However, the probability is likely to be subjective in nature—whereas, the impact of the risk is likely to consist of only a rough estimate. When numbers are used to estimate risk severity as in the case of the probability-impact assignment and the placement on the probability-impact matrix, the risk analysis is subjective and qualitative. Under what circumstances would numeric risk analysis be truly quantitative? If, for example, the probability estimate and the likely value of the impact were generated from actual historical data, then the resulting analysis would be considered quantitative.

Numbers Can Mean Different Things

When considering the use of numbers in risk analysis, it bears remembering that there are different classes of numbers that may be used in different applications—not all of which are quantitative. Imagine, for example, going to a restaurant with a friend and each of you order a numbered selection from the menu. If you ordered #10, and your friend ordered #15 off the menu, it would make no sense to inform the waitress that, as a compromise, your table will simply average the menu selections and each order "#12.5". This obviously makes no sense—but, the reason it doesn't make sense is that these numbers are simply acting as names and are not intended to be employed in calculations. As such, these numbers are referred to as *nominal*.

Another type of number reflects the ranking of different elements. For example, major cities in the United States may be ranked as #1, #2, #3, and so on. The rank in terms of relative size is clear—yet, the interval between each number is not defined. For instance, New York may be larger than Los Angeles in terms of population—but, the ranking does not inform regarding how much larger one rank is compared to another. These numbers are referred to as *ordinal*. The next category of numbers does have a fixed interval between each number. For example, when counting integers from 1 to 10, each integer increases by exactly 1. These numbers are referred to as *interval*. Finally, numbers that include not only fixed intervals—but also a zero—are referred to as *ratio* numbers. Given the categories of numbers and the amount of mathematical information they do or do not contain, project managers should be aware of what kind of numeric information they are working with so that it will be clear to what degree the analysis of any kind—including risk analysis—is truly quantitative or qualitative (Figure 9.4).

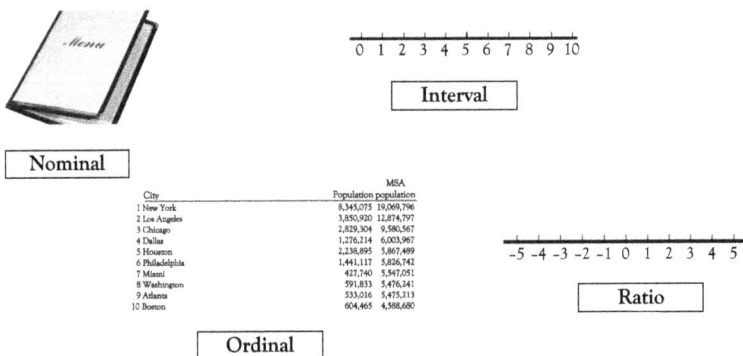

Figure 9.4 Number types—NOIR (nominal, ordinal, interval, ratio)

Risk Simulation

Often after the initial qualitative analysis is conducted, further detailed analysis using historical data or probabilistic simulation is employed. One method commonly available in many current project management software packages is Monte Carlo analysis. This analysis evokes the image of the roulette wheel within a casino. This is not far from the actual methodology employed by Monte Carlo analysis. In this type of probabilistic analysis, duration and cost values are chosen at random from a range of inputs (drawn from three-point estimates) to the project schedule. After several thousand runs, the analysis arrives at a probability duration of schedule completion dates as well as costs. The thousands of runs could be considered a long-run simulation of the project (Figure 9.5). This type of quantitative risk analysis informs project managers of the possible range of project outcomes calculated to be likely given the cost and schedule input data created from the risk brainstorming process.

Risk Planning and Bayes' Theorem

Risk simulations associated with Monte Carlo analysis and risk estimates using the weighted averages of PERT analysis are useful tools for predicting what is likely to happen in the future of the project.

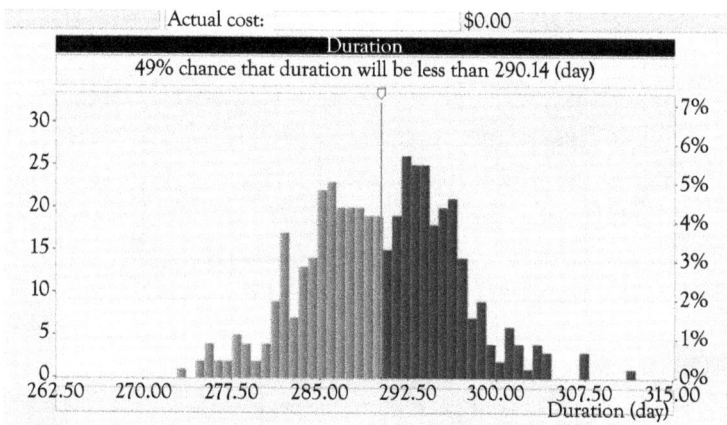

Figure 9.5 Monte Carlo analysis

However, the problem with such approaches is that they are "frequentist" in nature. That is, the simulations and averages will provide significant information about the long-run outcome possibilities of the project—but will not say much about a "one time only" undertaking. Simulation outcomes produce statistical distributions, and PERT analysis produces probabilities associated with weighted averages. Unfortunately, all projects are "one time only" and are not typically undertaken several thousand times. So then, project risk planners should well wonder if the project has a chance at being on time or not. An alternative to the frequentist approach to predicting project outcomes is to employ Bayes' theorem.

Bayes' theorem provides a formal method of making an educated guess that considers the prior probability estimates about a specific project outcome. This is following updating the guess with new evidence and arriving at an improved or posterior probability. Bayes' theorem uses the following formula:

$P(G\backslash E) = (P(E\backslash G) *P(G))/P(E)$

Where:

$P(G\backslash E)$, (or "G given E") is referred to as the posterior probability— or the new probability calculated by including new evidence,

PEG) is the conditional probability of "E given G" (or "Evidence given the guess"),

$P(G)$ is the prior probability of the "guess" or "hypothesis"—or probability of G determined prior to including updated evidence, and finally $P(E)$ is the prior probability E, or "Evidence."

What this formula states in everyday language is:
"The probability of your guess given the evidence is equal to the probability of the evidence given the guess, multiplied by the probability of the guess being true, and divided by the probability of the evidence." Understanding and applying Bayes' theorem and using it within a project

risk management plan may be a bit tricky. For starters, the formula will likely be confusing to project managers and even understanding the formula can be challenging. Also, it is not entirely clear how to determine the values for the equation to arrive at the revised probability. Finally, it is difficult to think about how to frame a project scenario so that Bayesian analysis may be applied. It is easier to understand how to apply Bayes' theorem by carrying out a simple visual project example. Also, project managers will find Bayesian analysis much easier to use by incorporating a shorthand, visual method for making risk assessments.

A Bayes' Theorem Example

Assume that the project manager has attended a team midpoint project review and has been informed of the latest status of the project. Further, the project team has conducted a PERT analysis and adjusted the schedule so that a 95 percent project duration is achieved. The team further announces that the project will be on time based on the evidence of the adjusted schedule and the PERT analysis. Upon hearing this information, the project manager wants to believe that the project will be on time, but wonders is it true that the schedule has a 95 percent probability of being achieved? Is there any additional evidence that could be collected to improve the understanding of the likelihood that the project will be on time?

It could be said that $P(E|G)$, the probability of the evidence given the guess that the project will be on time, is 95 percent based on the PERT analysis presented at the project review. The reported probability is 95 percent, but this probability is only a portion of the overall Bayes' probability calculation. What additional evidence could be collected to improve the understanding of the risk? Two questions could be asked to obtain a better picture of the actual likelihood. They are:

1. Historically, what percentage of projects was delivered on time?
2. What percentage of projects that presented a 95 percent PERT schedule at the midpoint project review was delivered on time?

The answer to question #1 provides the value for $P(G)$, and the answer for question #2 is the value for $P(E|G)$.

Assume that it has been determined that historically projects have been on time only 30 percent of the time. Therefore, the probability of the guess that the project is on time, or *P(G)*, is 30 percent. Finally, the project team has analyzed previous records of projects that exhibited a 95 percent probability at the midpoint project review—and determined that this evidence was present in 60 percent of the occasions where the project was on time, and 40 percent when the project was late. Using these values *P(E|G)* is determined as (.6 * .3 + .4 * .7) or .46. Putting the elements of the formula together, we have:

$$P(G\backslash E) = (.6 * .3)/.46 = .39 \text{ or } 39\%$$

This informs the project team—based on evidence and prior probability—that the PERT 95 percent schedule reported at the midpoint project review in the case of the organization in this scenario is—in reality—a schedule with only a 39 percent probability of success.

Visual Aids Make a Difference

Identification and keeping track of the formula elements may seem like an impossible task. The good news is that it is not necessary when a visual Bayes' template is used. Bayesian project risk analysis is then easily applied using a series of steps involving visual aids as follows.

Step 1: Create a diagram illustrating the basic probability categories under examination. In this case, the diagram illustrates the overall probability of projects being on time versus being late (Figure 9.6).

What percentage of projects are historically on time?

On-time: 30%   Late: 70%

	On-time	Late
Prior probability	30	70
New evidence		
Updated probability		

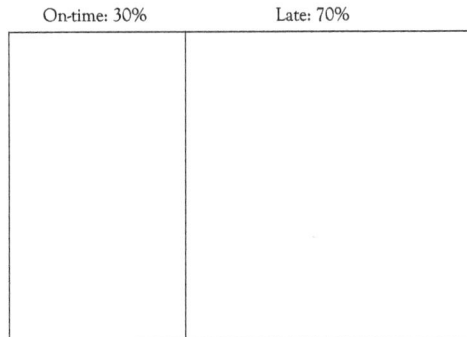

Figure 9.6 Step 1—identifying the basic probability categories

Next, use the table to shade in the probability value of interest. In the case of this scenario, it is the on-time versus late probability of projects that reported a 95 percent schedule probability at the project midpoint. Once this is completed, the Bayes' formula elements may be directly plugged in (Figure 9.7). (Note that the chart makes it easy to determine $P(E)$ by 0.6 * 0.3 + 0.4 * 0.7. This figure represents the total shaded area.)

Finally, there is a simpler shorthand method for calculating Bayesian probabilities that does not require the plugging in of values to the Bayesian equation. In this method, use the shaded areas to complete the probability table. Then, multiply each column to arrive at the updated probability. What results is the odds ratio 1800:2800 or 18:28. What are the odds of being on time using this method? It is calculated by determining the ratio of 18 out of the total (18 + 28). The ratio is 18/ (18 + 28) which is .39 or 39 percent. This is the same probability as calculated using the Bayes' formula directly (Figure 9.8).

Bayesian analysis is an important tool for updating the project risk outlook as new evidence becomes available. Because of its value, it is a methodology that is recommended to be included in the risk management plan.

Risk—What Should We Do About It?

Once risks are identified and analyzed, project managers next consider what should be done to address these risks. Each risk identified and

	On-Time	Late
Prior Probability	30%	70%
New Evidence	60%	40%

What percentage of projects presenting 95% PERT schedule at midpoint project review historically were delivered on time?

On-time: 30%   Late: 70%

60% of on-time projects presented 95% PERT schedule at midpoint

40% of on-time projects presented 95% PERT schedule at midpoint

$P(G|E) = (.6*.3)/.46 = 39\%$

Use visual as a guide to plug-in numbers into Bayes' equation

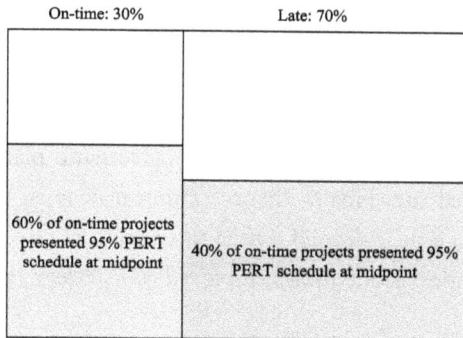

Figure 9.7 Step 2—shade in probabilities and plug into Bayes' formula

What percentage of projects presenting 95% PERT schedule at midpoint project review historically were delivered on time?

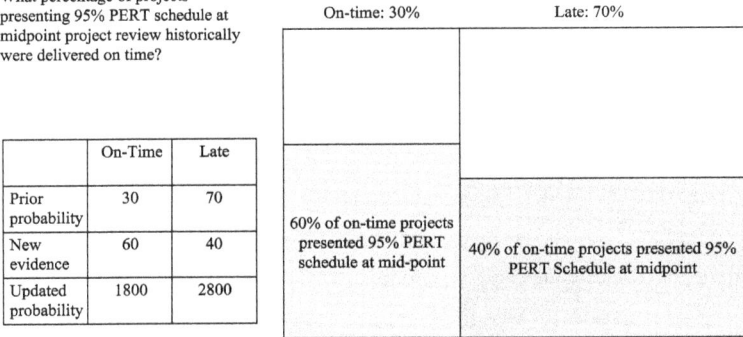

On-time: 30%   Late: 70%

	On-Time	Late
Prior probability	30	70
New evidence	60	40
Updated probability	1800	2800

60% of on-time projects presented 95% PERT schedule at mid-point

40% of on-time projects presented 95% PERT Schedule at midpoint

...or odds of 18:28 meaning 8/(18+28) or 39% chance of being on-time..

Figure 9.8 Bayesian analysis shorthand method

ranked in the risk register is linked to an accompanying response strategy. There are four generic approaches to dealing with risks that each has its associated pros and cons. The four approaches may be recalled easily using the acronym "MART" for *Mitigate, Avoid, Retain,* and *Transfer.*

Mitigate

The first inclination of the project team is to take some action that would minimize the possibility of the risk becoming an issue and—if it does—to minimize its impact. This generic approach is referred to as risk mitigation. The advantage to this approach is that it is an active strategy that directly seeks to counter any potential negative impact. The disadvantage is that a mitigation strategy will likely require the creation of a project subplan that will need to be staffed and funded. If mitigation is selected as a strategy, then there must be a reasonable expectation that mitigation will successfully counter the risk. Often, potential for mitigation success can be evaluated by employing scenario planning and, in some cases, a trial run. Finally, the mitigation plan must be less taxing to the project than the risk itself. Often this is not the case, and this explains why mitigation is not always employed as a strategy (Figure 9.9).

Avoid

When the risk is too significant to address via mitigation, it may be prudent for the project to *avoid* taking on project scope that is associated

Mitigate	Avoid	Retain	Transfer
Take steps to minimize risk	Select an alternative path	Accept the risk and live with it	Pass risk to third party

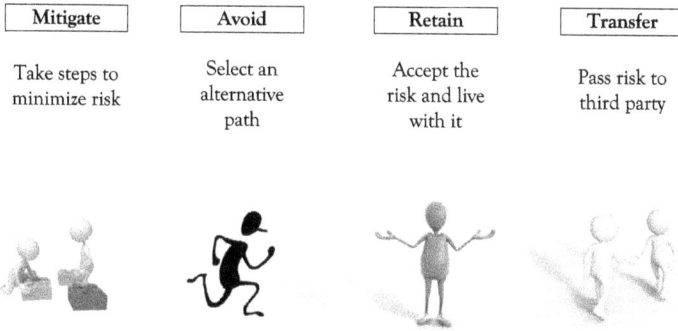

Figure 9.9 Risk response strategies

with the risk. When a project team chooses this approach for a given risk, then it forgoes the opportunity to complete some of the work that the project was chartered to accomplish. Unfortunately, for the project team, this strategy is not always possible. The client may insist on the completion of the project as it was originally scoped. In this case, if the avoid strategy is still the optimal strategy, then the team could consider approaching elements of the project scope in a different manner. For example, the original risk may have been linked to the implementation of a given technological solution. An avoidance strategy, in this case, would involve the selection of an alternative technological solution rather than foregoing an element of project scope altogether.

Retain

There are some cases when the identified risk is significant enough to monitor, but not significant enough to neither take immediate action nor avoid altogether. Under this circumstance, the project team may decide to proceed according to the plan and address the risk only if it becomes an issue. Such a risk strategy is referred to as a *retain* strategy. When a risk is retained by the project, the "chips fall where they may" and the project team deals with the issue should it become necessary to do so. The advantage of the retain strategy is that it takes little effort to implement beyond monitoring the risk. The disadvantage of this approach is that it is possible for the risk to be underestimated and the resulting issue may result in much higher cost and effort than originally expected. Finally, even when risks are addressed by other response options, it is rare that the risk will be completely addressed. There is usually some level of remaining or residual risk. The residual risk is likely to be retained by the project as further risk responses may not be possible—or, at minimum, be too expensive compared to the value of the risk itself.

Transfer

Risk *transfer* is employed when the project team shifts the responsibility for some, or all, of the risk impact to another party. Risk transfer is often used outside of the project domain using the mechanism of insurance. When a firm purchases insurance, the insurance company is compensated for taking over the monetary responsibility for the insured loss. Insurance may be used in some circumstances in the context of a project; but more commonly, the transfer of risk is carried out using contractual arrangements. For example, it is not uncommon for software and hardware component suppliers to contribute resources to the project team as a means of sharing the project risk. In this type of risk-sharing arrangement, it pays for the project manager to remember the phrase "no risk–no reward." This is because those vendors who participate in a resource-based risk-sharing arrangement will be likely to specify in the contract that the intellectual property that is jointly created will be owned by both parties so that both parties to the contract may benefit in the future.

The Elements of Uncertainty Management

What elements should be included in uncertainty management? Overall approach: How will risks be identified and assessed?

1. Roles and responsibilities: Who within the project team is responsible for the risk management process?
2. Categories: What categories of project risk will be targeted for focus?
3. Ranking and reporting: How will risk be ranked, reported, and revised on a periodic basis?
4. What risk response methods will the project team employ?

CHAPTER 10

Tailoring

Performance Domains and the PMI Framework: It Is All About Getting Work Done!

The performance domains of PMBOK 7 closely mirror the process groups and knowledge areas of previous editions of the PMBOK, including PMBOK 6. An interesting element of the performance domains is *tailoring*. Tailoring considers that the way things are done in one company are likely to differ from another. This is reflected in the culture of the company and its internal processes. These are traditionally referred to as Enterprise Environmental Factors (EEF) and Organizational Process Assets.

Tailoring may mean that the life cycle selected for managing projects may be unique. Additionally, the approach to planning may take a novel form. This may carry over into the specific tools and techniques employed by the project, the metrics used for project tracking and assessing risks, and finally the approach taken for closing projects. While all this may be true, projects from wildly different organizations and industries must be started, planned, and completed. Along the way—regardless of the specific form adopted—multiple subplans will be developed to address the wide array of components touched upon by the project including quality, scope, schedule, stakeholders, resources, and the like. While the performance domains provide a general "10,000-foot view" of the project, they are best understood as a companion for the processes found in PMBOK 6 and the PMI Standards + site. The abbreviated set of performance domains (PMBOK 7) loosely maps to some of the knowledge areas and process groups (PMBOK 6). An abbreviated approach may be desirable given the proliferation of PMBOK processes over time. However, the process framework presented by PMBOK 6 and previous generations of standards—in addition to having the essence captured in the performance domain—may be easily grasped once the big picture of how the processes flow together is developed (Figure 10.1).

Stewardship					
Value	System for value delivery				
Systems thinking					
Leadership					
Tailoring	Adaptability	Resiliency	Change	Complexity	
	Development approach/life cycle				
	Initiating	Planning	Executing	M & C	Closing
Integration		Planning	Project work	Measurement	Delivery
Scope		Planning			
Schedule		Planning			
Cost		Planning			
Quality	Quality	Planning			
Resources	Team	Planning	Team		
Communications		Planning			
Risk	Risk	Planning	Uncertainty		
Procurement		Planning			
Stakeholders	Stakeholders	Planning	Stakeholders		
	Methods/models/artifacts				

Figure 10.1 Project performance domains

Understanding the Legacy Process Framework

Project management professionals are known for their ability to get things done. Aspiring project managers may wonder why this is said to be the case when they scan the pages of the PMBOK. What they encountered in PMBOK 6 is a matrix of 49 processes that, at first glance, seems to defy understanding (and that also seems to grow with every revision of the PMBOK!). What is it about a table of processes that leads to such success in achieving goals? Is there an underlying logic to the table?

Although the table of processes in the PMBOK guide may seem daunting at first, there is an underlying logic to it that, which once understood, will go a long way toward demystifying it.

As a first step, consider that the PMBOK includes both a content as well as a process view of project management presented in a very compact manner. Because of its compactness and abbreviated tabular representation, it may be difficult at first glance for a novice to understand where to begin. The project performance domains in PMBOK 7 may be an easier entry path for understanding the process framework. Before even starting to understand the table of processes, a novice project manager should first understand that project management is a discipline that has evolved to support getting a specific type of work done. The work that a project manager does is temporary. A project is designed to produce specific deliverables and then terminate. This is very different from work that is done in the context of ongoing operations. Until this is understood, the rationale for even using the apparently complex system of processes may be unclear. Fully appreciating the logic behind the PMBOK first requires an analysis of what it means to carry out work and manage it outside of ongoing operations.

Projects Versus Ongoing Operations

Projects exist for one reason—and that is to produce specific deliverables. Once the deliverables have been delivered and accepted by the client, the project is over. By way of contrast, ongoing operations seek to achieve long-term goals as they execute against the strategy and mission of the company. What gets done therefore in ongoing operations are activities that contribute to the constant production of products or services for clients and returns for shareholders and stakeholders of the company.

Because of the temporary nature of projects, project organizations exist outside of the normal ongoing operation. A temporary project team operating within a larger organizational context therefore needs to be authorized, staffed, and funded, and also provided with a clear scope. This requires policies, procedures, and processes that may not exist to the same degree as it does within an ongoing operation. The special nature of projects, including the highly tangible and short-term focus, has therefore led to the development of a supporting project management process framework. The PMBOK performance domains therefore begins to make more sense when it is understood why it is needed.

The short-term focus of the project manager on producing deliverables also leads to the view of project managers as being highly task-oriented. Leaders of ongoing organizations get things done too—but often within the context of a much longer time horizon. Further, many of the activities carried out in ongoing operations may produce more intangible contributions that support its mission and vision. The longer time horizon and the absence of tangible deliverables provide a contrast to the short-term specific targets of the project manager.

Digital Versus Analog

Beyond the comparison of projects with operations, it could also be said that project management represents a different way of thinking about getting work done. This way of thinking mirrors the way that the world has changed in terms of how we communicate and carry out our jobs and professions within the information age in which we live. Consider for example how telecommunications have shifted from analog methods to digital techniques. Why this transition happened provides a useful framework for thinking about the how and why of project management.

During the old days of analog communication—if one person wanted to speak to another person, the telecommunications system would need to set up a dedicated connection from one speaker to another for communication to take place. Setting up a connection tied up resources to support the call during the entire duration of the call. This same situation applied when setting up and carrying out video conferencing. The Internet and the associated digital methods of transporting calls overtook analog communications in its various forms due to the increased efficiency of digital communications. Instead of tying up dedicated lines and communications channels, the conversation—be it audio or video conferencing—would be broken into pieces or packets, numbered according to its sequence, addressed to its destination, and routed through a nearly endless series of nodes. The resulting pieces of the conversation—or packets—were then reassembled at the call destination and presented to the receiver. As a result, no dedicated resources were engaged, multiple calls could be processed using the same resources, and, as a result, the tightly controlled disassembly, routing, and reassembly—made possible by new thinking and new technology—created vast improvements in telecommunications efficiency.

Likewise, traditional organizations and operations in the era of mass production could be viewed as essentially "analog" or continuous rather than discrete in their approach to doing work (Figure 10.2). Such operations excelled at doing one thing—and doing it well over a long period of time. The organization was dedicated to its primary function and was limited in its ability to manage multiple product lines and lacked flexibility to adapt to changes. The assumption of an ongoing operation was stability. In a stable market—dedicating an ongoing operation to primarily

Continuous   Discrete

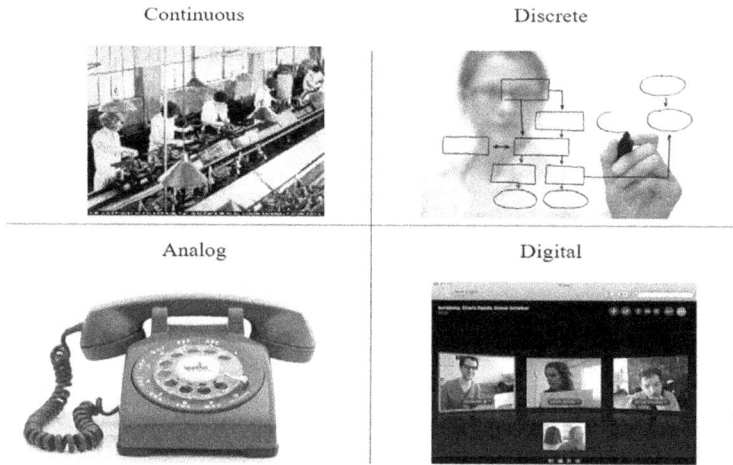

Analog   Digital

Figure 10.2 Project management as discrete business processes

one thing was a realistic business model since the cost of the overall organization could be allocated to the mass production of one major product
for an extended period.

In a similar manner, using the analogy of the dedicated circuit in telecommunications, the old telecommunications business model functioned
well so long as the users of the dedicated line were willing to absorb the
higher cost. Today, this is no longer the case.

Likewise, in the information age in which we live, price pressure is
intense and product life cycles tend to be quite short. Operations may
be required to launch multiple products at one time and as well, launch
different products throughout the year to survive and compete. Further,
product launches may be accompanied by software and services deliverables. This shift in the business model of companies delivering products
and services makes it impossible for companies to fund an operation that
makes only one primary product and relies on the sales of the product for
an extended period.

By way of contrast with the ongoing operations, and traditional analog technology, project management is a "digital" or discrete method of
carrying out work. Projects begin and then end once the deliverables
are produced. Further, as in the case of digital communications, work
is broken down into smaller pieces, carefully quantified, labeled, and
assigned by means of the work package, and then routed to resources in

the organization that can execute the pieces of work. The work that is completed by organizational resources is assembled into the final project deliverables. The thinking behind this discrete approach to getting work done mirrors the underlying philosophy of digital communications. Organizational resources are not occupied by being dedicated to the development and manufacture of a single product. Rather, organizational resources are assigned as needed to complete work packages and then freed up to do other work as work packages are completed. The act of breaking down the work into small pieces and assigning it by means of clearly described and closely managed work packages maintains tight control over the work activities. Further, this method of doing work enables the close monitoring of progress and resource usage.

As is the case in the digital communications infrastructure that we use every day—the tailoring approach to doing work made available by project management processes leads to increased efficiency and organizational flexibility. Project management is therefore a management discipline designed for an age of great change and instability in the market—rather than that which existed during more stable times of the mass production era. Project management as a discipline could well be described as the set of business processes for doing the work of the dynamic and rapidly changing work environment of the information age.

References

PMBOK Guide. 2013. "Guide to the Project Management Body of Knowledge, 5th ed.

PMBOK Guide. 2017. "Guide to the Project Management Body of Knowledge, 6th ed.

PMBOK® Guide. 2021. "The Standard for Project Management and the PMBOK® Guide, 7th ed." PMI Talent Triangle. Retrieved from www.pmi .org/-/media/pmi/documents/public/pdf/certifications/talent-triangle-flyer .pdf

Porter. (2008). The five competitive forces that shape strategy. Harvard Business Review, 86(1), 78–137.

About the Authors

Dr. James W. Marion is an Associate Professor with Embry-Riddle Aeronautical University—Worldwide. He is currently the Chair of the department of decision sciences. His experience includes leading large organizations in multiple product launches in the United States, Europe, and Asia, as well as significant experience with Japanese companies including NEC and Panasonic. Dr. Marion has a PhD in Organization and Management with a specialization in Information Technology Management (Capella University). He holds an MS in Engineering (University of Wisconsin-Platteville), a MSc and an MBA in Strategic Planning, as well as a Postgraduate Certificate in Business Research Methods (The Edinburgh Business School of Heriot-Watt University).

Tracey Richardson is an Associate Professor of Project Management at Embry-Riddle Aeronautical University—Worldwide. She has a Doctorate of Organizational Leadership from Argosy University's School of Psychology and is a certified Project Management Professional and a Project Management Institute (PMI)-Risk Management Professional. Tracey is a retired United States Air Force USAF Aircraft Maintenance Officer.

Index

Concise and Applied Business Books

www.ingramcontent.com/pod-product-compliance
Lightning Source LLC
Chambersburg PA
CBHW050456190326
41458CB00005B/1310